JUST GET OUT OF THE WAY

JUST GET OUT OF THE WAY

HOW GOVERNMENT CAN HELP BUSINESS IN POOR COUNTRIES

•

ROBERT E. ANDERSON

CATO
INSTITUTE
Washington, D.C.

Library of Congress Cataloging-in-Publication Data

Anderson, Robert E. (Robert Edward), 1944-
    Just get out of the way : how government can help business in
    poor countries / Robert E. Anderson.
        p. cm.
    Includes bibliographical references and index.
    ISBN 1-930865-54-6 (alk. paper)
        1. Industrial policy—Developing countries. 2. Free enterprise—
    Developing countries. 3. Privatization—Developing countries.
    4. Banks and banking—Government policy—Developing countries.
    5. Developing countries—Economic policy. I. Title.

    HD3616.D452A53 2003
    338.4'8'091724—dc22

                                                              2003065583

Cover design by Elise Rivera.

Printed in the United States of America.

CATO INSTITUTE
1000 Massachusetts Ave., N.W.
Washington, D.C. 20001
www.cato.org

Contents

Acknowledgments

I would like to thank two people for their help and inspiration in writing this book. Ian Vásquez at the Cato Institute supported the publication of this book, devoted considerable time and effort to reviewing drafts, and suggested many improvements. Gerhard Pohl, during our work together at the World Bank, inspired me with his unique insights to think "outside of the box" and not automatically accept the validity of current paradigms for economic development. The conclusions and recommendations in this book, however, are entirely my own.

1. Government Failure versus Market Failure

This book is based on two beliefs. First, economic growth is essential for reducing poverty in third world or developing countries. Second, an efficient, dynamic, and growing private sector is the only way to increase the rate of economic growth. This book then takes the next step and asks what governments can do to help develop the private sector.

The main conclusion is that the government often does too much. Many government programs and policies designed to help the private sector actually impede its development. The major reasons are the low level of ability or competence in most government institutions, the high level of corruption, and the influence of special-interest groups. Though private markets often fail to provide perfect outcomes, the ability of the government in poor countries to fix these failures is limited.

This conclusion reminds me of what my exasperated father told me many years ago when I was attempting to help him carry out a home improvement project: "Son, if you can't help, at least get out of the way." The best that governments can do in many poor countries is just get out of the way. The following chapters analyze which government policies intended to help the private sector are likely to succeed and how they can be designed to compensate for the government's poor ability to implement them.

Government Corruption and Incompetence

I first became concerned about government corruption and incompetence in 1991 when I went to work for the agency that managed privatization in Russia (the State Property Committee). Previously, I had worked on the privatization program in New Zealand managed by the Treasury. Though I was a U.S. citizen, the New Zealand Treasury recruited me along with a number of other foreign citizens to be regular members of the New Zealand civil service. The Treasury

1

felt it needed additional expertise to help with the Labour government's ambitious economic reform program under the leadership of the minister of finance, Roger Douglas.

After having worked in the U.S. government, I was impressed with the quality of the New Zealand Treasury staff and the dedication of the Labour politicians to reform. Though the civil service in New Zealand is skilled and honest and the political system is generally free from corruption, the policy of the Labour government supported by the Treasury was that many of the activities carried out by the government should be transferred to the private sector. In addition, the government should eliminate burdensome regulation of the private sector as well as subsidies and incentives designed to promote its development. These reforms in New Zealand are discussed in more detail in Chapters 6 and 9.

Later, when I went to work in Russia in 1991, I had lengthy discussions with the bright young team (some Russian, some expatriate) recruited to devise and implement a privatization program. After I expounded at length on my "brilliant" proposals to privatize the thousands of state-owned enterprises in Russia, one of the Russians on the team told me that my proposals did not take into account a fundamental fact of life in Russia. They would have to be implemented by the Russian bureaucracy.

Though a relatively small number of new people could be brought in to help organize the program, the bulk of the work would have to be done by existing officials in various agencies and state-owned enterprises. The Russian team member then told me that most officials are incompetent, corrupt, or both. Russia needed to design a privatization program that could be implemented by such officials. This team devised a program for the larger enterprises that was a complex mixture of management-employee buyouts and voucher privatization unlike anything previously used in rich countries. However, the program accomplished its main goal of rapid privatization resulting in the transfer of roughly 70 percent of large and medium-sized enterprises to private owners between 1992 and 1994. Many of the remaining large enterprises were privatized later using other methods.

This accomplishment was illustrated in a presentation by an official of the Russian State Property Committee at a conference where representatives of the various privatization agencies in Central and

Eastern Europe met to share their experiences. Some of the speakers from Poland and Hungary were critical of the Russian privatization method and implied that their countries were doing it better. The Russian representative countered by observing that Margaret Thatcher had privatized about 40 enterprises in the 11 years that she was prime minister of Great Britain. He then looked at his watch and said that in the 10 minutes since he began speaking, Russia had privatized at least that many.

Many have criticized Russian privatization for not achieving some theoretical ideal. However, the early program was probably the best that could have been implemented quickly given the limitation of the existing Russian bureaucracy and political system. More justified is the criticism of later programs, such as the loans-for-shares program, in which state-owned assets were awarded to financial supporters of the government at give-away prices.

Russia could have delayed privatization for years or even decades until government institutions and the civil service were improved and modernized. The choice for the government in the early 1990s was not between some inferior, second-best method of privatization and some theoretical, best method as determined by western experts. The choice was between a second-best method that could be implemented quickly by existing Russian officials versus delaying privatization for many years. This is a difficult choice about which reasonable people may disagree, but it is not obvious or clear-cut that the government made the wrong choice in spite of criticism from western experts. This argument about Russia reminds me of an old saying, "Don't let the perfect be the enemy of the good."

How to Develop the Private Sector

The *private sector* is a shorthand term for those economic, commercial, or business activities that are *not* carried out by the *public sector* and are instead carried out by privately owned businesses and individuals. I would also include nonprofit organizations and community-based organizations in the private sector. These are usually referred to as *nongovernmental organizations* or NGOs. In contrast, the public sector includes government ministries, agencies, and state-owned enterprises.

It is often easier to define the extent of the private sector by examining what the public sector does. Everything else is carried

3

out by the private sector. In many poor countries, the public sector provides health care; education; utilities (electricity, telephone, natural gas, water and sewer); transportation (roads, rail, ports, airlines); banking; insurance; mutual funds; wholesale and retail trade (particularly in agriculture); energy (coal, petroleum); and finally manufactured products.

Developing the private sector has two main components. The first is to transfer more of these economic activities from the public to the private sector. The second is to create the complex structure of government policies, laws, and institutions, hereafter referred to as the *business environment*, which will encourage the private sector to function efficiently and to grow by creating more jobs and higher incomes. There is a growing acceptance that the public sector has done poorly in carrying out these economic activities, and that the private sector can do better in the right environment.

Considering the poor experience of the communist countries and other countries that relied on state-led economic development, greater reliance on the private sector seems self-evident to me. If you don't already believe that the private sector will perform these activities better than the public sector or that developing the private sector is essential for economic growth, then an attempt by me to demonstrate this to be true will probably be unsuccessful. The purpose of this book is to analyze how best to develop the private sector and thus increase the rate of economic growth—not to prove that developing the private sector will increase the rate of economic growth and reduce poverty.

First, Do No Harm

Unfortunately, government policies intended to help the private sector are too often similar to the attempts of the medical profession of 200 hundred years ago to improve health. In those days, a visit to the doctor or hospital was likely to make you worse rather than better. Governments would be wise to follow the oath taken by physicians, which is "First, do no harm."[1]

The outcome of a government policy will fall into one of three categories. First, the best outcome occurs when the policy actually improves the performance and functioning of the private sector, and the benefits of the policy outweigh the budgetary cost. The second outcome occurs when the government tries to help the private sector but actually accomplishes little or nothing. Though not a desirable outcome, at least the damage is restricted to the wasted government expenditures. The third, and worst, outcome occurs when the government policy actually harms the performance of the private sector. The government expenditure is not only wasted, but the private sector would also have been better off if the policy had never been implemented.

As an example, let me describe the outcome when the government created a Board of Investment in Bangladesh. Initially, everyone had high hopes that this policy would fall into the first category. The actual outcome today is in the second category, and there is a risk that it could fall into the third category.

The government created the Board of Investment to encourage foreign companies to invest in Bangladesh. The chairman told me that the Board would try to help foreign investors find their way through the thicket of government licenses, permits, and regulations. He hoped that it would become a *one-stop shop* for government permits.

I asked the chairman how successful they were. He admitted that it was difficult. Most of his staff were transferred from the now defunct Ministry of Industry. They had never worked in the private sector and had little understanding of the needs of businesspeople. Moreover, their whole careers had been spent regulating and controlling the private sector, which was the function of the old ministry. It was difficult for them to change their thinking.

I was disappointed but tentatively concluded that the outcome was not too bad. Admittedly, the Board was unlikely to be of much help to the private sector, in this case, foreign investors. However, if foreign investors did not find the Board helpful, they could just refuse its assistance.

Unfortunately, what the chairman next told me suggested that the outcome could become much worse. He was concerned about foreign investors who were dishonest or did not have a good plan for investing in the country. He proposed that the Board approve the qualifications of foreign investors and review the quality of their business plans before they would be allowed to invest. This action would keep out dishonest and incompetent investors. His objective was to protect consumers, suppliers, and banks that might be harmed by those investors.

He was not impressed by my argument that consumers, suppliers, and banks might be in a better position to protect themselves without help from the Board. I hoped to convince him that his plan was bad by taking it to its logical extreme. I suggested that if his plan was good for foreign investors, why not extend it to domestic investors as well? The Board should review the qualifications and business plans of all investors, both domestic and foreign. I suggested that domestic investors were even more likely to be unqualified or dishonest. To my horror, he seemed to think that I had a good idea. Thus, instead of helping foreign investors, the Board was likely to become just another obstacle.

The Importance of Competition

At this point, the reader might think that I am some naive ideologue who believes that the private sector can do no wrong. A private sector without government intervention, controls, or regulation is some ideal economic system that cannot be improved upon. I am like Pangloss, the hero of Voltaire's *Candide*, and believe that an unregulated market economy is the "best of all possible worlds." Actually, I view a private market economy in the same way as Winston Churchill viewed democracy. A private market economy is the worst economic system except for all others that have been tried.[2]

The impact of competition on the behavior of private companies is the main reason a market economy is a better economic system. This insight is one of the oldest ideas in economics dating back at least to 1776 when Adam Smith wrote the *Wealth of Nations*. Smith argued that, because of competition, private companies in pursuing their own self-interest (namely, higher profits) would actually help the entire society.

Private businesspeople are not inherently more honest or more capable than government officials and politicians. However, competition encourages them to be honest and capable or else they will be driven out of business. Competition pressures a private company to produce high-quality products and services at reasonable prices. Similarly, competition pressures the company to treat its customers, workers, and suppliers honestly and fairly. If not, they will vote with their feet and do business or seek employment with another company.

Although this theory explains why a competitive market economy should perform well, we all know that the practice never entirely lives up to this ideal. We can all give examples of companies that cheat their customers and suppliers, sell unsafe products, charge excessively high prices, underpay and mistreat their workers, pollute the environment, and so forth. However, I despair about the ability of governments in most poor countries to improve this economic system and fix its weaknesses.

In contrast to private companies, the only pressure on governments to perform better is that the politicians might be voted out of office at the next election. Unfortunately, democracy in many poor countries is weak, and poorly performing governments stay in power for decades.

Private-Sector Rent Seeking

Most of the current impediments to the growth of the private sector are the result of past government policies intended to help the sector. At a minimum, any government policies have to be designed to take into account the low level of competence in many government agencies and ministries, the high level of corruption, and the likelihood that special-interest groups will end up distorting the policy for their own benefit.

The worst of these special-interest groups is the private sector itself. Perhaps the greatest weakness of the private sector in any country is its persistent attempt to manipulate and control the power and resources of the government for its own benefit. Economists have come up with a term for this kind of behavior that is certainly not one of the best examples of technical jargon, but I will use it anyway. Economists call this *rent-seeking behavior*. Though not a widely used meaning of the word *rent*, economists use the word in this context to mean above-normal or excess profits. Thus rent-seeking behavior by private businesspeople means that they are trying to use the government to earn excess profits.

Examples of such rent seeking in both rich and poor countries could fill many books. No country is immune. Every day when I pick up the newspaper in my own country (the United States), I become enraged when I see more examples of private firms, farmers, or labor unions using the power of government to enrich themselves at the expense of everyone else.

Governments can increase private profits in many ways. They can provide subsidies both for the products and services that private companies produce and for the inputs that they buy. Governments sell state-owned resources such as land or natural resources to private companies at below-market prices and buy goods and services from them at above-market prices. Governments provide low-interest loans from state-owned banks. Governments offer tax breaks for favored industries or companies. The general public pays for these higher profits through higher taxes or reduced government spending.

In addition, governments have a source of power not available to any other institution. Governments can pass laws or regulations that reduce competition and thus result in high profits for favored private firms and enforce those laws using the police and courts. For example, governments place high tariffs on imported products or limit imports in other ways so that domestic companies can charge high prices free from foreign competition. Governments refuse to allow foreign companies to set up operations in the country in competition with domestic companies. Governments use their power to license new companies so as to restrict their entry and thus limit competition even among domestic companies. The general public pays for these higher profits through higher prices or lower quality products and services. A recent book, *Saving Capitalism from the Capitalists*, argues that the biggest enemies of capitalism are business executives who use their influence to reduce competition.[3]

A better term than rent-seeking behavior grew out of the recent financial and economic crisis in East Asian countries—*crony capitalism*. This term succinctly describes how friends, associates, and relatives of the political leaders in some East Asian countries enjoyed a privileged economic position (the Philippines and Indonesia are often cited). These cronies received government subsidies, tax breaks, cheap loans, lucrative contracts to supply goods and services to the government, and protection from competition. Crony capitalism was blamed at least in part for the economic crisis in these countries.

Labor Unions

Labor unions often assist private companies in their rent seeking. If a company is protected from competition, it is more likely to grant wage increases to union workers in exchange for labor peace. The company knows that it can pass on the higher wages to consumers in the form of higher prices and not suffer reduced profits because it faces little competition. As a result, workers in these companies receive wages and benefits substantially above those of other workers. Labor unions know that increased competition will make it harder for them to demand higher wages. Not surprisingly, labor unions are the biggest opponents of globalization because globalization results in increased competition from foreign companies.

Labor unions are often more effective in rent seeking because they claim to be protecting poor, downtrodden workers even though only a minority of workers in most countries belong to unions. In both poor and rich countries, union members usually make up less than 35 percent of nonagricultural workers and often much less.[4] For example, in India only about 5 percent of nonagricultural workers are union members. If one includes agricultural workers, the percentage is even smaller. Unions often argue that increased competition will force private companies to lower wages or fire workers. Politicians are reluctant to appear to be hurting ordinary workers even though unionized workers are not ordinary. In contrast, rich businesspeople in expensive suits driving around in chauffeured limousines have a harder time gaining the sympathy of politicians.

The higher wages of union workers are borne by the rest of the public in the form of higher prices for the products and services produced by these workers. Labor unions would have us believe that they transfer income from rich capitalists to poor workers. In fact, they mostly transfer income from the large number of nonunion workers to a small number of relatively well-off union workers. In most poor countries, union members are usually the elite of the labor force with high-paying jobs in state-owned enterprises or government agencies. No evidence exits that industries with strong unions also have low profits. The actual choice for politicians is whether to encourage competition resulting in lower prices and higher quality goods for all citizens or whether to protect the privileged position of a few private companies and their union workers.

Pervasive rent seeking is the strongest argument for the government to minimize its involvement with the private sector and to just get out of the way. Government policies to fix perceived weaknesses in private markets will likely end up doing more harm than good because the government is *captured* (another term from economic jargon) by special-interest groups, most important, private businesses and labor unions. Though these policies may have been well intentioned, the end result is harmful.

Paradoxically, the best way for the government to help the private sector is not to help the private sector. Instead, the government should force it to survive without subsidies, tax breaks, and cheap loans and to face fierce competition from both domestic and foreign companies. What I mean by helping the private sector is usually not what the private sector wants when it asks for help from the government. Advice from the private sector and labor unions on how to manage the economy should always be viewed with suspicion because it is often rent seeking in disguise.

Pressure for Government Intervention

Assume for the moment that the main conclusion of this book is correct, namely, that too often government policies designed to help the private sector in poor countries are either ineffective or become an obstacle to its development. The question then is, Why do governments persist with such policies and programs? Don't they see the error of their ways?

There are a number of answers. First and foremost, many government officials and politicians are not really convinced that a large and dynamic private sector is the best way of promoting economic growth. They persist in believing that many important economic activities should remain in government hands and that the government must assist, direct, control, regulate, and guide the small private sector that does exist. In my experience, many politicians and government officials will say they support the development of the private sector because they know that this is the currently popular belief, but they have secret reservations.

For example, I was working with the agency in Russia responsible for promoting competition in private markets. One would assume that officials in this agency would be convinced that competitive private markets free of government regulation and control are generally good for economic growth. After I became friends with a high official in the agency, he admitted his deepest fear about the new market system in Russia.

10

He described how thousands of private companies were now producing whatever products and services they wanted and selling them anywhere and to anyone at unregulated prices. No one in the government knew what they were doing or had any control over them. He said this was complete chaos, and the government must intervene and bring order and stability. He did not see that under this surface chaos was in fact an ordered economic system enforced by the discipline of competitive markets.

Perhaps this is an extreme example because that official spent most of his life living under an entirely different economic system. Officials in many other poor countries, however, have also spent most of their lives working in economic and political systems that were fundamentally opposed to a large independent role for the private sector.

Nehruvian Socialism

Government dominance in economic development lasted for about 40 years, roughly from 1950 through 1990. This type of economy gained widespread acceptance after the Second World War when Soviet control spread over the countries of Central Europe, the Communist Party took control of China, and many former colonies in Asia and Africa gained their independence. It did not end until about 1990 when most of the former communist countries, admitting that communism had been a failure, decided to create private market economies.

Although the example of the Soviet Union and China influenced the leaders of many poor countries in this period, I think that the example of Jawaharlal Nehru in India was more important at least for the former colonies in Asia and Africa. After struggling for decades, Nehru achieved his objective of an independent India in 1947. This was the first major non-Anglo-Saxon colony to gain independence in the 20th century. As India's first prime minister, Nehru had to decide on an economic model that was most likely to bring economic development to the new nation and reduce poverty.

He saw two existing models from which to choose. Although many criticized the communist political system, many experts, including those from Western countries, reluctantly admitted that the communist economic system was achieving high rates of economic growth. As late as 1985, the famous U.S. economist Paul

Samuelson in his introductory textbook argues that the Soviet planning system was a powerful engine of growth.[5] Even the U.S. Central Intelligence Agency was known for exaggerating the growth of the communist economies. As an extreme example, a 1979 World Bank study of Romania concluded that its economy had grown at the phenomenal rate of almost 10 percent per year for 25 years. The 1988 speech by Soviet President Gorbachev in which he stated that the Soviet economy had not grown for 20 years was a shock to many observers of the communist economies.[6] Nehru took pride that India was the world's largest democracy and was unwilling to accept the communist political system, but he found its economic system appealing because he, along with many others, thought it would result in fast economic growth.

The alternative economic model was the capitalist system exemplified by Great Britain, the former colonial master of India. Though Nehru favored the British political system, he had little faith in its economic system and believed that it had exploited India and kept it poor. He saw little reason to adopt an unregulated, private market economy open to world trade and investment. This would just allow the rich capitalist countries to continue to exploit India. Economic imperialism should not be allowed to replace political imperialism. A similar view seems to be held today by those who oppose globalization though it is not easy to determine what their views are.

Instead, Nehru believed that he could devise a new economic system that combined the best of the communist and capitalist systems. As in the communist countries, the government would own the large, important industries and the financial system—the commanding heights of the economy. He emphasized self-reliance and minimized international trade and foreign investment and ownership. Domestic industries would make products previously imported—a strategy of *import substitution*. However, Nehru would not make the same mistake as Russia did and attempt to nationalize agriculture or small businesses. Government planners would regulate, guide, and direct both the state-owned sector and the remaining small private sector. The Indian economy under Nehruvian socialism would be a happy compromise between the extremes of the communist and capitalist models.

One theoretical advantage of state-owned enterprises is that they can combine various commercial and social objectives in a way that private companies would not. While a private company would be only interested in increasing profits, a state-owned company could also pursue desirable social objectives. For example, it could reduce unemployment by hiring more workers, subsidize prices paid by the poor, invest in industries or regions of the country identified as high priority by economic planners, provide higher wages and better working conditions, and minimize environmental pollution.

Unfortunately, the practical result is that state-owned enterprises did not achieve either their social or commercial objectives very well. This confused mixture of objectives meant that it was impossible to measure the performance of the enterprise. For example, was the enterprise losing money because it was poorly managed or because it was keeping prices low and investing in backward regions of the country as required by the government? It is revealing that perhaps the worst pollution in the 20th century was caused by government agencies and state-owned enterprises in the former Soviet Union. It is common practice when buying real estate in Russia to first check it with a Geiger counter to make certain that no one has used it as a dumping ground for radioactive waste.

Nehru's economic beliefs also fit nicely with his political beliefs, namely, nonalliance in the international conflict between capitalism and communism. He was one of the leaders of the nonaligned movement and believed that poor countries should be independent of both the communist block led by the Soviet Union and the western capitalist countries led by the United States.

As other colonies gained their independence in the 1950s and 1960s, they too had to choose an economic model. Since the weaknesses in the Communist model did not become apparent to many until the 1980s, their natural choice was to follow the example of Nehru and India.

Latin America

The history of economic development in Latin America took a somewhat different course because countries in that region had won their independence in the early 19th century, but the end result was similar to India's and that of the former colonies in Africa.[7] Views on economic development in Latin America were shaped primarily by the experience of those countries during the Great Depression of the 1930s rather than by their experience as colonies. In the 1930s, they relied heavily on the export of agricultural products and raw materials whose prices fell the most during the Depression.

This reliance led to the belief that their economies were too dependent on selling raw materials to the rich countries in order to buy their finished products (this theory came to be known as *dependencia*). The rich industrial nations at the center of the world's economy would always be able to exploit the countries on the periphery that only supplied the raw materials. Import substitution was encouraged by protecting domestic industry using high tariffs and quotas. Domestic industry was further encouraged through government ownership, subsidies, and regulation. The key qualification of a successful businessman was his ability to exploit government controls and regulation rather than to sell high-quality products at reasonable prices. Until the early 1970s, this strategy of import substitution seemed to work. Incomes doubled from 1950 to 1970. However, with the debt crisis of the 1980s, views began to change.

East Asian Miracle Countries

Under a strategy of import substitution adopted by most poor countries after the Second World War, a country increases the production of industrial products primarily to meet domestic demand rather than for export. This strategy reduces the importance of foreign trade as both exports and imports decline. Some countries in East Asia, notably Japan, Singapore, South Korea, and Taiwan, adopted a different strategy that emphasized the export of industrial products or what came to be known as export-led growth.[8] Governments encouraged some of their industries to compete in international markets, and many became world class by taking market share from industries in the United States and Europe. Various policies were introduced to favor those industries that the government thought could best compete internationally, sometimes called "picking winners." As a result, those countries had some of the highest rates of economic growth ever seen.

The East Asian financial crisis in the 1990s, however, exposed at least two weaknesses in this strategy. One weakness, discussed in Chapter 8, is that businesses producing primarily for the domestic market were protected from competition. An undervalued exchange rate that encouraged exports also discouraged imports. These economies tended to have a dual economy—highly efficient and modern businesses that could compete in world markets but high cost, backward, and inefficient businesses that sold their products and services domestically. A second weakness is that government policies designed to encourage specific industries led to crony capitalism in which politicians used these policies to benefit relatives, friends, and political supporters. Often policies designed to support rapidly growing industries ended up supporting declining industries with political influence.

For example, the ability of the Japanese Ministry of International Trade and Industry (MITI) to guide business and industry toward faster economic growth was widely accepted both within Japan and in other countries that were encouraged to follow this example. Recent studies have been more skeptical: an economist at the University of Tokyo and a professor at Harvard Law School argue that this myth was created by government officials who wanted to justify their pork-barrel politics and by Marxist economists who dominated university economics departments in Japan and favored government planning over private markets.[9]

Economic Power Is Political Power

Government officials and politicians in countries that did follow the Nehruvian socialist model find it difficult to admit that they were backing the wrong horse in the race between economic systems. There is a saying that new ideas don't replace old ideas—instead new people replace old people. We may have to wait for a generational change in the officials and politicians of poor countries before there is wholehearted acceptance of the role of the private sector.

In addition to their doubts about the merits of a private free-market economy, government politicians and officials have more selfish reasons for not reducing government ownership and control over the economy. Economic power can be used to sustain political power.

The party in power that controls large parts of the economy through state ownership or regulation can use its control to keep that party in power. The party can give political supporters jobs in state-owned companies or in bloated government agencies. The party can assist private companies owned by supporters of the party with lucrative government contracts, subsidized loans from state-owned banks, and protection from competition.

Again, examples of this kind of behavior are numerous. Let me give just two from Sri Lanka. First, the minister in charge of the country's ports forced the port officials to hire thousands of new employees from the minister's region of the country. This action was designed to help the minister win the next election. Unfortunately, it undercut attempts to restructure and privatize the ports.

Second, before an election, the government would often hire thousands of recent college graduates to be schoolteachers. These graduates did not have the training necessary to obtain good jobs in the private sector and had been waiting months or even years for a job to open up in the public sector. Unfortunately, they were not trained to be schoolteachers, which not only led to a decline in the quality of education but also to an increase in the number of graduates without the skills needed for a modern economy.

To add insult to injury, the government for the most part does not allow private schools to compete with the government schools. Therefore, children have no choice but to attend the low-quality public schools. The popular belief seems to be that instead of at least some children receiving a good education from private schools, all children must receive the same bad education from public schools in the name of promoting equality.

In addition to keeping their political power, politicians and officials often use control over the economy to enrich themselves personally. Instead of the government's offering a *helping hand* to the private sector, it is often a *grabbing hand*.[10] Numerous politicians and officials who have spent their entire careers working for modest salaries in the public sector somehow manage to own huge homes, drive expensive cars, and give lavish weddings for their daughters. In Russia, one game of foreign advisers was to count the number of low-paid government officials wearing expensive Rolex watches.

Unfortunately, the low salaries paid to government officials guarantee that they must become corrupt, at least to some extent, to survive. A private-sector businessman in Pakistan compared for me the salary he has to pay qualified managers for his factories with what the government pays senior civil servants with even greater responsibilities. Though the businessman railed against the pervasive corruption in government, he understood why it occurs.

One strategy to improve the quality of government and to reduce corruption is to reduce government activities to only those that are absolutely essential for the government to carry out. This strategy would allow the government to get rid of incompetent officials, pay the remainder a competitive salary, and then crack down on corruption. Misguided government policies intended to help the private sector are certainly at the top of the list to be eliminated.

Poor Expert Advice

Another reason why some poor countries continue with harmful policies is the poor advice given by experts from rich countries. When an expert from the United States, Germany, Great Britain, or another rich country is asked for advice on policies and institutions to develop the private sector, the expert is likely to recommend what he knows, namely, the policies and institutions that exist in his home country. Too often, the expert may not be aware of approaches used in other countries or take into consideration the weaknesses in the governmental, legal, and political systems of the poor country that will make it difficult for that country to successfully implement his recommendations.

Even experts from poor countries may make the same mistake. Often they have been trained at universities in rich countries (Harvard, Oxford, University of Paris, and so forth). These universities naturally emphasize the policies and institutions that exist in their countries. I am amazed, for example, how U.S. thinking about economics, policies, and institutions dominates the thinking of World Bank staff even though only a minority are citizens of the United States.

Although I am a U.S. citizen and educated in the United States, I readily admit that the policies and institutions of my country are often not appropriate for poor countries. An example that I discuss in more detail later is the system of corporate ownership in the United States. Large U.S. corporations typically have thousands of owners (shareholders) none of whom own more than a few percent of the total shares of the company. Some experts hold this example up as the ideal to which other countries should strive. One reason given is that it results in a large stock market. I question whether it has worked well in the United States and certainly do not believe that it is the best model for most poor countries because of their inability to create the institutions needed to protect the rights of small shareholders.

Unfortunately, government officials and politicians in poor countries often accept this poor advice from international experts out of a sense of national pride. If these policies and institutions are considered the best for the United States, Germany, or France, then these officials and politicians want to have only the best for their own countries as well. They are unwilling to admit that their countries may not be able to successfully implement these policies and institutions. If a foreign consultant recommends that government officials in a poor country adopt policies different from those in rich countries because these officials are ineffectual or corrupt, he is not likely to be popular or selected for any future consulting contracts.

The concept of *appropriate technology* is widely accepted in discussing poor countries. Similarly, the concept of appropriate government policies and institutions should have greater acceptance. As an example of appropriate technology, farms in rich countries often use large tractors capable of quickly plowing hundreds of hectares because the farms are large. It is well recognized that given the small size of farms in many poor countries, this is not an appropriate technology for them. Instead, farmers should probably use small motorized tillers appropriate for a farm of a few hectares or less. In the same way, government policies and institutions appropriate for rich countries may not be appropriate for poor countries, so other policies need to be developed that suit their circumstances.

In this regard, examples from the past in rich countries may be more appropriate for poor countries today. Today's rich countries were once poor countries. Policies and institutions that existed then may be better models to follow by today's poor countries. Economic historians may have more to say about the best policies and institutions in today's poor countries than other experts.

Market Failures

The economics profession is also to blame for encouraging poor countries to intervene in the private sector. Economists study the weaknesses as well as the strengths of a private market economy. Economists call these weaknesses *market failures*. Too often, the unstated assumption is that governments should adopt policies to fix these market failures once they are identified. Clever economists theorize at length about the existence of these failures and devise subtle and sophisticated government policies that will eliminate these failures.

As just one example, the well-known economist Joseph E. Stiglitz presented an influential paper titled "The Role of the State in Financial Markets" before a conference at the World Bank in 1993. Stiglitz was then a member of the Council of Economic Advisers to the President of the United States. He later became chief economist and vice president of the World Bank and a winner of the Nobel Prize in economics.

According to Stiglitz, "[t]his paper reexamines the role of the state in financial markets and identifies seven major market failures that provide a potential rationale for government intervention."[11] These are

1. monitoring as a public good,
2. externalities of monitoring, selection, and lending,
3. externalities of financial disruption,
4. missing and incomplete markets,
5. imperfect competition,
6. pareto inefficiency of competitive markets, and
7. uninformed investors.

I won't attempt to further describe these failures, in part because I am not certain that I fully understand them.

Stiglitz then goes on to discuss government policies that might correct these market failures. Since his reputation as an economist, including the granting of the Nobel Prize, is based on his research into these market failures, it is perhaps not surprising that he believes governments should adopt policies to correct the market failures that he has discovered. Some of the policies he seems to favor include various forms of financial market regulation, directed credit schemes, limits on the interest rates that can be paid to bank depositors, financial repression to lower interest rates charged to borrowers, and limiting competition from both domestic and foreign banks.

In only one place does he briefly mention that governments may not have the ability, resources, or incentives to actually implement these subtle and sophisticated policies. If I could be certain that someone as honest, smart, and capable as Stiglitz had the authority and resources to implement these policies, I might be willing to accept his advice.

Instead I am inclined to accept the conclusions of another expert at the conference who commented on the Stiglitz paper, Jaime Jaramillo-Vallejo from Colombia. He states, ". . . Stiglitz is asking us to assume that governments all over the world—especially in poor countries—are wise, fair, and efficient enough to carry out the kind of 'perfect' intrusive intervention suggested by him. It is as if . . . we had not learned from the experience with the different forms of government intervention that we have seen in this century."[12]

In the balance of this book, I analyze government policies proposed to help develop the private sector, and I conclude that many of these policies are not appropriate for poor countries. Where possible, I suggest policies that are more suited to these countries and argue that more research needs to be done to find appropriate policies. In subsequent chapters, I discuss government policies in the areas of privatization, banking, capital markets, corporate governance, regulation and licensing, competition policy, and bankruptcy.

2. Economic Growth: The Only Way Out of Poverty

The only way to reduce poverty around the world is to increase the rate of economic growth. The only way to increase the rate of economic growth is for governments to put in place policies and institutions that encourage the private sector to become more efficient and productive and to grow faster. In this way, the private sector will expand production, increase employment, and pay higher wages and salaries. This is how the rich countries achieved high incomes for most of their citizens. I see little reason to believe that today's poor countries will be able to reduce poverty in any other way.

I believe that this linkage between the development of the private sector and reducing poverty is obvious and indisputable. Much of the recent debate about how to help the poor, however, plays down this linkage or ignores it entirely.

Millennium Development Goals

An example of minimizing the importance of economic growth and the role of the private sector is the recent United Nations Millennium Development Goals adopted by a resolution of the General Assembly in September 2000.[1] A simplified version provided later in a report by the secretary general includes the following eight goals:

1. Eradicate extreme poverty and hunger.
2. Achieve universal primary education.
3. Promote general equality and empower women.
4. Reduce child mortality.
5. Improve maternal health.
6. Combat HIV/AIDS, malaria, and other diseases.
7. Ensure environmental sustainability.
8. Develop a global partnership for development.[2]

21

The target date for achieving these goals is the year 2015. These goals seem to have been adopted by a number of international organizations, including the World Bank, the Organization for Economic Cooperation and Development, and the International Monetary Fund, as the basis for their future activities.

Higher incomes brought about by faster economic growth would certainly help to achieve most of these goals. Even achieving the goal of environmental sustainability is helped because citizens with higher incomes begin to demand a cleaner and safer environment in which to live. The very poor cannot afford this luxury.

The original resolution of the General Assembly establishing these goals does not mention economic growth or the role of the private sector. The private sector is only referred to in a derogatory way in the statement, " . . . the central challenge we face today is to ensure that globalization becomes a positive force for all the world's people. For while globalization offers great opportunities, at present its benefits are very unevenly shared, while its costs are unevenly distributed."[3] This statement seems to support the critics of greater international trade, economic liberalization, and foreign investment who argue that economic growth has not helped the poor and has only helped either the rich countries or international companies.

Later when the secretary general lays out a plan to achieve these goals in a report to the General Assembly, he does mention briefly, "[i]n order to significantly reduce poverty and promote development it is essential to achieve sustained and broad-based economic growth."[4] He only mentions the role of the private sector in achieving this growth by pointing out how foreign capital can supplement the domestic resources of a nation but then goes on to point out the dangers of foreign capital because it may be short term and volatile.[5]

As another example, the World Bank has a Web site devoted to achieving the Millennium Development Goals.[6] It also gives little emphasis to economic growth and the private sector as a way to achieve these goals. Growth is only mentioned in the discussion of the first goal of eradicating extreme poverty and the eighth goal of developing a global partnership but not the other goals.

Is More Aid the Answer?

The primary emphasis of these discussions of the Millennium Development Goals is that aid from the rich to the poor nations must be increased. For example, the World Bank has estimated that aid must be increased by $40–$60 billion per year to achieve these goals by the year 2015.[7]

How this aid will be used to achieve the goals is unclear. Will this aid be used to finance an international welfare program in which the rich countries supplement the income of the very poor and pay for their health and education? Will this welfare program continue forever because economic growth remains low, and thus incomes in poor countries do not increase? Alternatively, will this aid be used to increase the rate of economic growth so that the income of the poor is increased and thus they can pay for more food, better health and education, less pollution, and so forth? After incomes have been increased, the aid from the rich countries can be reduced or eliminated.

The World Bank study that estimates this required increase in aid is contradictory about the use of the aid.[8] First, the study says that all of this aid will be needed to increase domestic investment and thus increase the rate of economic growth. Second, the study says that this aid will be needed to pay for better education, health care, and environmental protection.

I am not complaining about increasing aid from the rich to the poor countries if it is used effectively to increase the rate of economic growth. The rich countries can easily afford an increase of $40–$60 billion. This aid would amount to less that 0.2 percent of the annual income of an average resident of a rich country or a paltry $60 annually. When people in rich countries drive cars as big as the houses in poor countries, the rich can easily afford this modest help to the poor of the world.

There is considerable disagreement, however, over whether an increase in aid results in higher economic growth. The history of foreign aid to poor countries is not encouraging. Countries that have received large amounts of aid for decades have failed to grow. Some experts argue that aid actually reduced the rate of economic growth in poor countries.[9] Even the World Bank, the largest supplier of aid, now argues that aid only helps in those countries with good institutions and policies.[10] Thus, more and more aid from international development institutions is provided only if governments adopt the policies that these institutions think will increase the rate of economic growth. The theme of this book, however, is that governments cannot effectively implement some of the policies designed to help the private sector recommended by these institutions and that other policies are better.

If the World Bank study is correct and $40–$60 billion of additional aid will be effective in increasing the rate of economic growth and an equal amount is needed to pay for minimum levels of health care and education, I would gladly support an increase in aid of twice this amount and thus meet both needs. I am concerned, however, about how little emphasis in the discussion of the need for this aid is given to the role of economic growth and the private sector in reducing poverty and how to use this aid to increase the rate of growth.

Unless one can show that aid directly benefits a specific poor person (for example, providing him or her with food or paying for education and health), then many seem to believe that aid is not really helping the poor. Though increasing the rate of economic growth is an indirect way of helping the poor and identifying exactly who benefits is not easy, it will have a much larger and more permanent benefit to the poor.[11]

Why do some international institutions play down the role of economic growth in helping the poor and instead emphasize direct assistance? Perhaps these institutions do not believe that people will understand the indirect connection between economic growth and reducing poverty. It is no accident that charities requesting donations show a poor child living in a slum and imply that any aid will go to that child. In other words, emphasizing direct help to the poor instead of economic growth is good advertising and good public relations.

Also given the recent complaints about globalization and economic liberalization, emphasizing economic growth through development of the private sector may be seen as supporting big companies, the rich, and the powerful at the expense of the downtrodden poor. It is not obvious to many people why increasing productivity at a large company helps poor people, in particular, if it means a reduced workforce at the company.

An Example: India

Attempts to reduce poverty without economic growth are doomed to failure in most poor countries. This belief contrasts with what seems to be the belief of a growing number of people who oppose what they call *globalization*. Though the opponents of globalization have a variety of views, one is that economic growth mostly helps the rich and that economic growth should be made more pro-poor.

In the absence of growth, the only way to reduce poverty is to take income from the relatively rich in the country and give it to the poor, in other words, the Robin Hood plan for poverty reduction. However, this plan will do little to reduce poverty in most poor countries simply because the total income of the country is not adequate to raise people out of poverty even if it were possible to distribute income equally among all citizens. When the total size of the pie is small and the number of eaters is large, cutting the pie into more equal pieces still leaves everyone hungry.

I can understand the rage and injustice that people feel when they see a few rich people living in the midst of millions of very poor people. However, redistributing the income of the relatively small number of rich people to the vastly greater number of poor people will do little to help the poor. India, for example, has a population of more than one billion and thus has many rich people even though they amount to only a small percentage of the population. The rich include large landowners, business executives, owners of private companies, and corrupt politicians and government officials. However, because of the vastly greater number of poor people, taking away all of the income of the rich and giving it to the poor will not help the poor very much.

Many Indians now live in abject poverty. Roughly 80 percent of the population live on less than $2 per day or $730 per year (converted into dollars at purchasing power parity exchange rates). Even worse, 35 percent live on less than $1 per day or $365 per year (see Table 2-1). The benchmark of $1 per day is a generally accepted international standard for determining the level of extreme poverty in a poor country. At the other end of the income spectrum, the 10 percent of the population with the highest incomes have an average level of consumption of $6,213 per year.[12] (Note that in my discussion of Tables 2-1 and 2-2, I am being somewhat imprecise by using the terms income and consumption interchangeably as if they are always equal. This is probably true for a poor person, but the income of rich people may be greater than consumption because they are able to save part of their income.)

I agree that the government in such a country as India should try to do what it can to redistribute income to the poorest, but I am not

25

Table 2-1
THE RICH AND POOR IN INDIA—2001
(PURCHASING POWER PARITY)[1]

Population (millions)	1,032
Gross National Income ($ billion)	$2,913
Household Consumption ($ billion)	$1,914
Government Expenditures ($ billion)	$507
POOR ($1 per day benchmark)	
Share of Population with Consumption Below $1 a Day	34.7%
Poverty Gap %[2]	8.2%
Total Poverty Gap ($ billion)[3]	$31
Total Poverty Gap as Percent of Government Expenditures	6.1%
Average Poverty Gap Per Poor Person	$86
POOR ($2 per day benchmark)	
Share of Population with Consumption Below $2 a Day	79.9%
Poverty Gap %[2]	35.3%
Total Poverty Gap ($ billion)[4]	$266
Total Poverty Gap as Percent of Government Expenditures	52.5%
Average Poverty Gap Per Poor Person	$323
AVERAGE (all citizens)	
Average Consumption Per Year	$1,855
RICH (10% of population with highest incomes)	
Number (millions)	103
Share of Consumption	33.5%
Total Consumption ($ billion)	$641
Average Consumption Per Year	$6,213

SOURCE: World Bank, *World Development Indicators* and International Monetary Fund, *International Financial Statistics*.

[1] Values in dollars calculated at purchasing power parity exchange rates using a conversion factor of 7.8 rupees/dollar.

[2] See Table 2.6 of *World Development Indicators* for a definition.

[3] The total increase in consumption by the poor necessary to raise them to the $1 per day benchmark. Equal to 8.2% × $365 × 1,032 million.

[4] The total increase in consumption by the poor necessary to raise them to the $2 per day benchmark. Equal to 35.3% × $730 × 1,032 million.

optimistic that the government can do much. Given the limited revenues of the government in a poor country, it simply does not have the money to provide much help. Even worse, what money that is provided to help the poor is often wasted because of incompetent and corrupt politicians and government officials. As discussed in more detail below, these same problems are a major factor in determining what the government can do to help the private sector.

How much would it cost the government of India to substantially improve the lot of the very poor by raising their income up to a minimum of $1 per day? In the case of India, the government would have to redistribute about $31 billion per year (again measured in purchasing power parity dollars) from the rest of the population to those poor living on less that $1 per day to raise their income up to this benchmark (see Table 2-1). I refer to this as the Total Poverty Gap.[13] On average, a poor person living on less than $1 per day would have to receive $86 per year from the government to raise him or her out of poverty by this definition. Although $31 billion is a large sum of money, it amounts to only 1 percent of gross national income in India.

This additional expenditure to help the poor, however, should be compared with the current level of government expenditure and tax revenue to see whether such an increase is feasible. In other words, how much would taxes have to be raised on the nonpoor to pay for this redistribution of income to the poor? The additional government expenditure required for this transfer of income would amount to about 6 percent of current expenditures, and taxes would have to be increased by the same proportion.

A similar calculation can be done for the $2 per day or $730 per year benchmark. In this case, the average poor person living on less than $2 per day would have to receive about $323 per year from the government to raise him or her up to this benchmark. Because so many more people fall below this benchmark (about 80 percent of the population), the total amount required would be $266 billion (Total Poverty Gap). This equals more than half of current government expenditures.

Thus, at first glance, if the government had the political will to do so, it might be possible to redistribute enough income to eliminate the worst poverty in India using the $1 per day benchmark. Only a 6 percent increase in government expenditures and taxes would appear to be needed. To raise everyone above the $2 per day level, however, seems impossible because it would require a 50 percent increase in government expenditures and taxes.

Another option might be to convince the rich countries to provide some of the money in the form of foreign aid. The foreign aid would be directly distributed to the poor as a cash payment rather than used to fund specific projects such as health care or activities such as building schools. The total foreign aid now being given to poor countries, however, seems small by comparison to the need. The total is about $50 billion per year (UN Secretary-General Kofi Annan and World Bank President James Wolfensohn have called for aid to be doubled to $100 billion a year). Thus, $50 billion might be enough to raise the very poor in just one country, India, above the $1 per day benchmark (as calculated above, $31 billion would be the minimum needed). It would certainly not be adequate for all the poor countries of the world.

Targeting Help for the Poor

This simple calculation, however, ignores the fact that no income redistribution or welfare program can be perfectly targeted. This calculation assumes that government officials know exactly the current level of income for every poor person and thus how much additional income they need to raise them to the benchmark. Although a poor person needs $86 per year on average to rise up to the $1 per day benchmark, the actual amount could range from $1 to $365 depending on each person's individual circumstances. For the income redistribution program to be perfectly targeted, no person should receive $1 more or $1 less than required to raise him or her up to the benchmark.

Even if the government knew the current incomes of the approximately 350 million people in India living on less than $1 per day, attempting to transfer just the right amount of income for each person to raise him or her up to the benchmark would completely destroy any incentive for a poor person to work and earn income. If a poor person earned an additional dollar of income, the payment from the government would be reduced by exactly $1 under a perfectly targeted welfare scheme. This is like a tax rate of 100 percent on additional income. If this were the case, a poor person would say why work at all.

So as not to destroy incentives to work, the reduction in the payment from the government must be less than the increase in a poor person's income from other sources such as farming or laboring. For example, the payment from the government could be reduced by $0.50 for each additional dollar of income earned from other sources. This means that payments would have to be made to those whose income exceeded the benchmark of $1 per day unless the initial payment for someone who has no other income is much less than the $365 required to reach the benchmark. As a consequence, even the best designed scheme for redistributing income will cost a great deal more than the simple calculation of $31 billion given previously because the government must make payments to those whose income is above the benchmark. If not, the redistribution of income will fail to raise all of the poor up to the benchmark.

Wasted Help for the Poor

Based on past experience, government schemes to redistribute income to the poor are likely to suffer from other problems as well. Too often, government policies and programs that are intended to help the poor often benefit mostly the middle and upper classes. One reason is corruption.

A poor villager in India told me a story supposedly first told by Rajeev Gandhi, a former prime minister and grandson of Nehru. The story is that the government sends an elephant from New Delhi to help the poor in a remote village. By the time it gets there, nothing is left but the tail. Corrupt government officials and politicians are often the major beneficiaries of these programs. This story seems to reflect a widespread belief by the poor in India and elsewhere about government attempts to help them.

Another Indian villager told me about a government program to build concrete houses in his village to replace the mud huts covered with thatched roofs. He showed me the houses. After the houses were built, the villagers complained about the poor quality of the concrete and that the houses were immediately beginning to crumble. The private construction company that built the houses was honest about the cause. By the time the company paid bribes to government officials to obtain the contract to build the houses, the company had to skimp on the quality of the concrete to make a profit.

Even if corruption were not a problem, programs or policies to help the poor often are diverted to help the middle and upper classes, in other words, a subsidy for the relatively well-off. This is not surprising because higher income individuals are usually better educated, live in the capital city or other major cities, are more engaged in politics, and more likely to influence government decisions. Also politicians and government officials themselves benefit from these subsidies, and this increases their popularity in parliament.

Many government officials in poor countries say that they try to help the poor by subsidizing the prices of products and services that the poor buy. The usual result, however, is that the middle and upper classes consume far more of these subsidized products and services and thus receive most of the benefit. The cost to the government of these programs is high, and yet they do not help the poor very much.

To give just a few examples, kerosene is often subsidized based on the argument that the poor need cheap fuel for cooking and lighting. In fact, the very poor mostly use sticks, straw, or dried dung for cooking because they cannot afford kerosene even at subsidized prices or there is no distribution system to supply kerosene in remote areas. Most of the subsidized kerosene is actually bought by the middle and upper classes.

Health care often receives large subsidies from the government, but most of the subsidies go to the few modern hospitals in the large cities serving the urban middle and upper classes. Little goes to the primitive clinics in remote villages where most of the poor live. Similarly, electricity and telephone service is often subsidized, but typically a high percentage of the poor live in rural areas that do not have access to these services. Even in cities, the poorest often live in shantytowns that are not served by the state-owned power and telephone companies.

Schools that serve the children of the relatively well-off receive a large share of total government expenditures on education compared with what the rural schools that serve the poor receive. For example, Figure 2-1 shows for various countries the percent of total public spending on primary and secondary education received by the richest 20 percent of the population and the poorest 20 percent. In only two countries (Romania and South Africa) do the poorest 20 percent actually receive more than 20 percent of the total. In most countries,

Figure 2-1
PUBLIC SPENDING ON PRIMARY AND SECONDARY EDUCATION FOR
THE RICHEST AND POOREST 20 PERCENT OF POPULATION
(PERCENT OF TOTAL SPENDING)

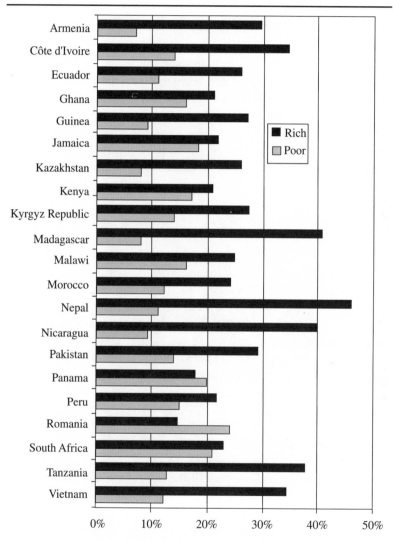

SOURCE: World Bank, *World Development Report 2000/2001: Attacking Poverty* (Oxford University Press, 2000), Table 5.1, p. 80.

31

the poor receive substantially less than 20 percent while the rich receive more than 20 percent. If spending on higher education was also included, the imbalance would be even greater.

Is Equal Poverty Better?

Even if I am completely wrong in my arguments about the feasibility of redistributing income to help the poor, there is still one incontrovertible argument in favor of economic growth as the only way to reduce poverty. Again using India as an example, suppose that all of the problems I have described in redistributing income could be overcome. The government could raise the necessary revenues through higher taxes, the income redistribution program could be efficiently targeted to the poor without greatly reducing incentives to work, and corruption or diversion to the relatively rich could be kept to a minimum.

Though incomes might be more evenly distributed, the people of India would still be relegated to an average level of consumption per person of only about $1,855 per year (see Table 2-1). Though this level is certainly better than the $1 or $2 per day benchmarks, the average person in India would still be poor. Even worse without economic growth, there is no hope that the average person will be better off tomorrow than today. India may have a more equal distribution of income, but the result is that everyone is equally poor. I would not like to be the person who tells Indian citizens that they can never expect to be better off than they are today.

Does Growth Help the Poor?

Those who give little importance to economic growth as the solution to poverty seem to believe that growth will mostly improve the incomes of the rich and not benefit the poor. Even if this were true, which I don't believe, the total pie is bigger and thus it is more feasible to redistribute income from the rich to the poor. Even those who favor redistribution of income to help the poor should also favor economic growth because there is more total income to redistribute.

Part of the debate about whether economic growth helps the poor may be the result of how one defines helping the poor. Again using

Table 2-2
HYPOTHETICAL EXAMPLE OF HOW GROWTH RAISES
INCOME/CONSUMPTION

Person	Old	New	Increase
Rich	$6,213	$7,456	$1,243
Average	$1,855	$2,226	$ 371
Poor	$ 365	$ 438	$ 73

India as an example, Table 2-2 shows how economic growth hypothetically might increase income and consumption for three persons—the average person in the richest 10 percent of the population, a person with just the average level of consumption for the entire nation, and a poor person living on just $1 per day. Someone with a mathematical inclination might immediately spot that the level of income for each of these three persons has increased by exactly 20 percent though the absolute amount of the increase varies greatly.

A critic of growth as a way to reduce poverty will argue that this example proves that most of the benefit of growth goes to the relatively well-off and little goes to the poor. The $1,243 increase in the income or consumption for the rich person is 17 times greater than the $73 increase for the poor person.

A defender of growth, however, will argue that the percentage increase in income is exactly the same for all people. In other words, growth has benefited everyone proportionately. Growth has not worsened the distribution of income, nor has it improved the distribution. Without economic growth, the rich person had an income about 17 times greater than the poor person. With growth, the ratio is still the same, but both are better off.

A study by the World Bank suggests that growth benefits both rich and poor by about the same proportion. This study of 92 poor countries finds that the income of the poor typically rises in proportion to overall income.[14] For some countries over some time periods, the income of the poor grew at a rate somewhat faster than overall income, but in other countries over other time periods, it grew slower. There seems to be no consistent pattern. In other words, the percentage increase but not the absolute value of the increase in income is roughly the same for all income classes. This hypothetical example from India is typical of most countries.

33

I would prefer growth to increase the income of the poor relatively more than the rich, thus making the distribution of income more equal. The state of economic science, however, is such that no one really knows which government policies will result in this type of growth. Economists have a hard enough time determining what will increase the overall rate of growth in a country much less channeling that growth to a particular group in the country, in other words, how to create more pro-poor growth.

The same World Bank study also tried to see whether certain government policies were likely to result in more pro-poor growth. Unfortunately, the authors could not find any evidence of this. We can hope that economists someday will learn which government policies will make growth more beneficial to the poor compared with the rich.

Helping the Rich in Poor Countries Is Not So Bad

Though I would favor pro-poor growth policies if they could be found, I would not want to completely discount or place no importance on increasing the income of even the relatively rich in a country like India. The reason is that most people who might be considered rich in India are still poor by the standards of a rich country.

In India, the average rich person has an income and level of consumption about three times higher than the average person and 17 times higher than a poor person living on just $1 per day. However, the per capita level of income or consumption of this average rich person ($6,213) would still be small compared with the average income or level of consumption in a rich country.

In the United States, for example, the average private consumption per person is about $23,000 per year. The U.S. government would officially classify an individual with an income of only $6,213 per year as poor. In the United States, the official benchmark to determine whether a single person is poor is about $9,000 per year (higher levels apply to couples and families). This hypothetical rich person in India would still be considered poor in the United States. Thus policies that raise the income of someone considered rich in India may still reduce poverty in the world by using other definitions of poverty.

Growth Has Reduced World Poverty

Recent evidence suggests that growth has lowered poverty by more than generally believed. Surjit Bhalla argues that data on poverty provided by the World Bank understate the decline in world poverty resulting from economic growth.[15] On a global level, he concludes that economic growth has been pro-poor during the last two decades of globalization. Using the $1 per day benchmark, Bhalla finds that 44 percent of the world's population in 1980 was poor. Using the same benchmark two decades later in 2000, only 13 percent were poor. In contrast to the popular belief that faster economic growth caused by globalization over this period did not help the poor very much, Bhalla concludes that the decline in world poverty has been much greater over these two decades than during the previous three decades following the end of the Second World War.

3. Large Companies: Heroes or Villains?

A Local Family-Owned Business

Not far from my home in a suburb of Washington, D.C., sits a modest, red-brick office building on a street with similar buildings. In the other buildings are banks, real estate agents, doctors, law offices, construction companies, and other businesses typical of a residential community. In the red-brick building is a business owned and managed by two brothers now around 70 years old. Their sister is also employed in the family business. They inherited the business from their father and grandfather. The two brothers are sometimes seen walking up the street to a snack bar for lunch and then returning to work. They live not far from their business. The odd thing about this building is that there is no sign or other indication of the name or type of business located inside.

Few people realize that this building is the international headquarters of the world's largest candy company—Mars, Incorporated. Almost everyone has used or seen its products. These include candy bars (3 Musketeers, Milky Way, Mars, M&M's, and Snickers), packaged foods (Uncle Ben's rice), and pet food (Whiskas and Pedigree). The company competes with other international giants such as Hershey and Nestlé and with many local candy companies around the world. It has annual sales of about $15 billion, 30,000 employees, and offices in more than 60 countries.

The two brothers (John Franklyn Mars and Forrest Edward Mars) and their sister (Jacqueline Badger Mars) are among the richest people in the world. According to a list compiled by *Forbes Magazine*, they are tied for number 21 in the list of the world's richest for 2003 and each has a net worth of about $10 billion. Their family wealth approaches $30 billion. This figure exceeds the annual gross national product of many countries.

This company is secretive. Because it is a privately held company and none of its shares are publicly traded on a stock exchange, it is not required to disclose information about its operations to the general public. For example, it does not issue an expensively printed annual report containing its financial statements as well as photos of happy and smiling shareholders, customers, and workers. Though the company advertises its products, the company does not have a public relations office to promote its public image by issuing press releases or holding press conferences describing what wonderful things it does for the community.[1]

The company, no doubt, provides financial information to the tax authorities as required by law in the various countries in which it operates. It may also provide financial information to its creditors such as banks so that they will loan the company money, though I have no way of knowing whether it actually has borrowed any money.

The company also abides by laws and regulations concerning the treatment of its workers, health and safety of its products, and protection of the environment; or, at least, I have never read any complaints that it does not. It must pay competitive salaries and treat its workers well or else it would not be able to attract 30,000 capable and motivated workers and managers that make it a successful company. The two brothers and their sister cannot expect to run such a large company without qualified help.

Though this company is certainly unusual compared with other large international companies, is there anything wrong or bad about how the company chooses to organize itself and operate? This type of family-owned company is common in most poor countries. When one reads much of the criticism today about large companies, particularly international, closely held, and family-owned companies, this criticism seems to apply to Mars, Incorporated.

Large companies, according to their critics, should focus on such objectives as fairness, transparency, accountability, and social responsibility in addition to or instead of the traditional objective of maximizing profits.[2] These critics might complain that the Mars company fails to achieve any of these objectives except maximizing profits. It is owned entirely by a powerful, rich family, which these critics would regard as unfair. Ordinary people are not allowed to own any shares in the company or influence its operations. If all companies had this type of ownership, stock markets would cease to exist because they exist primarily to allow small investors to trade their shares.

Critics might further complain that this company is secretive and certainly not transparent in its finances or operations. This family controls vast economic resources but is not accountable to anyone else for their use. It shows no social responsibility other than that required by law. It seems to believe that its only social responsibility is to pay its taxes and comply with government laws and regulations. The company's only objectives are to manufacture high-quality products, sell them at competitive prices around the world, and earn a profit for the owners.

In the last few years, there has been a growing concern about the role of large companies in poor countries and debate about what must be done to ensure that they promote the welfare of the entire nation rather than just the interest of the owners or managers of the companies. There seems to be at least three related reasons frequently given as to why large companies have performed badly in poor countries:

- Corporate governance is weak in many poor countries. For example, weak corporate governance was a major cause of the East Asian financial crisis.
- Ownership of large companies in most poor countries is concentrated in the hands of a few investors. More widespread ownership of companies will develop capital markets, in particular, by encouraging trading of shares on the stock market.
- Companies fail to behave in a socially responsible manner, and they should adopt one of the newly proposed standards of social responsibility.

In this chapter, I examine these alleged reasons for poor performance to determine the extent that they are valid. Analyzing these reasons is not easy because critics of large corporations often mean different things when they refer to corporate governance, stock market development, social responsibility, and corporate ownership.

Admittedly, there are numerous cases in which companies have failed to perform well. The objective of this book is to examine the important reasons for poor corporate performance and what governments should do about them. However, as one might guess from my use of the Mars company as an example, I conclude that the three reasons listed are not important. Even worse, focusing on them diverts attention from the important reasons and shifts the blame for poor performance to the owners and managers of companies rather than to where it belongs, namely, various laws, policies, and institutions created by governments.

Types of Corporate Ownership

Much of the debate about the performance of large corporations involves who owns these companies. Are they owned by other corporations, financial institutions such as banks or pension funds, a single individual, a family, a small group of investors, many shareholders, or the state? It will help to clarify the following discussion if I first define the various types of ownership and present data on who owns corporations in both poor and rich countries to the extent that data are available.

It is useful to distinguish between three types of company ownership:

- *Closely Held*: All of the shares are held by only one investor or no more than a few investors each of whom owns a substantial percentage of the shares.
- *Controlling Investor*: A controlling block of shares but not all shares are held by a single investor or a small group of investors with similar interests and objectives. Such an investor could be a rich individual, a family, or a large financial institution located where such ownership is permitted by law, another company, or the state. This investor is sometimes referred to as a *strategic investor*. The remaining shares are widely held by many investors none of whom owns more than a small percentage of the total. These investors are referred to as *portfolio investors* because this company is just one of many they hold in their portfolios or as *passive investors* because they do not take an active role in the management of the company.
- *Widely Held*: All of the shares are held by many portfolio investors each of whom owns only a small percentage of the total. This type of ownership is also referred to as widespread or dispersed ownership.

I will mostly use private businesses with the legal form of a corporation or company to illustrate my arguments because large businesses typically have this legal form. However, it must be recognized that businesses frequently have other legal forms, for example, a partnership or individual proprietorship. In most countries and in poor countries in particular, the businesses that are not organized as corporations are large in number and account for a large share of private business activity, but individually they tend to be smaller in size and are not usually the focus of concern about their functioning.

In the three types of company ownership described, a key issue is who controls the company, in other words, who makes important decisions about hiring and firing the senior managers and the overall business strategy of the company. In the first type of company (closely held), the single owner or a small group of owners clearly control the company. They may be the managers of the company themselves or sit on the board of directors of the company and closely supervise the managers.

In the second type of company (controlling or strategic investor), a single investor or small group controls the management of the company. The many portfolio investors who own the rest of the shares have little influence. What constitutes a controlling block of shares may vary from country to country and from company to company, depending on the laws, regulations, and corporate charter.

In the analysis that follows, I use the definition of a controlling block adopted in previous studies, namely, 20 percent of the outstanding shares. If a single investor or connected group of investors (for example, members of a family) owns more than 20 percent of the shares and all other shareholders own no more than a small percentage each, then that investor or group of investors will likely control the company; and the other shareholders have little influence.

In the third type of company (widely held), there is considerable debate about who controls the company. As I will discuss in more detail below, one outcome is that the managers may control the company because no individual shareholder or group can marshal enough votes to elect their own members of the board of directors or in other ways challenge the senior managers of the company. The senior managers may largely determine who sits on the board of directors even though they own only a small proportion of the company's shares.

Another way to categorize companies is whether they are listed on a stock exchange and are publicly traded. If so, they are sometimes referred to as a public company as opposed to a private company (a public company should not be confused with a company owned by the government referred to in later chapters as a state-owned company or enterprise). Government regulatory agencies and stock exchanges usually require a public company to meet certain requirements concerning the treatment of its shareholders for the purpose of protecting investors.

If a company is of the first type (closely held), it is unlikely to be a public company whose shares are listed and traded on a stock exchange. The few investors who own shares in the company rarely sell them. If they do sell them, it is probably not done through the stock exchange but through a private transaction in which one large investor sells his shares in a block to another large investor at a negotiated price.

If a company is of the second type (a controlling or strategic investor), it is most likely a public company. The many small shareholders will trade their shares on an organized stock exchange. The controlling or strategic investor, however, is more likely to keep his shares for a long time. If he does decide to sell them, he will likely do so through a private transaction with another investor who wants to control the company. The price of the controlling block often sells at a premium price compared with the other shares.

If a company is of the third type (widely held), it is almost certainly a public company listed on a stock exchange. Most shares will be traded on the exchange.

Who Owns Large Companies?

I know of three studies that have tried to determine the relative importance of the various types of company ownership in both rich and poor countries. Unfortunately, data are only readily available for publicly traded companies listed on a stock exchange because their ownership is a matter of public record. As noted earlier, such companies are most likely to be of the second or third type (controlling investor or widely held). Data on the importance of the first type of company (closely held companies) are rare.

Thus, in reviewing the results of these studies on corporate ownership, it is important to note that they do not reflect the importance of closely held companies because such companies are not included in their data. Particularly in poor countries without a stock exchange or with only a few publicly traded companies even if there is a stock exchange, closely held private companies carry out most business activity. Because publicly traded companies are rare in many poor countries, the existing studies shed light on who own companies in only a few of the poor countries.

For example, businesses not listed on a stock exchange (closely held) account for 60 percent of economic activity (measured by value added) even in the United Kingdom that has one of the largest stock markets relative to the size of its economy of any country. This activity increases to 75 percent in Japan and more than 90 percent in Thailand and Poland.[3] In other words, publicly traded companies probably account for a small percentage of economic activity in poor countries. Admittedly, many of the businesses not listed on a stock exchange are small, but others can be quite large, for example, the Mars company.

Concerning public companies that are listed on an exchange, the first study (see Figure 3-1) measures the proportion of the largest 20 public companies that are widely held in 27 countries, only a few of which would be classified as poor or developing. A company is classified as widely held if no single shareholder owns more than 20 percent of the shares.

Probably many believe that widely held public companies dominate the economies in most rich countries. We hear a great deal about corporate giants such as General Motors, Sony, or British Petroleum each having thousands of shareholders.

This study, however, suggests that the importance of widely held corporations is exaggerated even in rich countries. Of the large public companies, the proportion that is widely held is not high except in the United States, United Kingdom, and Japan. In these three countries, the proportion is 80 to 100 percent. In other countries, the proportion is smaller, for example, 60 percent in Canada, Switzerland, and France; 50 percent in Germany; and 10 percent or less in Hong Kong, Austria, Belgium, and Greece.

A high proportion of even the large public companies in most rich countries are in the second category of having a controlling or strategic investor. Again, let me emphasize that these data exaggerate the importance of widely held companies because large publicly traded companies are more likely to be widely held than any other type. I suspect that widely held companies are much less common among smaller companies and nonexistent among those companies that are not publicly traded.

Figure 3-1
PERCENTAGE OF 20 LARGEST PUBLICLY TRADED COMPANIES THAT ARE WIDELY HELD—1995

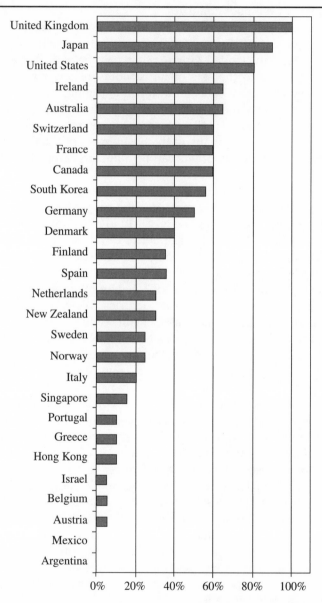

SOURCE: Rafael La Porta, Florencio López-de-Silanes, and Andrei Shleifer, "Corporate Ownership Around the World," *The Journal of Finance* 54 (No. 2): 471-517, Table II, p. 492.

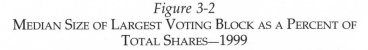

Figure 3-2
MEDIAN SIZE OF LARGEST VOTING BLOCK AS A PERCENT OF
TOTAL SHARES—1999

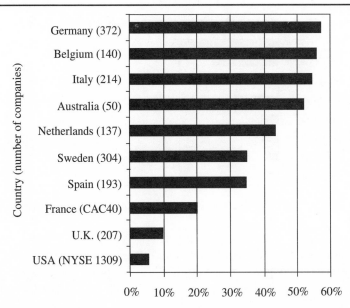

SOURCE: M. Becht and C. Mayer, "Introduction," in Fabrizio Barca and Marco Becht, eds., *The Control of Corporate Europe* (Oxford University Press, 2001), Table 1.1.

The second study looked at the size of the largest block of shares under one investor's control in large public companies in Europe and the United States. This is referred to as a voting block because an investor may control more shares than he owns. Figure 3-2 shows the median size of the largest voting block (the largest block in 50 percent of the companies was greater than this number while smaller in the other 50 percent).

This study demonstrates that the typical pattern of ownership even for publicly traded companies in rich countries is that a single investor controls a large voting block of shares and thus effectively controls the company. The only exceptions seem to be the United States and the United Kingdom, which again demonstrates that widely held companies without a controlling investor are common only in a few countries.

45

Figure 3-3
PERCENTAGE OF PUBLICLY TRADED COMPANIES IN EAST ASIA
THAT ARE WIDELY HELD—1996

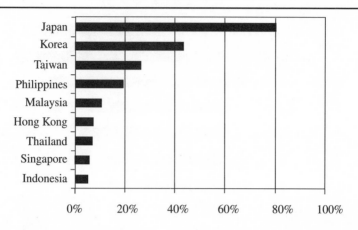

SOURCE: Stijn Claessens, Simeon Djankov, and Larry H. P. Lang, "Who Controls East Asian Corporations?" World Bank Policy Research Working Paper 2054, February 1999, Table 2, p. 80.

Because of the controversy surrounding the performance of large companies during the East Asian crisis, a third study examined the ownership of companies in this region.[4] This study includes a much larger sample of publicly traded companies, almost 3,000, in nine countries. The same standard is used to classify a company as widely held, namely, no shareholder owns more than 20 percent of the shares.

The interesting result of the third study (see Figure 3-3) is how unimportant widely held companies are in these nine countries of East Asia except for Japan (80 percent are widely held) and possibly South Korea (43 percent are widely held). In the other seven countries, the proportion of publicly traded companies that are widely held ranges from 5 to 26 percent.

Though these studies do not analyze the many closely held companies not listed on a stock exchange, I think it is safe to say that the dominant forms of ownership in East Asia are either closely held companies or companies with a controlling or strategic investor. In other words, most companies in these countries are more like the

Mars company than General Motors or British Petroleum. I suspect that this conclusion is even more valid for most of the poor countries of the world. An important question discussed below is whether these two types of ownership are somehow inferior to widely held ownership, and whether countries should emulate the example of the United States and the United Kingdom by adopting policies that encourage widely held corporate ownership.

Because experts from the United States and the United Kingdom often advise governments in poor countries and a high proportion of the staff of international development institutions have been trained in the prestigious universities of these countries, the importance of widely held companies may be exaggerated or is held up as a model for poor countries to follow. In my own conversations with experts from these two countries, I have noticed that many seem to believe that their economic system (sometimes referred to as the Anglo-Saxon model) is the most advanced and that other countries should aspire to their high level of economic development. Though I too may be biased by my citizenship and education in the United States, I also believe that the economic system in these two countries is the most developed in many ways. I am not convinced, however, that widely held companies with no controlling investor are superior to other types of ownership or provide a model that other countries, particularly poor countries with weak institutions, should attempt to copy.

Corporate Governance—Broad Definition

Recently, many have criticized large companies in poor countries for having weak *corporate governance*. The definition of this term that became popular after the East Asian financial crisis seems to include anything that influences the behavior or performance of a company. This new definition is different from the conventional definition that focuses primarily on the relationship between the dispersed shareholders and the professional managers of widely held public companies.

This new definition is a tautology. The statement that poor company performance is caused by weak corporate governance is obviously true and indisputable because weak corporate governance is defined to be everything that causes poor company performance.

Such a statement, though true, is almost useless in analyzing what should be done to improve company performance.

This new definition of corporate governance grew out of the controversy surrounding the causes of the East Asian financial crisis. A widespread belief was that the poor performance or misbehavior of large companies in these countries caused or at least contributed to the crisis, for example, the chaebols in Korea or the companies owned by relatives and cronies of Suharto in Indonesia.

Critics of these companies found it convenient to argue that poor corporate governance caused the crisis. I suspect that this term became popular in part because it was similar to the other use of the term governance, namely, to refer to the political and governmental system in a country. For example, James Wolfensohn, president of the World Bank, is quoted as saying, "The governance of the corporation is now as important in the world economy as the government of countries."[5]

Following this lead, a major World Bank report on corporate governance states, "[t]he economic crises in East Asia and other regions have demonstrated how macro-economic difficulties can be exacerbated by a systemic failure of corporate governance. . . . "[6] A similar report by the Asian Development Bank states, "[c]ountries that suffered dramatic reversal of fortune during the Asian financial crisis have identified weaknesses in corporate governance as one of the major sources of vulnerabilities that led to their economic meltdown in 1997."[7]

Both reports then go on to define weak corporate governance as almost anything that causes companies to perform badly. Some of the causes of poor corporate performance discussed in the reports include weak competition, banking systems, bankruptcy laws, protection of minority shareholders, and legal and regulatory systems.

Corporate Governance—Conventional Definition

In contrast, the conventional and narrower definition of corporate governance grew out of concerns 70 years ago about dispersed corporate ownership in the United States. In their 1932 classic book, Berle and Means observed that large U.S. companies are controlled by a new professional class of managers who own few or no shares in the company.[8] Instead the shares of the company are widely held by thousands of shareholders each of whom owns only a small fraction of the shares and may have little influence over how the company is managed.

This pattern of widely held corporate ownership resulted in what came to be known as the separation of ownership from control. More recently, economists have called this an *agency problem* or *principal-agent problem*. The managers of the company are entrusted with the responsibility to make the company as profitable and valuable as possible for the benefit of the owners. However, the owners (*principals*) may have difficulty in ensuring that the managers (*agents*) actually carry out this responsibility.

Thus, according to the conventional definition, corporate governance deals with how the many owners of a widely held company can monitor and control the managers to make certain that they are doing their utmost to maximize the value of the company.[9] By this definition, weak corporate governance means that the managers are not maximizing company value, and the many owners seem to be incapable of doing anything about it, for example, by firing the managers. Countless studies have examined corporate governance issues in the United States and to a lesser extent in other countries. I review below in more depth the weaknesses of corporate governance in the United States when I discuss whether or not poor countries should follow the example of the United States and encourage widespread ownership of companies.

Using the conventional definition of the term, corporate governance may be a serious problem in the United States but is a minor problem in most poor countries. The reason is that widely held corporate ownership that results in a principal-agent problem is still rare in poor countries. Instead, as the studies discussed previously show, businesses are typically owned or controlled by an individual, a family, or a small group of investors. In other words, ownership is closely held or there is a controlling investor. The owners are often also the managers or at least are capable of controlling the managers. There is little reason to think that the managers are not carrying out the wishes of the owners. Similarly, I doubt whether corporate governance according to the conventional definition was a major problem in the countries of East Asia that experienced a financial crisis in the 1990s or was an important cause of this crisis.

Business Environment

When James Wolfensohn made his statement about the importance of corporate governance, he must have been using the new definition; but I believe it is misleading to define corporate governance in this way. If one wants to use a shorthand term to refer to everything that influences the behavior or performance of a business, a better term is *business environment*. This term refers to all of the laws, regulations, government policies, and institutions that encourage businesses to perform well.

Improving the business environment is the main subject of this book, and therefore I obviously believe it is important. This book covers some of the major reforms needed to improve the business environment involving banking, competition policy, privatization, and bankruptcy. Thus, I agree with the thrust of Wolfensohn's statement though I don't agree with his terminology.

The reader might think that I am being pedantic to argue that the term business environment should be used instead of corporate governance. The term used for a concept or idea, however, is important because all words carry with them certain meanings or implications. Using the term "corporate governance" instead of "business environment" gives a misleading impression as to the causes of poor business performance. Emphasizing corporate governance implies that one should look at the internal structure, ownership, or management of the company to find the cause of its poor performance. At the extreme, corporate governance could imply that companies perform badly because their owners and managers are greedy, evil, rich people who have no concern for the welfare of their country.

After the East Asian financial crisis, it was common to point the finger of blame at the rich individuals and families that owned the important companies in these countries. This reaction is similar to what occurred in the United States during the Great Depression in the 1930s. People wanted someone to blame for their economic hardship. An easy target for their anger were the rich individuals, large corporations, banks, and other financial institutions sometimes referred to as "malefactors of great wealth." The result was new government policies and laws in the United States designed to curb the perceived misbehavior of these companies, some of which were misguided and created more problems than they solved.

Implying that poor performance of companies just like the poor performance of governments is caused by weak governance draws invalid parallels between private companies and government institutions. Critics of large companies demand that they be more like public or government institutions. These companies should be more transparent and accountable to society in general and not just to their owners. Their responsibility should be to advance the welfare of the entire nation and not just the interest of their owners. This goal is one reason why the concept of corporate social responsibility has become popular in recent years.

This concept runs counter to the traditional concept advanced so long ago by Adam Smith that private businesses in pursuing profits are in fact advancing the general welfare if the business environment gives them the proper incentives. As you might guess, I do not believe that making large companies into quasi-public institutions is the best solution for poor company performance. Instead, I favor improving the business environment that motivates companies and regulates their activities.

If instead one says that the cause of the East Asian crisis was a weak business environment, the finger of blame is pointed at governments rather than at companies. Governments through their policies, laws, and institutions created the business environment that led to poor corporate performance and thus should be blamed for the East Asian crisis.

A more sophisticated analysis suggests that either blaming only governments or blaming only the rich, powerful individuals and families that owned the large companies in East Asia is misleading. Both were responsible. The owners in many cases influenced the government to create a weak business environment that would enable them to earn high profits even though this was detrimental to the nation as a whole. In other words, the East Asian crisis was another example of rent-seeking behavior by the business community that has been the bane of most poor countries and many rich countries. This behavior, however, should not be called a problem of corporate governance. If anything, it is a problem of national governance in which the government represents the interests of only the rich and powerful.

For example, the government of Indonesia protected many large businesses from competition and thus could be blamed for their poor performance. However, these businesses were often owned by relatives and cronies of Suharto, who for all practical purposes was the government of Indonesia. Thus, the owners and the government were the same people.

51

I prefer the term "business environment" not because I want to blame the government for the poor performance of private businesses and absolve the rich elite from blame. I think it is a better term because it focuses attention on the external environment in which businesses function rather than on their internal structure and ownership. One should always keep in mind, however, that the owners and managers of businesses often can shape the business environment because they have undue influence with the government.

Investment Climate

I also do not favor another term that is sometimes used instead of business environment, namely, *investment climate*. For example, the World Bank recently said that improving the investment climate in poor countries is one of the two main pillars of its strategic framework that will guide its activities and programs over the next few years.[10]

The use of the term "investment climate" gives a misleading impression of the main contribution of the private sector to economic growth. Using this term suggests that the private sector only contributes capital for new investment and ignores the superior management and technical skills that private firms can provide compared with state-owned enterprises and government agencies, assuming that a good business environment is in place. Moreover, the implication is that the only thing needed to achieve faster economic growth is to increase the amount of private investment.

Using this term also supports the beliefs of many in government and elsewhere who do not favor an increased role for the private sector. Because of mismanagement of state-owned enterprises and the weak fiscal position of many governments in poor countries, neither the enterprises nor the governments can provide the capital to make needed investments in the industries or sectors dominated by the state. For example, only a small fraction of the population may have access to electricity, telephone service, or modern water and sewer systems.

Faced with the low quality of many services supplied by the government and state-owned enterprises, these governments admit that they cannot provide the capital for new investment and reluctantly agree that the private sector can provide this capital. These governments, however, are often unwilling to allow private firms to actually take control and improve the management of state-owned enterprises, for example, through privatization. Governments do not want private owners to take the politically unpopular steps necessary to improve the efficiency and profitability of these enterprises, for example, raising prices, eliminating theft, and laying off surplus workers. No prudent private investor, however, would normally be willing to invest in unprofitable and badly managed industries that he cannot control. This issue is discussed in more detail in Chapter 4 in the section dealing with private investment in new infrastructure capacity.

Providing capital for investment is one of the least important contributions of private owners. What they can do is make businesses (including privatized companies) efficient, well managed, and profitable. Once they are well managed, they will have no difficulty in attracting new capital. The problem in many poor countries is not a lack of capital but a lack of investment opportunities in profitable companies.

Causes of the East Asian Crisis

What was the cause of the East Asian financial crisis that primarily affected South Korea, Indonesia, Thailand, Malaysia, and the Philippines? Was it weak corporate governance as conventionally defined, a poor business environment, or something else? There is no single explanation of the crisis that all experts agree on. The cause will be debated for years just as the cause of the Great Depression in the United States is still being debated 70 years later. However, almost no expert blames the crisis on weak corporate governance as conventionally defined.

After reading some, but certainly not all, of the substantial research on this question, I find two schools of thought each supporting a particular cause.[11] The debate about the cause of the East Asian financial crisis is similar to the much older debate about the causes of domestic banking crises.

The East Asian crisis, however, was more complicated because it involved both a banking crisis and a foreign exchange crisis. Financial liberalization in the late 1980s and early 1990s encouraged a large expansion of the banking sector in these countries. For example, claims by domestic banks on private firms increased by more than

50 percent relative to the size of the economy in just seven years in Thailand, Korea, and Malaysia.

This increase in bank lending was financed only in part by an increase in domestic deposits. A large share was financed by capital inflows from foreign financial institutions and investors. East Asian banks borrowed large amounts of dollars, yen, marks, and so forth on a short-term basis from abroad and incurred an obligation to repay the loans in the same foreign currencies. These banks in turn loaned this money to domestic corporations. The consequence was a large increase in short-term liabilities by both the domestic banks and corporations that must be repaid in foreign currencies.

In Thailand, for example, the foreign currency liabilities of banks and other financial institutions rose from 5 percent of GDP in 1990 to 28 percent in 1995. In Korea, banks borrowed heavily overseas (foreign currency liabilities of banks tripled between 1992 and 1996) and then used those funds to lend to the large corporations (chaebols).[12]

The result was debt-to-equity ratios for many East Asian companies higher than in most other countries. The ratio of total debt (liabilities) to stockholders' equity in 1997 was 3.0 in Indonesia, 3.5 in Thailand, and 4.3 in Korea. It was at a more reasonable level of 0.9 in Malaysia and 1.5 in the Philippines.[13] In contrast, the debt-to-equity ratio of most companies in rich countries is less than 1.0.

The first school of thought, which I tend to agree with, says that the cause of the crisis was government guarantees. These guarantees encouraged excessive inflows of foreign, short-term capital and imprudent lending by banks, in other words, a problem of moral hazard.[14] Because foreign investors believed these government guarantees existed, domestic banks were able to borrow abroad at low interest rates, loan these funds domestically at high interest rates, and thus earn substantial profits while the government bore the risks. This situation is similar to the widespread domestic banking crises caused by government guarantees or insurance for bank deposits and other liabilities as described in later chapters on banking. In the case of East Asia, however, the government was guaranteeing bank liabilities held by foreign institutions and investors rather than domestic deposits.

To understand these guarantees, note that domestic companies could fail to repay these loans primarily for two reasons. The first reason is that the companies may have invested the loan proceeds unwisely in projects that turned out to be unprofitable. There is some evidence of this, such as an investment boom in real estate and the stock market, which increased the prices for these assets to unreasonable levels. In other words the availability of foreign capital may have caused a speculative bubble in some assets that burst, causing large losses for companies and the banks that lent them the money.

The second and more important reason is that the currency may be devalued. Since the bank loans were typically denominated in a foreign currency (for example, Japanese yen), devaluation would increase the amount of the loan in local currency (for example, Thai baht) that the companies would have to repay. Since company revenues in local currency are unlikely to be increased proportionately to a devaluation, the companies may not be able to repay these loans. The local companies and in turn the banks were taking on substantial exchange-rate risk by borrowing in foreign currencies. Banks may have thought that they were passing this exchange-rate risk to their corporate borrowers by requiring them to repay the loans in foreign currencies but did not seem to recognize that most of their borrowers could not do this if a large devaluation occurred.

The foreign financial institutions must have known that lending to the domestic banks was inherently high risk and made these loans only because they believed that the governments in these countries implicitly or explicitly guaranteed the liabilities of these banks and even the liabilities of the companies that borrowed from the domestic banks. Because of this assumed guarantee, the interest rates charged by foreign creditors were low, and thus banks could profit from the difference between the rates of interest at which they borrowed money internationally and the rates at which they loaned money domestically.

Foreign creditors seemed to believe that the governments in these countries provided two types of guarantees. First and most important, they believed that the governments would not devalue their currencies because they had a long history of fixing or pegging their exchange rates. In other words, the government was guaranteeing the exchange rate. Second, even if the government did devalue its currency, foreign creditors may have believed that the government would not allow large, powerful domestic companies and banks to default on their foreign liabilities and was in effect guaranteeing these liabilities.

In contrast, the second school of thought, which I do not find convincing, emphasizes the inherent instability of financial systems, systemic risk, herd behavior, contagion, and bank runs. The crisis was the result of a self-fulfilling panic by foreign investors who simultaneously wanted the domestic banks to repay their foreign, short-term liabilities. As in a domestic run on banks, all the banks cannot simultaneously pay off all their liabilities. More importantly, the government's foreign currency reserves were not large enough to cover the immediate repayment of all the foreign liabilities. Advocates of this cause of the crisis believe that, if the foreign creditors had only been patient and not panicked, banks could have repaid their foreign liabilities over time because the banking system and the economies were fundamentally sound.

Theoretical economists have coined a new term for this inherent instability. It is referred to as a problem of *multiple equilibria* in which the economy can suddenly shift from one equilibrium to another if investor expectations change. A frequently mentioned solution to this instability is the creation of an international lender of last resort. This institution, perhaps the International Money Fund, would lend to countries that are facing a run on their currency but are otherwise financially sound.[15] This is similar to the role that central banks are expected to play if there is a run on banks by their domestic depositors.

I am inclined to support the first school of thought because of the prominent role that fixed exchange rates played in the crisis. In effect, fixed exchange rates mean that the government is guaranteeing the exchange rate. As long as all parties believe that the government is able to honor this guarantee, banks will be able to borrow from foreign creditors at low interest rates and, in turn, make foreign currency loans to domestic companies. The foreign creditors believe that the risk is small that the nation's currency will be devalued and cause both domestic companies and banks to default on their foreign liabilities.

If, however, foreign creditors begin to doubt whether the government will be able to honor this guarantee of the exchange rate, they have an incentive to quickly demand repayment of their loans to the domestic banks before devaluation occurs and threatens the ability of the banks to repay. If the amount of these foreign liabilities of the banking system grows large relative to the government's foreign currency reserves, it becomes less likely that the government will be able to honor its guarantee of the exchange rate. Recognition of this fact by foreign creditors encourages them to be the first to obtain repayment in advance of devaluation. In other words, if many foreign creditors demand simultaneously that the government honor its guarantee of the exchange rate, then the government cannot honor it for everyone and only the first in line will be paid.

The financial systems in these countries were unstable, but only because foreign creditors lost confidence in the government's guarantee of the exchange rate. Without a government guarantee (for example, the government adopts a flexible, market-determined exchange rate system), all parties would have been more likely to recognize the exchange-rate risk of borrowing in foreign currencies. Foreign creditors would have demanded higher interest rates on their loans to domestic banks in recognition of this risk. The high bank profits resulting from borrowing at low interest rates abroad and lending at high interest rates domestically would have been eliminated. As a result, the amount of foreign short-term liabilities of the banks and their loans to companies would not have increased to dangerous levels.

Regardless of which of these two causes of the East Asian crisis is correct, neither has much to do with corporate governance as conventionally defined. Both the banks and the companies seemed to be responding to the system of incentives that the government created. If banks could make large profits by borrowing abroad and then lending these funds at home because of government guarantees, they had an incentive to do so.

If companies borrowed large amounts from banks that resulted in high debt-to-equity ratios, they were using leverage to maximize the return on equity. Companies in rich countries may attempt to do this, but are usually stopped by banks and other lenders who insist on prudent debt levels. The banks in East Asia failed to do this. These banks seemed to suffer from many of the problems discussed in the later chapters on banking.[16]

It has been claimed that some companies, notably Korean chaebols, were engaged in empire building by investing in many different industries using borrowed funds rather than making only those investments that would maximize profits. If true, this activity would be a problem of corporate governance as conventionally defined because the companies were pursuing objectives other than maximizing profits, such as enhancing the size and prestige of the company. This claim is plausible because Korea has the highest proportion of widely held companies in the region other than Japan. In such companies, corporate governance as conventionally defined can be a serious problem. This problem may have been true to some extent, but no one seems to argue that it was the primary cause of the East Asian financial crisis.

The cause of the crisis was weaknesses in the business environment that allowed or even encouraged banks to borrow excessively overseas and companies to borrow excessively from the banks. If you believe the first school of thought on the cause of the crisis, the weakness in the business environment was government guarantees. If you believe in the second school of thought, the weakness in the business environment was the inherent instability of financial systems that can only be corrected by an international lender of last resort.

Widespread Corporate Ownership: A Risky Objective

Some argue that poor countries should encourage their corporations to have a more widespread ownership. In other words, these countries should move away from companies that are closely held and move toward either companies that are widely held or at least companies with a controlling investor coupled with widespread ownership of the balance of the shares. One argument is that companies with widely held ownership are dominant in some rich countries, notably the United States, and thus this type of ownership must be superior to other forms. A related argument is that widely held ownership will encourage the development of capital markets; in particular, it will increase trading on stock markets; and larger stock markets are good for economic growth.

It is true that the United States probably has the richest and most developed economy, and a high proportion of its large companies are widely held. It does not follow, however, that this type of corporate ownership contributed to the development of the U.S. economy or that other countries should encourage this type of ownership. I am inclined to believe that this type of corporate ownership actually hindered economic development in the United States, and this country became rich because of the many other strengths of its economic system, notably the intense market competition faced by U.S. businesses.

As with other issues, U.S.-trained experts seem to assume that the U.S. model of corporate ownership is automatically superior because it exists in the United States. Even if it is the best model for the United States, which I doubt, it is not clear that it is the best model for poor countries with weak political, government, and legal institutions. The inherent weaknesses of this type of ownership structure may have been reduced through a strong regulatory and legal system in the United States, but this would probably not be the case in most poor countries.

Implicit in much of the discussion of the system of corporate ownership in the United States is a sort of Darwinian theory of the survival of the fittest. Various types of corporate ownership have existed previously in the United States yet one became dominant. It must be superior to win out in the competition with other types of ownership. A review of the historical origins of this type of ownership, however, suggests that it became dominant because of government regulations and other policies that prohibited or discouraged other types of ownership rather than some process of natural selection or survival of the fittest. Many of these same regulations and policies are now being recommended for poor countries, which I think would be a mistake.

Professor Mark J. Roe of Columbia University has written extensively on the origins of the U.S. system of corporate ownership. The following is a summary of his views, which I believe are widely accepted:

> The distinctive ownership and governance structure of the large American corporation—with its distant shareholders, a board of directors that defers to the CEO, and a powerful, centralized management—is usually seen as a natural economic outcome of technological requirements for large-scale enterprises and substantial amounts of outside capital, most of which had to come from well-diversified shareholders. Roe argues that current U.S. corporate structures are the result not only of such economic factors, but of political forces that restricted the size and activities of U.S. commercial banks

and other financial intermediaries. Populist fears of concentrated economic power, interest group maneuvering, and a federalist American political structure all had a role in pressuring Congress to fragment U.S. financial institutions and limit their ability to own stock and participate in corporate governance.

Had U.S. politics been different, the present ownership structure of some American public companies might have been different. Truly national U.S. financial institutions might have been able to participate as substantial owners in the wave of end-of-the-century mergers and then use their large blocks of stock to sit on the boards of the merged enterprises (much as Warren Buffett, venture capitalists, and LBO firms like KKR do today). Such a concentrated ownership and governance structure might have helped to address monitoring, information, and coordination problems that continue to reduce the value of some U.S. companies.

The recent increase in the activism of U.S. institutional investors also casts doubt on the standard explanation of American corporate ownership structure. The new activism of U.S. financial institutions—primarily pension funds and mutual funds—can be interpreted as the delayed outbreak of an impulse to participate in corporate ownership and governance that was historically suppressed by American politics.[17]

Canada may illustrate what corporate ownership would have been like in the United States if it had been allowed to evolve without the many restrictions placed on share ownership by financial institutions. The two countries have similar economies, history, law, and geography and yet the systems of corporate ownership are very different. According to one study, most major Canadian firms are members of an interlocking group of companies and financial institutions dominated by one of the six large Canadian banks similar to the Japanese keiretsu.[18] Ownership of Canadian firms is far more concentrated than in the United States.

Weaknesses of Widely Held Companies

Companies with the second and third type of ownership structure described previously (companies that have a controlling investor with the balance of shares widely held and those that are widely held with no controlling investor) have serious weaknesses if the proper legal and regulatory framework is not in place. Even if the proper framework is in place, I believe that closely held companies are likely to perform better. Governments should be cautious in encouraging companies to have dispersed share ownership at the expense of closely held ownership.

A company is performing well if it meets two criteria. First, is it maximizing profits or the value of the company? And second, is it sharing these profits equitably with all shareholders? The major weakness of companies with a controlling investor is that this investor may divert the company's profits unfairly to himself at the expense of the many small and powerless shareholders. This is called a problem of *minority shareholder protection*. In this case, the controlling investor has an incentive to maximize the profits of the company and can effectively monitor and control the managers to achieve that objective. However, the controlling investor has an incentive not to share these profits with the other shareholders.

With weak legal protection of minority shareholders, the controlling shareholder of a company may divert profits to himself through transactions with his other businesses using nonmarket *transfer prices*. Such transactions could include selling assets, products, or services at below fair market prices or buying them at above fair market prices from businesses wholly owned by the controlling shareholder. Note that in this case the publicly reported profits and thus valuation of the company by the stock market would be low even though the company is well managed. Since, in effect, a significant share of the profits is being stolen, the company appears less profitable than it really is. This may partially explain why the controlling block of shares typically sells at a higher price per share compared with shares traded by minority shareholders on the stock market.

The greater the percentage of shares owned by the controlling shareholder, the less the gain from diverting profits to his other businesses. If the controlling shareholder owns 90 percent of the shares, then 90 percent of the profits would accrue to him even if distributed equally to all shareholders. The incentive for him to increase this amount is small. In contrast, if the controlling shareholder only owns 10 percent of the shares, he can potentially capture a much larger share of the profits, for example, through transactions with his other businesses.

The major weakness of companies with widely held ownership and no controlling investor is that the many shareholders cannot effectively control the managers to act in the interest of the shareholders. This type of ownership can have two outcomes. First, the managers may simply do a poor job of managing the company but cannot be replaced and thus its profits will be reduced. Second, the managers may divert some of these profits for their own benefit rather than paying dividends or reinvesting the profits in the company. Thus, in a widely held company not only are the shareholders likely to be denied their fair share of the profits, but total profits will also be less than they could be because of bad management.

Thus, I would rank the likely performance of companies with these three types of ownership as follows.

- A company that is *closely held* will likely do well by both criteria.
- A company with a *controlling shareholder* is likely to perform well according to the first criterion of maximizing profits but not the second criterion of sharing profits equitably with all shareholders.
- A company that is *widely held* is more likely not to perform well by either criterion. Profits are less than they could be because of bad management and some of these are diverted to the managers at the expense of the shareholders.

Empirical Evidence on Company Performance

Though this ranking of the three types of ownership may seem plausible, is there any empirical evidence to support it? The problem with measuring performance is the lack of data on closely held companies that are not listed on a stock exchange. Even when data are available for listed companies, it is difficult to determine why profits or stock-market values are low. For example, low stock-market value could be because either the company is badly managed or the controlling shareholder or managers are not sharing the profits equitably with all shareholders.

In spite of this problem of measuring performance, two interesting studies examine the performance of companies with a controlling shareholder. The first study examines the stock-market valuation of companies with a controlling shareholder in 27 rich countries. It shows that stock-market valuation increases as the percentage of shares owned by the controlling shareholder increases.[19] Keep in mind that the stock-market valuation is determined by the value that the minority shareholders place on the company's stock because they are the ones who trade on the exchange. The second study examines companies with a controlling shareholder in East Asian countries.[20] It also finds that the stock-market value of the company increases as the ownership of the controlling shareholder increases and, thus, is consistent with the first study.

This empirical result could have two explanations. First, if the controlling shareholder owns a large percentage of the shares, his ability to control the managers increases, and thus he can better ensure that the company is as profitable as possible. Second, as noted previously, the incentive for the controlling shareholder to expropriate for himself a share of the profits that exceeds his share of the ownership is reduced. In other words, as the ownership of the controlling investor increases, the company is both likely to be better managed and more profitable and to treat minority shareholders more fairly. This type of ownership increases the value that the minority shareholders place on the shares of the company.

Corporate Governance in the United States

As noted earlier, the United States has a high proportion of companies with widespread ownership and no controlling shareholder. Corporate governance in the United States is perhaps the most widely studied and analyzed. I will not attempt to provide a complete review of the corporate governance problems that exist in the United States.[21] I would like, however, to give a few examples of the problems that result from this type of ownership to illustrate why poor countries should be cautious in adopting this model.

The problem with this type of ownership is illustrated by the inherent conflict of interest in the board of directors. The primary duty of the board of directors is to represent the interest of the shareholders. Thus, the directors are supposed to be elected by the shareholders at their annual general meeting. However, because of the ability of the managers of widely held companies to influence this election process, many of the members of the board are also senior managers of the company or closely tied to the management. Because a conflict often exists between what is in the best interest of the shareholders and the managers, how can such board members honestly represent only the interest of the shareholders? They have an incentive to sacrifice the interest of shareholders for the interest of managers.

The most obvious example of this conflict of interest can be found in the commonly used title for the senior manager of a company in the United States. He typically holds dual titles—chairman of the board and chief executive officer. He is both the head of the board of directors, which is supposed to represent the interest of shareholders, and senior manager of the company. The United States places more emphasis on avoiding conflicts of interest than most other countries. Yet this obvious and serious conflict was until recently largely accepted with little question. It is unreasonable to expect that this person will honestly report to the shareholders about the performance of management and fairly determine the salaries and other compensation of managers when he is the most important manager. In other words, will he place the interest of the shareholders ahead of himself and other managers? If the company is performing badly, does anyone seriously expect that this person will argue that he should fire himself and replace himself with a better manager?

Because management dominates the board of directors, shareholders may be unable to remove poorly performing senior managers even though this action would increase the value of the company. A somewhat macabre study examined what happened to the share price of U.S. companies when their senior executives died unexpectedly, for example, because of a plane crash or a heart attack. One might think that this would cause the share price to fall because of lack of company leadership and concern over who the new senior executives might be. Surprisingly, the share price often increased after the deaths. This increase suggests that shareholders felt that the company was underperforming but could not replace the managers. After the deaths, there was a chance to install better managers.[22] Another example is the recent outbreak of financial scandals in large U.S. companies such as Enron and WorldCom. These scandals usually occurred because the senior executives were unfairly enriching themselves at the expense of the shareholders.

Over time, there have been increasing demands that the board of directors should include at least some members who are not managers of the company. These members are referred to as *outside directors* or *nonexecutive directors* as opposed to *inside directors* or *executive directors* who are also managers of the company.

Also, a growing practice is that the decisions of the board of directors causing the greatest conflicts of interest should be evaluated by special committees of the board composed largely of outside directors. These committees make recommendations to the full board concerning management pay (compensation committee), financial results to be reported to shareholders (audit committee), and the nomination of new members of the board of directors to be approved at the next annual meeting of shareholders (nomination committee).[23] These committees are an implicit recognition that the entire board of directors cannot be trusted to make decisions in the best interest of shareholders when the interest of managers is also at stake.

In spite of the special committee established by many companies to review management compensation, it is generally agreed that the level of compensation of senior managers in the United States substantially exceeds the levels in most other countries. Admittedly, it is difficult to measure the compensation of senior managers because it is often in forms other than a simple salary, for example, stock options, retirement benefits, memberships in exclusive clubs, housing allowances, entertainment allowances, or personal use of a company's fleet of airplanes.

One study surveyed the compensation of chief executives of manufacturing companies with approximately $500 million in sales in 26 countries (see Figure 3-4). The total pay and benefits of chief executive officers (CEOs) in the United States approached $2 million per year and was more than twice as high as those in any other country.

Similar studies are not available for larger companies. Many U.S. companies have sales substantially in excess of $500 million. However, far fewer such companies are in other countries, and no study provides detailed data comparing salaries between countries for these larger companies.[24] Anecdotal evidence does suggest that executives of large companies in the United States may be even more handsomely rewarded compared to similar companies in other countries perhaps because such companies in the United States are less likely to have large, influential shareholders. According to one survey, the remuneration of the CEOs of the 200 largest industrial and service companies in the United States averaged a record $11.5 million in 2001.[25] This is more than five times higher than the remuneration of CEOs of companies with only $500 million in sales.

This level of compensation has been growing rapidly over recent decades. One estimate is that in 1980, on average, the CEOs of the

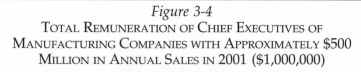

Figure 3-4
TOTAL REMUNERATION OF CHIEF EXECUTIVES OF
MANUFACTURING COMPANIES WITH APPROXIMATELY $500
MILLION IN ANNUAL SALES IN 2001 ($1,000,000)

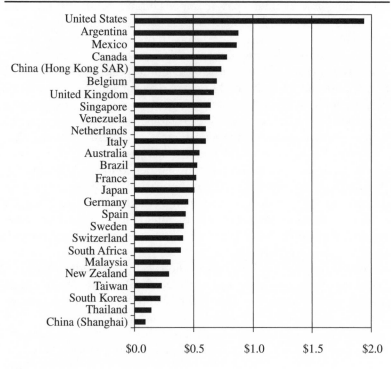

SOURCE: Towers Perin, "Worldwide Total Remuneration 2001–2002," p. 4, http://www.towers.com.

biggest U.S. companies were paid 40 times as much as an hourly wage earner at their companies. Today that number is approaching 500 times as much.[26]

In defense of the high remuneration of CEOs in the United States compared with the remuneration in other countries, it could be argued that their remuneration is more closely tied to the performance of their companies. This could provide a desirable incentive for CEOs to improve company performance. Though the remuneration of CEOs on average is high, the benefit to shareholders may be vastly greater if the executives have improved company performance.

A recent review of the theoretical and empirical evidence concludes that some of the high remuneration of U.S. executives can be explained as a reward for improving the performance of the company. However, a large part is probably due to the control that executives have over the board of directors of widely held companies. The study refers to this excess remuneration as an economic rent that the executives are able to extract from the owners of the company. The study concludes " . . . [p]rofessional CEOs hired by companies with more concentrated ownership and companies controlled by a large shareholder will therefore extract less rents than the CEOs of U.S. firms, whose shareholders are likely to be more dispersed and therefore less able to closely monitor the CEOs."[27]

Including stock options in the remuneration package of executives is frequently cited as a tool for rewarding executives if they can improve the performance of their companies. They are rewarded by the increase in the price of the stock above a certain level set by the board of directors, called the *strike price*. One unfortunate consequence is that managers have an incentive to exaggerate the profits of the company to increase the stock price. This tactic seems to have been a cause of some of the recent financial scandals in the United States, and was accomplished in spite of accounting firms auditing the financial statements. Poor countries with even less ethical accounting firms probably should not encourage public companies to grant options to managers.

Another explanation for the use of stock options is that managers favored this method because accounting rules did not require the company to report the value of these options as an expense and thus reduce profits reported to investors. In effect, the company could hide a large share of the compensation paid to managers even though the government allowed companies to deduct the expense for tax purposes. The managers had the best of all possible worlds— they could hide an increase in their compensation from the owners (shareholders) and yet it could still be used to reduce corporate income taxes.

Also, this type of option is not a very good method for creating incentives for managers to improve profits. Another option sometimes called an *indexed option* would be better. The usual type of option rewards a manager if there is a general increase in the stock price of most companies due, for example, to an improvement in the overall economy. This would be the result even if the management of the company had not improved. In other words, a rising tide lifts all boats. Alternatively, if the stock market falls, managers are punished even if the stock price of their companies does not fall as much as others because of improved management. In these situations, managers are rewarded for not improving the relative performance of the company and punished even if they do.

In contrast, an indexed option only rewards managers if the share price of the company increases more than the average increase in stock prices for other companies in the same industry or, alternatively, for all listed companies (the latter is a less desirable option). In other words, the strike price is tied to an index of other stock prices. Managers are only rewarded if the company's performance improves relative to similar companies and not just in absolute terms.

Another blatant example of this conflict of interest is found in the frequently used term *hostile takeover*. One of the reasons why the U.S. system of widespread company ownership has worked as well as it has is because of the ability of outside investors to take over control of a badly performing company. If the current managers of the company oppose this, it is known as a hostile takeover.

If a company is performing badly and its share price is low, there is an incentive for investors to buy up a controlling block of shares in the company from the existing owners, replace the managers, and attempt to increase the company's profitability. These moves would change the company from one with widespread share ownership either to one with a controlling shareholder or to a closely held ownership. The investors can be another company or a group of rich individuals.

Existing managers often oppose the takeover because they know that it threatens their jobs, and they will use whatever influence they may have to stop it. For example, existing managers often introduce various provisions in the company charter that make it difficult for the company to be taken over—so-called *poison pills*. I find it shocking that this opposition by existing managers is often considered normal and acceptable. What right do the managers of a company have to restrict the ability of the owners of the company to sell their property to other investors? The managers are only the employees of the owners but nevertheless have taken control of the company away from them.

Stock Market Development: The Tail Wagging the Dog

A frequently heard argument supporting widespread share ownership is that it *develops the stock market* and thus in turn increases the rate of economic growth. Proponents of this view seem to believe that a developed stock market is synonymous with a large stock market. In other words, a developed stock market is one in which many companies list their shares for trading (high stock market *capitalization*) and a large amount of trading of these shares takes place (high stock market *turnover*).

According to some experts, almost anything that increases the size of the stock market, including government policies that encourage widespread share ownership of companies, is desirable. They seem to assume that a large stock market is good for the economy without explaining why. For example, an important study prepared by the World Bank and Flemings (an investment bank) argues that privatization of state-owned enterprises by selling all or part of the shares to many small investors will result in a larger stock market. It then assumes without providing any evidence that this must be good for the economy and is one of the important benefits of this type of privatization.[28]

To understand the relationship between widespread share ownership and the size of the stock market, note that a formal, organized stock exchange is only needed when owners of small blocks of shares want to sell their shares. A stock exchange brings together many small buyers and sellers and enables a seller in one part of the country to trade anonymously with a buyer in another part of the country at low cost. The greater the number of small shareholders, the greater the trading on the stock exchange.

In contrast, shareholders who want to sell a large block of shares in a company often cannot use the stock exchange. If I were so fortunate as to own 20 percent of the shares of a large company, I probably could not call up my broker and place an order to sell my shares on the exchange. It would be difficult to find enough buyers on the exchange without greatly depressing the price, or the stock would have to be sold over a long period as buyers became available. Instead, sales of large blocks are often traded *off-market* in a negotiated transaction between large buyers and sellers though the agreed price may have to be reported to the stock exchange. Another reason why an owner of a controlling block of shares will sell them off-market is that a buyer is likely to pay a premium for the shares because he gains control of the company.

Thus, the size of the stock market in a country depends directly on the pattern of company ownership. In countries where many companies have widespread ownership such as in the United States or the United Kingdom, the stock market will be large. In countries where most companies are closely held or family owned, the stock market will be small. Thus some experts seem to advocate forcing companies to have widespread share ownership because it will result in a large stock market even if the legal and regulatory institutions are not in place to protect the many small shareholders. My view is that the legal and regulatory institutions should first be put in place, then let companies decide whether they want to sell shares to small investors, and let investors decide whether they want to buy shares in these companies. A country with good legal and regulatory institutions to protect small shareholders has a well-developed stock market even if the stock market is small. Over time, the stock market will grow.

A number of empirical studies do seem to suggest that a large stock market is associated with faster economic growth.[29] At first glance, they would seem to support the view that encouraging wide-spread share ownership and thus creating a larger stock market will result in faster economic growth.

One has to be careful, however, in interpreting the results of these studies. What they are really saying is that a well-developed stock market is associated with faster economic growth. Because data are readily available on stock market capitalization and turnover, these two measures of the size of a stock market are used as proxies for the degree of stock market development. By a developed stock market, these authors typically mean a well-functioning stock market with the proper legal and regulatory institutions in place, but they cannot directly measure the quality of these laws and institutions. For example, one study begins "Do well-functioning stock markets . . . boost economic growth?"[30] The study then goes on to use stock market turnover in countries around the world as a proxy for how well stock markets are functioning.

Those who stress the importance of developing stock markets imply that stock markets are an important source of capital for private businesses, but they almost never provide data to support that view. The reason is that selling new shares on the stock market is, in fact, a small and unimportant source of capital on average for private firms in most countries. The stock market is mostly a way to trade ownership of companies rather than as a source of capital. For example, the United States has the largest, most developed stock market, but on average the U.S. stock market is a drain on capital and not a source of capital for private firms. The reason is that many companies are using their capital to buy up existing shares of their company stock rather than issuing new shares to raise capital. In 2002, for example, nonfarm, nonfinancial corporations in the United States spent about $40 billion more in buying back existing shares of stock than in selling new shares.[31] As will be discussed in Chapter 6 on banking, by far the most important source of capital for private firms is retained earnings, in other words, their own profits and not bank loans or selling stock.

As an example of a poor country, India has a large stock market, but it is also a limited source of capital for private firms. One study estimates that selling new shares amounted to between 4 and 6 percent of funds raised by medium and large Indian firms and concludes that " . . . the role of the stock market as a source of finance is limited and remarkably similar for Indian and U.S. firms . . . " and that " . . . the development of stock markets is unlikely to spur corporate growth in developing countries, if the analysis is restricted to the role of the stock market as a source of finance."[32]

Though probably not an important source of capital in the aggregate, selling new shares may be an important source for some firms in some circumstances, and thus developing capital markets should not be ignored. However, the best way to do this is to create the legal, regulatory, and institutional infrastructure that requires companies to treat their shareholders fairly and thus encourages small investors to own shares. A well-developed market also means that companies can sell their shares for a higher price and thus are encouraged to do so to raise capital for investment. A well-developed market is likely to be a large one, but a large one is not necessarily well developed if various government policies have prematurely encouraged widespread share ownership.

I support government policies to create a well-developed stock market though this will be difficult in countries with weak governmental institutions and poor legal and regulatory systems. What I do not support is the idea that the government should encourage widespread share ownership just to cause more trading on the stock exchange and give the illusion of a well-developed stock market. This seems to be a good example of the tail wagging the dog. Widespread ownership of companies should be judged primarily on whether it will encourage companies to be well managed, efficient, and profitable and not whether it will increase the size of the stock market.

In the absence of a well-developed stock market, the government is exposing its citizens to substantial risk by encouraging widespread share ownership. In the case of companies with a controlling investor, small investors may be disappointed to discover that the controlling investor has appropriated an unfairly large portion of the profits for himself. In the case of companies with only small shareholders, they may be disappointed to discover that the managers are not doing a good job of managing the company and are also appropriating for themselves most of the profits that the company is earning.

Legal Protection of Shareholders

To improve the performance of companies with widely held ownership, governments can put in place various laws, regulations, and institutions to protect the interest of minority shareholders and thus develop the stock market. Drafting the laws and regulations and designing the institutions is not an issue in most poor countries. They can follow the models that exist in rich countries, for example, the United States. Technical assistance is readily available to help governments do this. As is the case with many other government policies to improve the functioning of the private sector, the problem is that the regulatory institutions are weak and possibly corrupt and do not enforce the laws.

An important protection of shareholder rights is the government requirement that companies must make financial statements available to the public. These statements must follow generally accepted accounting principles and be audited to ensure their accuracy. It is easy for countries to adopt good accounting principles because well-established models exist in rich countries, for example, the Generally Accepted Accounting Principles (GAAP) used in the United States or the International Accounting Standards (IAS) recently adopted in the European Union.

Again the problem is with implementing this requirement. Many poor countries have few well-trained accountants who can prepare such statements. One expert told me about visiting a poor African country to evaluate its accounting standards and procedures. The Ministry of Finance assured him that the government requires that all public companies follow IAS. The expert then tried in vain to find a copy of these standards anywhere in the country. Adopting these standards was easy. Implementing them was more difficult.

More important, the accounting firms that audit and certify these statements to be accurate are often poorly trained or, even worse, corrupt. It seems to be common knowledge in many countries that most accounting firms will, for a modest fee, certify the accuracy of any financial statement no matter how badly prepared. Even the accounting firms in poor countries affiliated with the big international accounting firms do not seem to be much better in this regard.[33] As a result, companies may be under little pressure to report accurate financial information.

Even if accurate financial information is made available to shareholders, it is of little value unless the many small shareholders can take action to change the managers if they are performing badly, in other words, have a voice in the control of the company. Otherwise, their only option is to sell their shares at a low price reflecting the poor company performance.

An important protection of small shareholders is if a large outside investor can take over control of the company if it is not performing well. The investor will typically offer the small shareholders a price for their shares higher than the current market price. In a poor country, foreign rather than domestic investors may be more likely to have the capital to purchase a controlling block of shares in an underperforming company. As seen in the United States, however, the existing managers will attempt to block a takeover if it threatens their employment.

In particular, the managers are likely to encourage nationalistic fears if the outside investor is foreign, and they will use their political influence with the government to block a takeover. This tactic occurs in rich countries as well. For 12 years, the European Union has been trying to reach an agreement on a takeover directive that would establish procedures for investors in one member country to take control of a company in another. Company management as well as unions, particularly in Germany, have blocked the adoption of the directive. Germany seems to be concerned that its largest automobile company, Volkswagen, might be subject to a takeover by investors from another European country.

Is Small Beautiful?

Though large companies are often criticized for their size, power, wealth, and influence, small businesses are viewed much more favorably. While government programs to help large businesses would be widely criticized as an example of their power and influence and cited as another example of rent-seeking behavior, government programs to help small businesses are widely supported.

Such small businesses are commonly referred to as SMEs, short for *small- and medium-sized enterprises*. Programs to help SMEs are common and seem to be popular both among international aid agencies and governments in rich and poor countries. My experience is that foreign donors and governments are almost falling over themselves to provide assistance to SMEs in many poor countries. This assistance can be in the form of subsidized loans, grants, information, and advice to help entrepreneurs run small businesses.

What is surprising is that it seems to be impossible to find convincing explanations as to why such assistance to SMEs is desirable while similar assistance to large businesses is not. Any other government policy that is so widely accepted usually has some empirical or theoretical support, but this does not seem to be the case for assisting SMEs. I once asked an official of a U.S. agency that provides support for SMEs to suggest something that I could read that would explain why this support is desirable. He could not recommend anything.

The World Bank has a department devoted to providing assistance to SMEs. The Web site for this department has a page that specifies the following three reasons this assistance is desirable:[34]

- Most businesses in poor countries are small.
- Small businesses may be a way for the poor to escape from poverty.
- Small businesses face a more difficult business environment than large businesses.

As suggested by the World Bank Web site, such assistance to SMEs may be popular because it is viewed as a direct way of helping poor people. Many seem to believe that the owners and employees of small businesses are more likely to be poor compared with owners and employees of large companies and, thus, more deserving of assistance. Being small is synonymous with being poor while being large is synonymous with being rich. Helping a small business seems to provide the direct link between aid and reducing poverty that many are looking for.

Assisting small businesses, however, may actually help the relatively rich in a country and harm the poor. Programs to assist SMEs typically define a small business to be one with 5 to 50 employees and a medium-sized business to be one with 51 to 500 employees. Thus aid to SMEs is actually helping the owners of a business that may have as many as 500 employees. It is hard to see how these owners qualify as being poor and deserving of special government assistance to operate their businesses.

If helping poor people to start a small business and thus escape poverty is the objective, then programs to help SMEs probably should be restricted to what are called *micro-credit* programs. These programs make small loans (e.g., $100) to help the borrower, for example, to buy a cow and sell the milk, buy a bullock for pulling a plow or hauling a cart, buy a sewing machine and start a tailoring business, buy a cell phone and set up a pay phone kiosk, or buy cooking equipment and start a tea shop. Some of these programs seem to be successful and the borrowers usually repay the loans. Others, however, have run into financial difficulties because too many of the loans are not repaid.

Perhaps the intention is to help the employees of small businesses rather than their owners. SMEs typically employ more workers per unit of output compared with big businesses. In the jargon of economics, SMEs are *labor-intensive* businesses. Thus, some argue that increasing the number of SMEs will do more to create jobs and reduce unemployment compared with increasing the number of large businesses.

Large firms typically use less labor per unit of output because they use more advanced production techniques, but they typically pay higher wages and offer better working conditions. Programs to increase the number of small businesses rather than large businesses may result in lower wages and not higher wages. These programs may actually reward the inefficient and backward businesses with low labor productivity and low wages rather than the efficient and modern ones with high labor productivity and high wages.

With regard to the claim that small businesses suffer the most from a poor business environment, why then are there so many small businesses and so few large businesses in poor countries? Even if the claim is true, the solution is to improve the business environment (which is the subject of this book) rather than to give special subsidies or assistance to compensate for the poor environment.

The fact that a poor country has mostly small businesses may be a sign of weakness, and such businesses should not be artificially encouraged. This misguided emphasis on SMEs was brought home to me by a conversation I had with an executive of a large company in Pakistan after the government announced a program to help small businesses. He could not understand why the government was doing this except to win votes in the next election. He said that Pakistan has many thousands of small businesses. There are dozens on every street. What Pakistan needs are large modern companies that can compete in the global marketplace and pay decent wages.

I am not arguing that government assistance should be provided to large businesses instead of the small. I think that most government aid to both types is a mistake. I suspect that programs to aid SMEs are popular in both rich and poor countries primarily because of political pressure rather than any sound economic justification. In pressuring the government for aid, owners of small businesses may have a political advantage compared with large businesses. First, the many owners of small businesses constitute a powerful voting block. Second, when they combine into industry organizations, they have the financial resources to influence governments. It is for the same reasons that farmers who comprise only a small percentage of the population in rich countries seem to have considerable political influence and are successful in pressuring governments to help them at the expense of the rest of the population. It is not only large companies that engage in rent-seeking behavior. Aid to SMEs can also be thought of as politicians using tax revenues to buy the votes of small business owners—a common practice in most countries.

Company Ownership Should Evolve Naturally

At first glance, companies with widespread share ownership have some appeal. They allow all of the citizens to be owners of important companies and not just a few rich, powerful families or financial institutions. It is suggested that this type of ownership would bring about a more equitable distribution of income, reduce crony capitalism, and create a more democratic society. I have even seen some politicians refer to selling the shares of state-owned companies to many small investors as *peopleization* rather than privatization. There is a romantic notion that capitalism will have a more acceptable face if companies are owned by ordinary citizens.

It is hard to find much evidence to support these claims. The country that has the most companies with widespread ownership, the United States, has one of the most unequal distributions of income. Companies with widespread ownership are also likely to use the powers of the government if they can to increase their profits, in other words, to engage in rent seeking. Crony capitalism is not restricted to just companies with closely held ownership. Encouraging the public to own shares in companies may reduce their support for a capitalist system when they discover that either the controlling shareholder or the managers have diverted a large share of the profits to themselves.

The ultimate form of widespread share ownership is government ownership. The government owns and manages companies supposedly for the benefit of everyone. As will be discussed later, the performance of state-owned enterprises has usually been poor. I am concerned that forcing companies to have widespread ownership will also result in poor company performance, particularly if the country's legal and regulatory institutions for these companies are not well developed. Even in the United States where these laws and institutions are perhaps the most developed of any country, there is considerable doubt as to whether companies with widespread share ownership are performing as well as they could.

I favor improving the legal and regulatory institutions for stock markets but not forcing companies to have widespread share ownership. The type of company ownership should evolve naturally in response to market conditions. As the economy grows, companies become larger, and legal and regulatory institutions improve. Companies may then move toward widespread ownership to attract capital. Small investors will then have confidence that they will be treated fairly and will be willing to purchase shares in companies.

Standards of Corporate Social Responsibility

The third criticism of large companies is that they fail to be socially responsible. A recent movement is for nongovernmental organizations to take over some of the traditional functions of governments to regulate the private sector and establish standards of corporate social responsibility. They then attempt to encourage or pressure large companies to abide by these standards.

Numerous sets of standards have been put forth. Some of the more important ones and their sponsors are listed in Box 3-1. As one can see from this list, a variety of different organizations, including the United Nations, groups of businesspeople, and environmental and religious organizations, have prepared standards.

The standards usually cover the same general issues but differ in the details. The main issues covered by these standards are as follows:

1. *Accountability*—A company should report to its various stakeholders on its compliance with the set of standards.
2. *Business Conduct*—A company should comply with all relevant laws, not engage in anti-competitive activities, and not bribe government officials.
3. *Community Involvement*—A company should assist in local economic development, employ underutilized workers, and give to charities.
4. *Corporate Governance*—A company should protect the rights of shareholders.
5. *Environment*—A company should protect the environment, including but not limited to meeting all relevant laws and regulations, protecting its employees from hazardous materials, and contributing to the development of public policy concerning the environment.
6. *Human Rights*—A company should protect the health and safety of its workers, not use child or forced labor, pay a living wage, allow workers to be represented by unions, and protect indigenous peoples.
7. *Consumers*—A company should not engage in deceptive advertising, should sell only high-quality and safe products and services, and should respect consumer privacy.
8. *Employees*—A company should not discriminate in hiring, salaries, or promotions and should provide training, child and elder

care, maternity or paternity leave, and assistance or severance for employees who are laid off.

Box 3-1
Standards of Corporate Social
Responsibility

1. *Caux Principles for Business* (1994) sponsored by the Caux Roundtable of senior business leaders.
2. *Global Reporting Initiative* (1999) led by the Coalition of Environmentally Responsible Economies.
3. *Global Sullivan Principles* (1999) written by the Reverend Leon Sullivan.
4. *OECD Guidelines for Multinational Corporations* (revised in 2000) prepared by the Organization for Economic Cooperation and Development.
5. *Principles for Global Corporate Responsibility—Benchmarks* (revised in 1998) prepared by several religious organizations from the United Kingdom and North America.
6. *Social Accountability 8000* (issued in 1998) sponsored by Social Accountability International, a nongovernmental organization.
7. *United Nations Global Compact* (issued in 1999) sponsored by the United Nations.

Source: Organization for Economic Cooperation and Development, "OECD Guidelines for Multinational Enterprises 2001, Focus: Global Instruments for Corporate Responsibility, Annual Report 2001," p. 60.

It is important to note that most governments already have laws and regulations in place that require private firms to comply with many of these standards but not all. For example, governments usually require firms to limit pollution, protect the rights of shareholders if the company is a public company (i.e., listed on a stock exchange), not engage in anti-competitive acts, not engage in bribery, provide healthy and safe working conditions, pay at least a minimum wage, sell only healthy and safe products, and so forth.

79

However, governments usually do not require private firms to meet some of these standards because they have concluded that this is not an appropriate responsibility of private firms. For example, it is highly debatable whether private companies should be required to provide special reports to various interest groups (stakeholders) other than their shareholders, to engage in local economic development activities, or provide child and elder care for their employees. The primary responsibility of private firms is to become more efficient, sell better products and services, and expand and grow. Competitive markets will provide them with the incentive to do this. The Nobel Prize–winning economist Milton Friedman said this better than I can more than 40 years ago: "There is one and only one social responsibility of business—to use its resources and engage in activities designed to increase profits so long as it stays within the rules of the game, which is to say, engages in open and free competition without deception and fraud."[35]

This book does not argue that governments should never intervene in the private sector to regulate the activities of private firms. To improve the business environment, governments may have to regulate some activities because of what economists call *market failures*. The more important failures are the result of *externalities* (for example, pollution) and *information asymmetries* (for example, inability of consumers to judge the safety or quality of products). Governments, however, need to carefully evaluate the impact of these regulations on various groups in society and determine whether the benefits exceed the costs. Moreover, this book emphasizes that governments should take into account their ability to implement policies impacting the private sector and to adopt those that they are capable of implementing.

Thus, the organizations that created or support these standards must believe that government laws and regulations regulating private firms are weak or that governments are not adequately enforcing them. Also, they seem to believe that private companies should meet certain standards in areas that governments typically do not believe are the responsibility of private firms. Thus, the organizations believe that they should take on a quasi-government role of establishing and enforcing standards to supplement what governments are doing. This role could begin to resemble vigilante justice in American cowboy movies where a posse of concerned citizens instead of the sheriff would capture someone they believe to be a criminal, and the posse instead of the courts would determine his punishment.

Private Enforcement of Corporate Social Responsibility

Organizations that created these standards and their supporters have used a number of ways to encourage or force companies to abide by these standards. Perhaps the most frequently mentioned is to convince companies that adopting these standards will increase their profits. Speeches and reports on corporate social responsibility often stress this point, which is probably not harmful, but it is rather naive and pointless.

I agree that companies pursuing higher profits and facing competitive pressure are likely to achieve many of these standards without government regulation. For example, the best way for a company to attract a stable, high-quality workforce is to pay competitive wages and to offer good working conditions. The best way to increase sales and profits is to sell high-quality products at reasonable prices. The best way to ensure a high stock price and raise equity capital is to protect the rights of its shareholders.

Long before any of these various standards were created, however, most companies were already aware of how they could increase profits by good treatment of their workers, consumers, and shareholders. It is unlikely that the organizations that have created these standards, for example, the United Nations, the OECD, or the World Bank, are able to teach companies anything new about how to increase profits.

Corporations are less likely to voluntarily follow these standards if doing so would force the company to raise prices or else suffer a large reduction in profits. For example, a company would have to raise prices to pay for expensive pollution control equipment that exceeds the standards currently established by the government or to raise wages to whatever level is defined to be a "living wage" if that exceeds the current competitive wage level in the country. Moreover, if the company is selling its products and services in a competitive market, raising prices when other companies do not will result in reduced sales, lower revenue, and possible bankruptcy.

Perhaps recognizing that companies will not voluntarily implement those standards that force them to raise prices, proponents of these standards have shifted toward mechanisms to pressure reluctant companies to implement them. One form of pressure is to organize a consumer boycott of products sold by firms that violate these standards. Another is to organize an investor boycott of the shares of these companies. For example, various investment funds in rich countries have been created that only invest in the shares of companies that they judge to be socially responsible. The hope seems to be that reduced investor demand will reduce the share price for companies that do not comply with these standards and make it difficult for them to raise capital.

Government Enforcement of Corporate Social Responsibility

I have no objection if individuals or private organizations encourage companies to follow particular standards of behavior. Consumers should have the legal right to join a boycott and not buy products or services from a company whose activities they oppose. In a market economy, consumers should be free to decide which products they want to buy based on whatever criteria they choose to employ. Similarly, investors should be able to invest in "socially responsible" funds or to buy shares in some companies but not others for whatever reason they think is important. But according to the same principal, companies should have the same right to adopt or to ignore these standards. They should not be under any legal obligation to follow them except to the extent that they need to comply with the various government laws that regulate the behavior of private companies.

My concern, however, is that some supporters of these standards of corporate social responsibility are proposing that governments use their legal power to force companies to abide by them. This is likely to violate basic democratic principals of government and impair the performance of companies.[36]

Some of the proponents of standards of corporate social responsibility seem to naively believe that everyone in society will benefit if companies adopt these standards and would support them if they only had a better understanding of them. No one would be harmed by enforcing these standards and there is no conflict or disagreement about adopting these standards. In fact, a particular standard will almost always benefit some groups but harm others. Since these standards are stated in general and imprecise terms, many people may support them. However, there is likely to be substantial disagreement when these standards are made more precise and detailed or are actually enforced.

To give just one example, it might seem at first glance than no reasonable person would object to companies paying a "living wage." But how do these organizations or companies determine the precise level of the living wage? Should it be the same for all countries and all types of workers? What is considered a living wage in France is probably much higher than in India. It would be economically impossible for companies in poor countries to pay a minimum wage comparable with that in the United States or Europe. The various sets of standards provide little guidance.

I know of no scientific or objective methodology for determining such a wage, and there is likely to be widespread disagreement about what the wage should be. Labor unions and existing workers will support a high level. Shareholders, however, may complain that this will reduce profits. Consumers may object because this increases the prices of the products and services that they buy. Young people may suffer because a high minimum wage can reduce the total number of jobs and make it difficult for them to find any job.

Most of the various standards of corporate social responsibility state that the company's board of directors and managers should somehow take into account the interests of all "stakeholders" who are affected by the company's operations and not just the owners of the company. In effect, these managers would have to take on the difficult job of balancing the conflicting interests of various stakeholders, including their shareholders. The standards do not say who these stakeholders are, but frequently mentioned are workers, consumers, children, the poor, young people, old people, women, racial or religious minorities, citizens concerned about the environment, disadvantaged groups, and so forth.

In a democratic society, government has the responsibility to balance the conflicting interests of all citizens, and it should not delegate this responsibility to the officials of these various organizations that created these standards or to company managers. They are not elected representatives of the people. Also, the various standards of social responsibility should not be given any legal status nor should the self-appointed organizations that devised the standards be given any legal authority to enforce them.

Moreover, any attempt to legally require companies to abide by such vague standards of social responsibility runs the risk of introducing into private companies the same confused mix of commercial, social, and political objectives that led to the poor performance of state-owned enterprises. Transparency and accountability are enhanced when these responsibilities are clearly divided between government and private firms. If it is accepted that private firms have a mandate to pursue a wide range of noncommercial objectives, I am afraid that politicians will begin to interfere in their operations in the same way they did with state-owned enterprises. For example, I can imagine a government minister telling the general manager of a private firm that he has a social responsibility to hire more workers to reduce unemployment before the next election, keep prices low to help the government control inflation, hire supporters of the political party in power, invest more in the minister's home district, or hire the minister's nephew.

A similar argument was made by Professor Michael C. Jensen at the Harvard Business School who states, " . . . stakeholder theory, argues that managers should make decisions so as to take account of the interests of all stakeholders in a firm (including not only financial claimants, but also employees, customers, communities, governmental officials, and under some interpretations the environment, terrorists, and blackmailers). Because the advocates of stakeholder theory refuse to specify how to make the necessary tradeoffs among these competing interests they leave managers with a theory that makes it impossible for them to make purposeful decisions. With no way to keep score, stakeholder theory makes managers unaccountable for their actions. It seems clear that such a theory can be attractive to the self-interest of managers and directors."[37] In other words, as was the case with state-owned enterprises, broad and imprecise objectives allow managers to escape responsibility for achieving any objective—multiple objectives mean no objective.

To a limited extent, a few rich countries have given private firms a legal mandate to pursue broad social objectives, but poor countries should not follow this example. Germany has tried to develop what it calls a "social market" economy. For example, Germany requires that a company must appoint a representative of the company's workers as a director on its supervisory board along with those who represent the interest of the shareholders. However, this means that only two out of the many stakeholders are represented on the board—shareholders and employees. If it is accepted that the board of directors should represent the interests of all stakeholders, the board would have to be expanded to include representatives of other stakeholders as well. The board of a company would begin to resemble the national parliament.

In some countries, governments are beginning to require companies to report on their achievement of social objectives in addition to normal commercial objectives. This requirement could be the first step in legitimizing the concept that private companies should be legally required to abide by one of these various standards of social responsibility in addition to the normal governments laws that regulate their behavior. For example, the Danish Ministry of Social Affairs has prepared a Social Index and published a 40-page guide to help private companies prepare the index. According to the guide, "The Social Index is a tool for measuring the degree to which a company lives up to its social responsibilities. It is a self-evaluation tool forcing the company to reflect on its social commitment and the results. It thus provides a platform for discussion of where the company scores and also where it can make improvements."[38] In the United Kingdom, an amendment to the 1995 Pensions Act requires pension funds to publish their investment policy (Statement of Investment Principles), and it must specify, among other things, the extent to which social, environmental, and ethical issues are considered in making investment decisions. France and Belgium have enacted similar requirements.

As noted earlier, governments have in place policies, laws, and regulations that, in effect, require private firms to abide by many of these standards of social responsibility though they are usually not described in this way. In enacting these laws, we expect governments to evaluate the various tradeoffs and balance the interests of all groups in society. Democratic governments are far from perfect in doing this, but to again paraphrase Winston Churchill, they will do this better than any other form of government or any other organizations in society.

In a democratic society, the organizations that have created these standards of corporate social responsibility are free to persuade companies to adopt a tougher standard from those specified in the law or additional standards not now specified in the law. The organizations are also free to convince governments that they need to change the laws or to enforce them better. However, it violates basic democratic principles for the government to give these or other private organizations any legal authority to establish and enforce such standards.

Large Companies Are Not the Problem

The recent criticism of large companies is misguided and diverts attention from the serious weaknesses in the business environment in most poor countries. Critics view large companies as powerful, secretive organizations owned by a few rich people that must be brought under the control of the public and forced to behave in a socially responsible manner. Their activities should be more transparent, and they should be accountable to all interest groups in society and not just their shareholders. In other words, they should be more like a government ministry or state-owned enterprise.

I find this thinking surprising given the miserable performance of both government ministries and state-owned enterprises in most poor countries. Private businesses in poor countries are the one type of institution that has the potential to become modern, well managed, and efficient and thus increase the rate of economic growth and reduce poverty. Turning them into quasi-public institutions with a confused mix of social and commercial objectives will destroy this potential. To achieve this potential, however, private businesses must operate in an environment that encourages them to improve their performance. Perhaps the most important challenge facing governments is to create such an environment, which is the subject of the balance of this book.

4. Privatization: Just Sell It

A central element of any program to develop the private sector is that the government should transfer commercial activities now carried out by state-owned enterprises or government agencies to the private sector. Since the early 1980s, many poor countries have *privatized* state-owned enterprises, in other words, transferred ownership to private investors. There is widespread agreement that state-owned enterprises have performed badly and that privatized companies have usually performed better. I will not attempt to summarize the hundred or more studies that provide empirical data that demonstrate this conclusion.[1] Few now argue, at least publicly, that privatization is a poor policy.

Given this acceptance of the need to privatize state-owned enterprises, one would expect that there is widespread agreement on both the objectives of privatization and the methods of privatization that best achieves those objectives. Instead, the voluminous literature on privatization contains a bewildering list of objectives. Similarly, numerous methods or techniques of privatization have been used, including trade sales, initial public offerings, management-employee buyouts, voucher privatization, and capitalizing pension funds.

In contrast to most other issues in economic development, international development agencies, consultants, and academics do not seem to have reached a consensus on what the objectives of privatization ought to be and what methods will best achieve those objectives. The prevailing view seems to be that each country is unique and the objectives and methods of privatization need to be tailored to the specific circumstances of each country.

The following is typical of what is written about privatization: "Privatization is neither a simple or a uniform process. Starting points differ; countries have varying objectives, face a wide and shifting range of problems and obstacles, and thus need to adopt different strategies and tactics to achieve their privatization objectives. There is no universally applicable approach to privatization, and the attempt to apply a 'one size fits all' has proved ineffective and counterproductive."[2]

The vast literature on privatization gives little guidance to countries on what the objectives of the privatization ought to be. However, it is recognized that countries should specify their objectives and then design a privatization program to achieve those objectives. For example, one World Bank study says, "A privatization strategy has to be assessed in light of the objectives pursued. Most privatization methods and techniques are not inherently good or bad, but merely more or less well suited to the pursuit of one or more specific objectives. The more objectives there are, the more complex the entire privatization process."[3]

The only feature of a privatization program that advisers seem to agree on is that the program should be *transparent*. In other words, the criteria and process used to select the preferred private owner should be easily understood and open to public examination. The purpose is to minimize corruption, for example, selling state-owned enterprises to favored buyers at low prices.

This unwillingness for international development institutions, experts, and advisers to provide guidance to poor countries on how best to privatize is puzzling for three reasons. First, it is in contrast to most other issues in development economics in which there is usually a recognized consensus on the best policy or practice. It would be surprising to see statements similar to those made about privatization made about other issues such as fiscal and monetary policy, trade reform, or bank supervision.

For example, concerning fiscal and monetary policy, I cannot imagine the International Monetary Fund saying that each country is unique and circumstances differ greatly from country to country. Thus, it is desirable for some countries to have large government deficits financed by printing money and thereby induce hyperinflation while other countries have a balanced budget to achieve stable prices. A country is free to choose either, depending on the objectives of the government. In fact, the IMF is quite willing to tell governments what the objectives ought to be and how to achieve them. Similarly, I cannot imagine the World Bank arguing that the system of bank supervision should vary greatly from country to country, depending on the special characteristics of each country. Concerning these issues, "one size does fit all."

Governments often like to believe that their countries are different from others, and thus a privatization program needs to be designed to fit their special features. In contrast, I am struck by the similarities between poor countries rather than by their differences. Except possibly for the former communist countries, I am hard-pressed to identify a particular feature of a country that would justify a special approach to privatization.

Second, in contrast to other issues, experts and advisers on privatization seem more willing to accommodate political opposition to privatization and to accept a privatization program that will be popular even if this sacrifices important economic and development objectives. Too often, discussions of privatization seem to start off with the goal of finding a popular method of privatization. If the government says that it needs to adopt a particular method of privatization to have it accepted by the public, this seems to be accepted with little disagreement.

Privatization advisers may support popular methods because they want to complete transactions quickly. For example, investment banks often advise on privatization, and they usually earn their fees only when a transaction is completed. They are unlikely to recommend a privatization method that is unpopular even if it better achieves the objectives of privatization.

A better strategy in my view is that advisers should recommend to governments what is best practice from the point of view of increasing economic efficiency and growth even if this is likely to encounter opposition. Governments then have two choices to deal with opposition. They can attempt to explain and persuade the public why the preferred method of privatization is, in the long run, the best interest of the nation. A frequent failing of privatization programs is that they do not include a well-thought-out public relations campaign to explain the benefits of privatization to the public.

If persuasion fails, then the government may be forced to modify their preferred approach to privatization to win public support. A second-best method of privatization is still probably better than no privatization at all. However, governments and their advisers should always keep in mind what is best practice and what is being sacrificed to win public support.

Third, the various studies of the impact of privatization surprisingly do focus on just one criterion for measuring the success or failure of privatization. This criterion is the extent to which the operating efficiency or productivity and thus profits of the enterprise have improved after privatization. A variety of data are used to measure the improvement, including production costs, quality of products, labor productivity, sales revenue, and investment. Though many other objectives are often given for a privatization program, these studies rarely consider them. They seem to implicitly accept that the primary objective of privatization is improving economic efficiency. There seems to be little agreement about the *ex ante* objectives when designing a privatization program, but there is wide agreement *ex post* when evaluating the success of a program.

In the rest of this chapter, I will argue that there is only one primary objective of privatization and that a best-practice method of privatization exists to achieve that objective. In brief, the objective is to increase the economic efficiency or productivity of the enterprise and thus increase profitability. The best-practice method is to open up the bidding to buy the enterprise to all possible investors, both foreign and domestic, and to choose the winning bidder based only on the highest cash price offered. In other words, governments should follow the normal practice in the private sector of selling an asset. This method is also simple, transparent, and within the capabilities of most governments to implement. I do admit, however, that special circumstances in the former communist countries may require a different approach to privatization, and I will discuss those circumstances. However, they are the exception and not the rule.

Objectives of Privatization

One World Bank publication lists 37 possible economic, social, and political objectives for a privatization program. For the complete list, see Box 4-1. An unfortunate implication of such a lengthy list of objectives is that governments can freely choose from this list, any objective is as important as any other, and there are no conflicts between the objectives. Though there is no conflict between some of these objectives, there is a serious conflict between others and the primary efficiency objective. Should the efficiency objective be sacrificed to achieve these other objectives?

In almost all cases in which there is a conflict with the efficiency objective, these other objectives are unimportant, undesirable, or, if desirable, there are better methods to achieve them than through privatization. As an obvious example, few would publicly support one of the objectives in Box 4-1, namely, to enrich those managing or implementing privatization projects, though there are too many examples of which this was an objective of privatization. A less obvious example is the objective of developing a national middle class. Even if this is a desirable objective, privatization is not the best way of achieving it.

If the government adopts a lengthy list of objectives for its privatization program, I am concerned that it will repeat the mistakes that were made in managing its state-owned companies. Governments tried to use them to achieve a variety of economic and social objectives. This confused mixture, however, has usually meant that these companies did not achieve any of the objectives very well. Thus governments are now turning to privatization.

For example, a state-owned company was often expected to be efficient and profitable but nevertheless subsidize the sale of its product or service, hire large numbers of workers to help the government achieve its employment objectives, or, even worse, provide lucrative contracts or high-paying jobs to supporters, relatives, and cronies of the politicians in power. Government attempts to use the privatization process or privatized companies to achieve a similar mix of objectives will probably also fail.

The government should achieve its economic efficiency objective by transferring ownership of state-owned companies to private owners using the best-practice method described here. The government should then achieve its social objectives through other policies (for example, regulation, social welfare programs, subsidies, taxes), but not through its ownership of companies. Moreover, this separation of objectives will create greater transparency and accountability in achieving both economic and social objectives.

When I discuss below the various methods of privatization that deviate from best practice, I will describe the objectives that these methods are supposed to achieve and why these objectives are unimportant, undesirable, or can be achieved better through other means.

Methods of Privatization

A wide variety of different methods of privatization have been used. (To simplify the discussion, I am assuming that the government

Box 4-1
Possible Objectives of Privatization

1) *Efficiency and Development of the Economy*

   a) Create a market economy—the key objective in economies in transition
   b) Encourage private enterprise and expansion of the private sector in general
   c) Promote macroeconomic or sectoral efficiency and competitiveness
   d) Foster economic flexibility and eliminate rigidities
   e) Promote competition, particularly by abolishing monopolies
   f) Establish or develop efficient capital markets, allowing better capture and mobilization of domestic savings
   g) Improve access to foreign markets for domestic products
   h) Promote domestic investment
   i) Promote foreign investment
   j) Promote integration of the domestic economy into the world economy
   k) Maintain or create employment

2) *Efficiency and Development of the Enterprise*

   a) Foster the enterprise's efficiency and its domestic and international competitiveness
   b) Introduce new technologies and promote innovation
   c) Upgrade plant and equipment
   d) Increase productivity, including utilization of industrial plant
   e) Improve the quality of the goods and services produced
   f) Introduce new management methods and teams
   g) Allow the enterprise to enter into domestic and international alliances essential to its survival

(continued next page)

3) *Budgetary and Financial Improvements*

a) Maximize net privatization receipts in order to fund government expenditures, reduce taxation, trim the public sector deficit, or pay off public debt

b) Reduce the financial drain of the SOEs on the state (in the form of subsidies, unpaid taxes, loan arrears, guarantees given, and so on)

c) Mobilize private sources to finance investments that can no longer be funded from public finances

d) Generate new sources of tax revenue

e) Limit the future risk of demands on the budget inherent in state ownership of businesses, including the need to provide capital for their expansion or to rescue them if they are in financial trouble

f) Reduce capital flight abroad and repatriate capital already transferred

4) *Income Distribution or Redistribution*

a) Foster broader capital ownership and promote popular or mass capitalism

b) Develop a national middle class

c) Foster the economic development of a particular group (ethnic or other) in society

d) Encourage employee ownership (also important for efficiency reasons)

e) Restore full rights to former owners of property expropriated by previous regimes

f) Enrich those managing or implementing privatization projects (rarely an admitted objective)

5) *Political Considerations*

a) Reduce the size and scope of the public sector or its share in economic activity

(continued next page)

> b) Redefine the field of activity of the public sector, abandoning production tasks and focusing on the core of governmental functions, including the creation of an environment favorable to private economic activity
>
> c) Reduce or eliminate the ability of a future government to reverse the measures taken by the incumbent government to alter the role of the state in the economy
>
> d) Reduce the opportunities for corruption and misuse of public property by government officials and SOE managers
>
> e) Reduce the grip of a particular party or group (communist party, nomenclature, or labor unions, for example) on the economy
>
> f) Raise the government's popularity and its likelihood of being returned to power in the next elections.
>
> Source: Pierre Guislan, *The Privatization Challenge: A Strategic, Legal, and Institutional Analysis of International Experience*, World Bank Regional and Sectoral Studies (World Bank, 1997), p. 20.

is selling shares in a limited-liability or joint-stock company).[4] These methods have four important distinguishing characteristics:

1. which types of investors are permitted to purchase shares in the company,
2. whether the government is selling all or part of the shares in the company,
3. the criteria used to select the preferred investor, and
4. the extent to which the purchase is financed by debt.

The first characteristic is whether there are restrictions on the types of investors who are allowed to become owners or preferences given to some investors over others. In some cases, only domestic investors but not foreign investors are allowed to purchase shares. Preference is sometimes given to certain religious or ethnic groups in a country, for example, the Bumiputra in Malaysia or citizens of African countries that are not from Chinese or Indian ethnic groups. Managers and workers in a company may be sold shares on favorable terms and become the dominant or controlling owners in what is sometimes called a *management-employee buyout* (MEBO).

Some privatization programs have a preference for many small investors over a few large investors. Shares in a company may be sold to many investors either domestic or foreign with no single investor owning more than a small percentage of the total shares. This sale is done through an *initial public offering* (IPO), which is also called *share-issue privatization*. A variation is for the government to sell shares at a discount to small investors who do not usually own shares and thus encourage widespread share ownership. An extreme form of this method is to give shares to all citizens. This sale is typically done by allowing citizens to buy their shares using vouchers sold to them by the government for a small payment.

In other cases, most or all the shares are sold to a single large investor, sometimes referred to as *trade sale* or sale to a *strategic investor*. Shares may also be sold or even given to new or existing financial institutions such as pension funds or investment funds. Though usually not admitted publicly, preference may be given to politicians, their families, cronies, and political supporters.

The second characteristic is whether the government is transferring all or just part of the ownership of an enterprise and whether the transfer occurs all at once or in stages (sometimes called *tranches*). The simplest case is when the government transfers 100 percent of the ownership in a single transaction. In other cases, governments may sell only part of the shares of a company and keep the remainder indefinitely. Even if the government sells all of the ordinary shares, it may keep a special *golden share* that gives the government certain rights over the operation or ownership of the company after privatization.

Sometimes, the government sells part of the shares, called the first tranche, and then waits for some time to sell the remainder, the second tranche. The first tranche might be sold to a strategic investor, and the second sold to many investors in an initial public offering.

A related question is whether the government is selling new or existing shares in a company. Selling existing shares means that sales revenue accrues to the government as the owner of these shares. Selling new shares means that the revenue accrues to the company and thus becomes a source of capital for new investment. As a result, the ownership is split between the purchasers of the new shares and the government as the owner of the existing shares.

The third characteristic is how the government chooses which particular private investors will take over ownership. One approach is to sell all or part of the shares in a company to the investor who offers the highest purchase price. Sometimes, however, the government introduces other considerations, for example, the experience and qualifications of the investor and his plan for managing the business after privatization. An investor may be chosen because he promises to invest more in the company than other investors, retain more of the workers, bring in new technology, provide access to foreign markets, and so forth.

The fourth characteristic is the extent to which the sale is financed by debt, in other words, the degree of *leverage*. The higher the leverage, the less the purchaser will have to pay to take control of the company. Leverage can occur in three ways:

- First, before privatization, the state-owned company may already be partially financed by debt such as loans from banks. The greater the amount of debt on the balance sheet of the company, the smaller the value of the equity and thus the less the purchaser will have to pay for the equity.
- Second, the purchaser may borrow part of the purchase price from banks or other lenders.
- Third, the government may allow the purchaser to pay in installments over a number of years and thus, in effect, makes a loan to the purchaser for part of the purchase price.

Best Practice

Privatization should have one primary objective: to make the former state-owned companies as productive, well managed, and profitable as possible, in other words, the objective of economic efficiency. Which method of privatization will best achieve this fundamental objective? The best method has five main features. The government should

1. offer to *sell 100 percent* of the state-owned company in a competitive auction,
2. allow the auction to be *open to all investors* both domestic and foreign on equal terms,
3. place *no conditions* on how the new owner may operate the company except those resulting from laws and regulations that normally apply to private companies,

4. select the winning bidder based only on who offers the *highest cash price* to purchase the company, and

5. not permit highly *leveraged* sales, in other words, the amount of debt directly or indirectly financing the company or the purchase price should be within reasonable limits.

If this method is followed, the winning bidder is likely to be the domestic or foreign investor that has the best plan or strategy for improving the profitability of the state-owned company. For this reason, he is sometimes called a *strategic* investor. He will make the highest bid because he can make the company more efficient and profitable than any of the other bidders.

Another advantage is that this method is transparent and only one criterion is used to select the winning bidder, namely, the highest cash bid. There is little discretion on the part of the privatization officials and thus little chance that they can be accused of favoritism or corruption in selecting the winner. When the purchase price is the only criterion in selecting the winner, some privatization agencies open up the bids on national television and the winner is immediately announced, subject, of course, to the winner actually making the payment.

Though this method of privatization will best achieve the economic efficiency objective, it must be emphasized that a private company will only perform well if it operates in a good business environment. No method of privatization can compensate for a weak environment. Most of this book is devoted to how governments can improve the environment, for example, competitive markets, good regulation of banks and monopolies, a legal and regulatory environment suitable for private firms, and so forth.

In particular, the government may need to establish a regulatory regime before the privatization of those state-owned enterprises that are likely to remain a monopoly, for example, power and water distribution companies. These enterprises are often referred to as *natural monopolies* because the technology of production does not permit more than one supplier (for example, it is not feasible to have multiple power lines or water lines going down the same street). Many problems with such regulation have been identified (for example, cost-plus type regulation reduces incentives for the utility to keep costs low). During privatization, one problem is the uncertainty about how this regulation will be implemented. Naturally, investors will want to know the details of the regulatory regime before making a bid because the level of regulated prices will determine future company revenues. Investors are likely to be concerned that the government may change the regulatory regime to their detriment after privatization, and this *regulatory risk* will reduce the price investors are willing to pay or cause them to withdraw from the auction.

Maximizing Revenue

A secondary but still important objective of a privatization program is that the government should obtain maximum revenue from the sale of state-owned enterprises consistent with the primary objective of maximizing economic efficiency. This objective is important to make sure that privatization does not enrich a few people who purchased the company at the expense of the rest of the population. These assets belong to all citizens, and the government should obtain the maximum sales revenue for their benefit. This revenue can be used to reduce taxes, provide additional services, or reduce the government's indebtedness. This revenue objective could also be called the objective of social equity or fairness.

Achievement of the revenue objective, however, should not sacrifice the efficiency objective. For example, the government should not create a legal monopoly that will charge high prices to consumers just to obtain a higher privatization sale price.

The best-practice method of privatization just described will achieve this objective of maximizing government revenue from the sale of the enterprise. Opening the auction to all investors will increase the number of bidders and thus increase the likely sale price. Investors will bid an amount based on their estimate of the future cash flow from managing the company. As discussed below, other methods of privatization have been argued to increase the revenues to the government from privatization, but this is unlikely.

In more technical terms, private-sector investors will determine the highest price they are willing to pay by calculating the *present discounted value* of the future cash flow of the company (revenues minus costs and new investments). The discount rate used is the rate of return that investors require on investments of similar risk (sometimes called the *cost of capital*). Without going into the details, it can be shown that if the auction is competitive, the government will capture through the sale price any above-normal future profits that an investor might earn from owning the company. After paying the sale price, the investor will just earn a normal rate of return or profit on his investment.

Nonprice Criteria

Governments sometimes consider other criteria besides the highest bid in selecting the winning bidder. One reason is that the government wants to judge which investor is the most qualified to own the business or has the best plan for managing the business. Though not perfect, the highest bid is the best guide that the government has to determine the most qualified owner with the best business plan and there is no need to introduce other criteria.

Another reason is that the government wants to evaluate the proposed business plans based on the same confused mixture of economic and social objectives that was the downfall of state-owned enterprises. The government may attempt to rank or score the business plan according to such criteria as the extent of new investment, likely employment levels, increased sales, future prices, and so forth. Naturally, prospective bidders will construct a business plan that best achieves whatever social and commercial objectives are given high priority by the government. For example, if the government wants to keep prices low, the bidder will promise to do so. If the government wants the company to invest in backward regions of the country, the bidder will promise to do so. Whether or not the winning bidder actually fulfills these promises is another problem.

Governments fail to see the inherent contradiction between evaluating the proposed business plans and the basic reason why the government is privatizing the enterprise. In accepting privatization, the government is saying that it is not capable of managing a commercial business and wants to have this done by the private sector. Yet, the government insists on approving the business plan of the new owners and directing how the company is managed after privatization. If this is in fact a desirable practice, the government should extend this policy to all private companies and not just those that are privatized. All private companies would have to submit their business plans each year for the government to review and approve.

Why are only former state-owned enterprises selected for this special review of their business plans?[5]

One criterion sometimes used in evaluating the business plan is how much the new owner promises to invest in expansion and modernization. This criterion may be appealing because of the great need for new investment in the company. In some cases, an *investment auction* has been proposed in which the amount that the new owner promises to invest in the company after privatization is considered along with the purchase price in determining the winning bidder.

Though perhaps superficially appealing, such an auction is illogical. The investor is being judged on how much he is willing to invest in improving his own property. This is like selling your home to a new owner based on how much the new owner promises to spend after sale on repairing, modernizing, and improving the house rather than the price he pays to buy the house. As a home owner, I do not plan on adopting this method for selling my house.

Moreover, including an investment criterion can distort the bidding process and result in a less qualified investor taking ownership. This outcome is possible if the government selects a winning bidder who offers a lower purchase price but a higher future investment than another bidder. The bidding can turn into a liar's contest in which an investor promises large future investments if he can reduce his up-front purchase cost. Once the investor takes over ownership, he expects to delay or renegotiate the investment commitment. The government's ability to enforce such a commitment is weak. The end result may be that a better qualified and more honest investor was not selected because he refused to make unrealistic promises about future investment but was willing to pay a higher purchase price.

A better strategy for the government is to create a business environment that gives the proper incentives for the new private owners to invest in the privatized companies. New owners should choose to invest because it is in their interest to do so rather than because they are forced to do so by commitments or conditions of privatization.

Adopting complex criteria for judging the best owner reduces transparency and increases the chances of corruption. It becomes almost impossible to know whether the government is honestly and objectively evaluating the various bidders if multiple criteria are used to select the winner or whether the choice was influenced by bribes or preference given to relatives, friends, and cronies of the politicians in power.

Operating Conditions

For reasons similar to why governments sometimes want to consider nonprice criteria in selecting the winning bidder, they may also place conditions in the sales contract on how the new owner may manage the company. For example, the new company may not lay off workers or must invest so much each year.

The reason is that the government does not trust the new owner to manage the company well or wants to use the company even after privatization to achieve social objectives. Again, stipulating conditions runs the risk of re-creating the confused mixture of objectives that impaired the performance of state-owned companies. If a privatized company is expected to meet social objectives, this should be spelled out in public laws and regulations that apply to all firms and not in obscure clauses of a privatization sales contract that are often confidential.

The new owners of a privatized company should not be expected to do any more or any less to meet the needs of society than other private companies as provided for in laws and regulations. Imposing these social obligations through the privatization process is fundamentally anti-democratic because it bypasses the normal government process for enacting laws that regulate the behavior of private firms.

Such conditions will also reduce the purchase price offered for the company. Thus, they will impose a cost on the government. However, no one knows what the purchase price would have been in the absence of these conditions and thus the cost of these social objectives. The cost of using privatization to achieve these social objectives may be high, and the government would not have imposed these conditions if it knew the cost.

Strategic Companies

In deciding which companies to privatize, governments often label some as *strategic*. Such companies are kept in state ownership or are only partially privatized. The term strategic seems to suggest some national security concern or a strategic plan for the development of the economy, but it is rarely defined. Almost any reason why the government wishes to intervene in the management, place conditions on the new owners, or retain ownership or control of a company is classified as strategic and thus given an aura of legitimacy with little explanation or justification.

In the past, some governments had an industrial policy or strategy that was used to guide the development of the economy. The government would determine those industries with the greatest promise for growth and would then channel resources to those industries. This policy was sometimes used to justify why the government should retain ownership and control over the companies in those strategic industries.

The concept of an industrial policy or strategy, however, has fallen into disrepute, and most governments no longer attempt to "pick winners." Yet remnants of this concept still seem to be used to justify continued government ownership of so-called strategic companies. I find it surprising that privatization advisers or international development agencies often do not challenge or question governments when they classify a long list of companies as strategic and plan to keep them in state ownership.

Sometimes the government will sell a stake in a strategic company to an investor but retain the balance of the shares. This strategy is often viewed as a good compromise between the need to have a private investor improve the performance of the company and the need for the government to retain influence over its operations. If the share of ownership held by the government is more than 51 percent and thus the government can still control the company, the government may sign a management contract with the investor giving him control over the company.

It is rare, however, for the government to explain why it needs to retain influence over the company. The government may promise to sell the balance of its shares in the company some day in the future when it is clear that private ownership is superior to government ownership or after the need to protect some undefined strategic interest has disappeared.

Even if some form of government regulation over the company is needed, retaining an ownership stake is not the best mechanism to exercise this regulation. The government can use the full force of law if it needs to regulate the company. By mixing ownership with regulation, the government is once again mixing commercial and social objectives in a nontransparent way. Instead the government should specify in laws or regulations the noncommercial objectives that the company is expected to achieve and, if necessary, create a regulatory body to enforce this requirement.

Sometimes partial privatization is used only to attract private investment in the company with no intention of giving control over the company to private owners. Partial privatization is achieved by selling new shares in the company on the stock exchange to many small investors. Since these are new shares, the proceeds of the sale go to the company and not to the government. The government, however, still owns the original shares and effectively controls the company. Managers of state-owned companies may also favor this limited form of privatization because they are supplied with additional funds for investment or to cover the losses of the company and yet they remain in effective control of the company because of lax government oversight.

A partial sale of shares on the stock market seems to be the dominant method of privatization used in China for large state-owned enterprises. According to a recent study of 252 publicly traded companies, the government is still the controlling shareholder in more than 95 percent of these companies.[6]

In some cases, the government retains ownership of a special *golden share* while selling all of the ordinary shares to private investors. The charter or bylaws of the company specifies the special rights of the holder of the golden share. These rights can include the right to intervene in the management of the company in certain circumstances. For example, the golden share may give the government the right to approve of any new owner that takes control from the initial owner.

Though I am skeptical about the merits of the government keeping a golden share, it may be acceptable if the special rights of the government are narrow and clearly defined. For example, I can imagine a situation in which the government may want to prevent the ownership of a company from being transferred to an investor from an enemy country in time of war. If instead the rights granted by the golden share are broad and general, it could lead to undesirable government interference in the management of the company and the same problems created by state ownership.

Widespread Share Ownership

Other objectives in some privatization programs conflict with the economic efficiency objective. One such objective is to encourage widespread share ownership. Advocates of this objective argue that it will increase public support for privatization and develop stock markets because the many shareholders will frequently trade their shares. In contrast, selling the company to a strategic investor will not allow the ordinary citizens of the country to become owners, and such an investor is unlikely to trade shares on the local stock exchange.

Advocates of widespread share ownership often seem to have a romantic but unrealistic idea that it will reduce what they see as the weaknesses in a capitalist economy. Instead of a small, rich, capital-owning class exploiting everyone else, widespread share ownership will result in the *democratization of capital* and thus everyone will be an owner of capital. One class will not be exploiting another.

Of course, to be effective, this requires that all citizens own an equal share of capital, but this is unlikely because the rich will always own more than the poor. In my view, the best way to stop owners of capital from exploiting others is to expose companies to vigorous competition. Competition will ensure that companies sell high-quality products at low prices, pay reasonable wages, and do not earn excessive profits at the expense of consumers.

Another of the vague objectives of privatization mentioned previously is to create a middle class. If, as was the case in the former communist countries, the government owns many small businesses such as shops and stores, then selling them may result in a new class of small business owners who could be called middle class. In contrast, simply selling shares in large companies to many small investors does not create additional members of the middle class. To my knowledge, owning shares is not required to be middle class and is not sufficient by itself to classify someone as middle class.

If people had a better understanding of privatization, I believe that the vast majority would support it because it promises them lower prices, higher quality goods and services, more jobs, and higher incomes. Most people would consider these the main benefits of privatization and have little interest in owning shares.

A strategic investor can supply the necessary expertise to improve the management of the company. In contrast, thousands of small shareholders will have little influence over the existing managers of the company. For this reason, managers of state-owned companies often favor selling shares to many investors in the form of an initial public offering (IPO) because then no shareholder will challenge their control of the company. Investment bankers hired to assist governments with privatization also often favor this method because their fees resulting from an IPO are typically larger than a sale to a single strategic investor. As a result, however, widespread share ownership may mean that the operation of the company will be little changed from state ownership. Neither the government nor the shareholders may have any control over the managers.

As discussed earlier, such widespread share ownership does exist for large companies in some rich countries like the United States. However, such ownership creates serious problems of corporate governance. Over the years, these countries have established laws and regulatory institutions that compensate in part for the inability of thousands of small shareholders to control the managers and force managers to be at least somewhat accountable to their shareholders. If these laws and institutions are weak and underdeveloped in a poor country, forcing state-owned enterprises to have this type of ownership will result in poor company performance.

A hybrid method used by some governments is that a controlling stake is sold to a strategic investor while the balance is sold widely to the citizens of the country. This method is better than selling all of the shares to small investors but still detracts from the primary efficiency objective. The strategic investor must share any profitability gains with the other shareholders even though they contribute nothing to the management of the company. This requirement probably reduces both the share price that the strategic investor is willing to pay for the company and his incentives to improve its performance.

As discussed earlier, this hybrid also raises difficult issues of minority shareholder protection. Will the strategic investor attempt to capture more than his fair share of future profits to the detriment of other shareholders, for example, through transfer pricing with other companies owned by the investor? This is not an issue if the investor owns all of the company. Until effective measures to protect minority shareholders are in place, governments may be doing their citizens a disservice by encouraging them to become shareholders in a company controlled by a strategic investor.

Widespread share-holding schemes usually reduce revenue to the government and enrich a minority of the population at the expense of the majority. To attract small investors, governments typically sell shares at below their market value, in effect, a subsidy to the purchasers. However, only a small fraction of the population can take advantage of these schemes. They are usually the better paid, better educated, urban residents who have at least some savings to purchase these shares even at their reduced price.

For example, I recall officials proposing such a scheme in Tanzania where 80 percent of the population did not have access to electricity or a telephone much less access to a stockbroker to buy and sell shares. This would just be a subsidy to the relatively well-off urban elite.

As another example, Chile introduced a *people's capitalism* program in which citizens could purchase shares in state-owned enterprises using low interest rate loans from the government. However, to do so, they had to be taxpayers and current in their tax payments. This condition effectively ruled out the poorest groups in society.[7]

One argument for widespread ownership of shares is that it will buy the public's support for privatization. Without knowing the specific political circumstances in a country, it is hard to know whether this argument has merit. As noted earlier, such schemes usually benefit only a minority, though admittedly that minority may be the more influential segments of the population. A better strategy for a government would be to implement a public relations campaign to explain the benefits of selling a company to a strategic investor who has the expertise and incentives to make the company efficient and profitable. Buying the public's support through a subsidized sale of shares should only be used as a last resort.

Stock Market Development

Politicians often believe that widespread share ownership and thus a high volume of trading on the stock market is a sign of a rich developed economy, for example, the United States. The frantic trading on the New York Stock Exchange has come to symbolize a developed capitalist economy. The implication is that countries without a large stock exchange are backward and underdeveloped. By encouraging lots of trading of shares in recently privatized companies, the stock market and the country somehow become more developed.

In contrast, countries with smaller stock markets are those in which a typical company has a more concentrated ownership, and shares are held by a few large investors who do not trade the shares on an organized market, for example, Germany or Canada. Such countries, however, are not necessarily less developed and may be a better model for poor countries, especially those with weak legal and regulatory institutions for stock markets.

As discussed in Chapter 3, a large stock market with lots of trading is not synonymous with a well-developed stock market. Artificially increasing trading by selling shares in state-owned enterprises to many small investors may only give the illusion that the stock market is well developed. Even worse, it exposes these shareholders to a high risk that they will not receive a reasonable return on their investment and thus discredit the entire privatization program.

Restrictions on Foreign Investors

Restricting bidders to only domestic investors or giving them special preferences in the sale of state-owned enterprises reduces the pool of investors who can participate. This restriction may result in a lesser qualified owner taking control of the company and reducing the sales revenue to the government.

Fear of foreign investors is widespread in most countries, and thus restrictions on their participation in privatization are often popular. This xenophobia, however, is largely irrational and similar to other prejudices against people of different races, religions, and ethnic backgrounds. Unfortunately, opponents of privatization or domestic investors who want to buy state-owned enterprises cheaply often encourage this fear. There is little reason to think that a foreign owner will have objectives in managing a company different from a domestic owner. Both are interested in maximizing profits. In fact, a foreign owner compared with a domestic owner may be more cautious about taking actions that are perceived to be detrimental to the country because of this widespread fear. Instead of governments simply accepting these irrational fears, they should do more to change them.

It is surprising that such institutions as the World Bank that normally emphasize economic efficiency and growth seem to support the idea that domestic ownership should be emphasized over foreign ownership. A major publication of the World Bank rates the privatization programs in various African countries according to eight criteria. Though seven of the criteria are reasonable, the eighth criterion is whether the program resulted in broadening domestic ownership, which implies that there is something undesirable about foreign ownership.

The report attempts to explain why broadening domestic ownership is a desirable objective. It says that it is necessary to "garner political acceptance of privatization." Furthermore, "ownership by indigenous citizens is more palatable than outright sale to a foreign investor," and "fear of so-called 'economic neocolonialism' through privatization is a powerful force against foreign investment."[8]

Though the report does not appear to believe these fears about foreign investment are justified, it does seem to accept that the only option of the government is to accept these fears as unchangeable and to emphasize sales to domestic investors. The report then goes on to discuss various ways to broaden domestic ownership, including share-issue privatization, management and employee buyouts, and even voucher privatization.

Another reason given for limiting the role of foreign investors is that domestic investors need to have good, profitable companies to invest in. For example, a common method of privatization is to sell a large stake to a foreign strategic investor but reserve the balance for sale to domestic investors. The foreign strategic investor will ensure that the company is well managed and profitable and thus is a good investment for citizens.

Such a method, however, reduces the capital available for other domestic companies. By limiting foreign capital in privatization, some of the limited supply of domestic capital must be used to purchase shares in state-owned enterprises instead of used for investment by other domestic businesses. It seems foolish to limit foreign investment when domestic companies are often in desperate need of more capital.

Leveraged Sales

For a variety of reasons, governments are often tempted to allow the sale of enterprises to be financed in large part by debt. A common situation is that a state-owned enterprise is heavily indebted. It has borrowed from state-owned banks over the years to pay for operating losses. An objective assessment of its capital structure would show that the amount of debt relative to the market value of its equity vastly exceeds what is normal in private companies. In some cases, the size of the debt exceeds the value of the company's assets, and thus the market value of the equity may actually be negative.

Governments, however, are loath to remove any of this debt before privatization. If they do so, they admit how badly the company was managed under state ownership and the large amount of bad loans held by the state-owned banks. They hope in vain that a private owner will be able to pay off the debt.

Even if the company is not overindebted, governments sometimes allow the purchaser to buy the equity of the company in installments. In effect, the government loans the investor money to buy the equity. Another way of accomplishing the same thing is for the government to require or pressure state-owned banks to loan money to the investor to finance his purchase of the company's equity.

The government permits the investor to pay in installments because it may result in a higher apparent purchase price for the equity (ignoring the fact that this price may not actually be paid), and thus the government can claim a greater success for its privatization program. Also, it is one way of allowing domestic investors to buy the company rather than foreign investors who may have greater access to capital. Even worse, it may be a way to allow family, friends, and cronies of the ruling politicians to take control of state-owned enterprises without investing their own money.

Such leveraged sales, however, have serious problems. The incentives for the new owner will be distorted if he is able to gain control over assets by only paying a small amount of his own money while the balance of the purchase price is financed by debt.

Highly leveraged sales encourage the new owners to engage in a risky business strategy. If the strategy fails, most of the losses will be borne by the providers of the debt and not the owner because he has only a small amount of money invested in the firm. If the strategy succeeds, he will reap most of the gains while the suppliers of debt only receive their normal fixed interest payments. In the privatization auction, the investor with the high-risk business strategy is likely to bid more than a more prudent investor. Speculators rather than investors may win the bidding in a highly leveraged sale.

Even worse, a dishonest or unscrupulous investor may simply steal the assets because they are worth more than the small amount of cash he has invested in the company. He will leave an empty shell of a company that cannot repay its debts. As noted earlier, there are many ways of doing this, primarily through transactions between the privatized company and other companies owned by the investor.

To avoid these problems, highly leveraged sales require a skilled and experienced lender that will adequately supervise the owner to ensure that his business strategy is prudent and he is not stealing assets. This level of supervision is unlikely if the lender is either a state-owned bank or the government if it permits installment sales. When governments have permitted such transactions, the record of payment by the buyers has been poor, and actual revenues are probably less than would be received under the best-practice method.

To increase domestic ownership, a number of African countries (Ghana, Madagascar, Mozambique, and Uganda) have permitted installment sales. The privatization agencies, however, have often been unable to collect the required payments. As a result, at least one, Uganda, decided to give preference to noninstallment sales.[9]

As an example of outright theft of assets, Togo leased the assets of its state-owned steel company to a private company. Leasing is another way that investors can gain control of a company without making a large, up-front cash payment and is similar to a leveraged sale. Though on the surface the private company was doing well, the investors gradually milked the company and covered their traces with creative accounting techniques. In 1991, lenders and creditors were left with unpaid loans amounting to 3 billion CFA that could not be collected.[10]

I conclude that governments should sell companies with only a reasonable amount of debt financing on their balance sheets, especially if state-owned banks provide the financing. The question is, what constitutes a reasonable amount of debt financing? Based on the amount of debt financing in private companies, a rough rule of thumb is that the amount of debt should not exceed the market value of the equity. (Note that the market value may be higher or lower than the book value.) In this way, private investors will have to pay a purchase price for the company's equity equal to at least half of the market value of the company's assets.

Furthermore, the government should not increase the amount of leverage indirectly by allowing the investors to buy the equity in installments or requiring state-owned banks to loan money to the investor to buy the equity. Buyers should be forced to pay in cash for all of the equity of the company. However, I would have no objection if the buyer arranges for loans from private financial institutions to help finance his purchase because they are better able to monitor and control the buyer's behavior than are state-owned banks or the government.

If the amount of debt is high relative to the market value of the equity, governments should absorb some of the debt before sale. Governments may be concerned about having to absorb this debt, but they should keep in mind that the purchase price will be increased as a result. This increased revenue from privatization will offset in part the debt absorbed by the government. The simplest way of doing this is a debt-equity swap in which the government or the state-owned banks increase the nominal amount of their equity ownership in exchange for forgiving debt.

Two-Tranche Sales

Instead of selling all of the shares at one time, governments sometimes sell the shares in two tranches in the mistaken belief that this will increase the total revenue from the sale. For example, the government may first sell a controlling stake (the first tranche) to a strategic investor and then sell the balance (the second tranche) some years later. It is argued that this will increase the total sales revenue because the second tranche will command a high price after the strategic investor has made the company profitable.

It is true that the price of the second tranche will probably be higher than the first. However, this does not prove that the total revenue from a two-tranche sale will be greater than that from a one-tranche sale. For example, consider a two-tranche sale in which half of the shares are sold in each tranche. Further assume that the price of the first tranche will be $20 per share and the price of the second tranche will be $30 per share after the company's profitability has been improved, resulting in an average sale price of $25 per share. Supporters of a two-tranche sale implicitly seem to assume without any explanation that the price of all shares sold in a one-tranche sale will equal the lower $20 price. In fact, the price of shares in a one-tranche sale is likely to exceed $25 and thus generate more revenue than a two-tranche sale. Unfortunately, it is difficult to prove this conclusively because it is not possible to engage in a controlled experiment in which the same company is sold twice, first in a one-tranche sale and then again in a two-tranche sale.

I believe, however, that an investor is likely to pay a higher price per share in a one-tranche sale compared with the *average* price in a two-tranche sale for at least three reasons:

- The investor will have a greater incentive to improve profitability if he can capture all of the future profits instead of sharing them with future purchasers of the second tranche.
- The investor does not have to worry about the government remaining a large shareholder until the second tranche is sold and possibly interfering in the management of the company.
- The investor does not face the risk of who purchases the second tranche and whether they will challenge his control of the company.

Methods of selling an asset that seem impractical or even ridiculous in a private transaction somehow appear desirable to many in a privatization transaction. A two-tranche sale is like a farmer attempting to sell half of his farm but with one condition. The buyer has to agree to improve the productivity of the entire farm and not just his half. Afterward, the farmer will sell his remaining half to another buyer at a higher price. Most people would doubt whether this complicated method of sale will result in greater total sales proceeds because the first buyer will simply reduce his purchase price to reflect the cost of improving the half of the farm that does not belong to him.

Management-Employee Buyouts

Sometimes governments give special preferences to the workers and managers in the privatization of a company, and they become the controlling or majority shareholders. This preference is often in the form of permitting a highly leveraged purchase. Workers and managers are allowed to borrow a large part of the purchase price from state-owned banks or to pay in installments over a long period, and thus they do not have to make a large initial cash payment.

In evaluating a sale to employees, one should distinguish between the cases when employees become the majority or controlling owners versus when they are only minority owners. I am particularly concerned about the case when they become controlling owners in a highly leveraged transaction. I am not so concerned when governments allow employees to buy, for example, up to 10 percent of the shares either at no cost or on concessionary terms as an incentive for them to support privatization of their company. The balance of the shares could still be sold to a strategic investor who takes over control and management of the company. Though I question the fairness of providing such a benefit to employees and not other citizens, I have to admit it may be desirable if it reduces employee opposition to privatization.

Various reasons are given to justify privatization methods that encourage employees to become the controlling or majority shareholders. As noted, it may reduce opposition of the managers and labor unions to privatization. In countries with a socialist tradition, it may seem fair to allow the workers to become the owners of the company because their labor created the company. Also, some believe that companies with a high degree of ownership by their employees will perform better.

If the political strength of the workers and managers is such that privatization to outside investors is impossible or no outside investors are interested, then I admit that a highly leveraged, management-employee buyout may be the only option. Even a weak or a second-best method of privatization is probably better than no privatization.

I question, however, whether it is fair to the rest of the citizens to give managers and workers special preferences in privatization. These assets were paid for by the entire nation, not just the workers; and the entire nation should benefit from their sale. Also, the workers at state-owned enterprises are typically some of the highest paid and enjoy better working conditions. They have already benefited substantially from their employment in state-owned enterprises, and it is unfair to give them additional compensation or rewards.

Thus, I conclude that managers and employees should be allowed to participate in the auction of their companies but only on the same terms as other investors. If, in fact, companies owned by their managers and workers actually perform better, then the managers

113

and workers should be able to outbid other investors in purchasing the company. Even if they do not have the capital to buy the company, they could join together with outside investors who could provide the capital. In the United States, there are a number of examples in which outside investors have teamed up with the senior managers to buy the company from its current owners (called a management buyout), and the performance of the company improved as a result. Naturally, these investors will have to be convinced that the managers and employees will be able to improve the performance of the company. As discussed next, the empirical evidence seems to suggest that selling state-owned enterprises to their employees generally leads to less improvement in company performance compared with other methods of privatization.

Empirical Evidence

The preceding discussion provides theoretical arguments as to why one method of privatization will best achieve the economic efficiency objective. What empirical evidence supports this theory?

Though many studies show that privatized companies perform better than state-owned companies, only a few examine which methods of privatization best improve company performance. Part of the reason is that data on company performance are only readily available for companies that are privatized using one particular method of privatization, namely, share-issue privatization. These companies are listed on a stock exchange, and their financial statements are available to the public. State-owned enterprises that are sold to a strategic investor, however, are more likely to be private companies not listed on an exchange, and thus financial information is not easily available.

In spite of this limitation on data, a number of studies support the conclusion that the best-practice method of privatization described previously will be more likely to achieve the economic efficiency objective. In an earlier chapter that discussed widespread share ownership, two studies were cited that show concentrated ownership results in a higher market value for the company. The logical extension is that selling a state-owned enterprise to a single investor— the most concentrated form of ownership—is likely to result in the most improvement in company performance.

The variety of privatization methods used in the countries of Central and Eastern Europe also provides useful insights. A recent survey summarizes the main conclusions reached by 34 studies of the effect of different methods of privatization.[11] Though these studies measure company performance in a variety of ways, they generally conclude that widespread shareholding results in little improvement in company performance compared with companies having either a single owner or a few large shareholders (block holders). Also, these studies suggest that companies whose ownership was transferred to employees performed worse than companies with outside investors.

It is argued above that opening up the privatization auction to more investors, in particular foreign investors, will result in a higher purchase price because the investor with the best plan for managing the company is more likely to be included. In support of this argument, a study of 361 companies privatized in Mexico using various methods shows that eliminating restrictions on who can participate does increase the purchase price.[12] This study also shows that selling only minority stakes in a company reduces the sales price per share.

A study of 79 privatizations in poor countries shows that selling a controlling ownership stake to a private investor will result in a greater improvement in performance than if the government sells only a minority stake and thus keeps control.[13] Another study of 118 privatized firms in 29 countries found that the increase in performance after privatization was reduced as the level of employee ownership increased.[14] The study also found that higher foreign ownership led to a greater improvement in performance while higher residual state ownership resulted in a smaller improvement.

Privatization of New Infrastructure Capacity

A frequent result of poor management of state-owned utilities (for example, electric power, telecommunications, and water and sewer systems) is lack of capacity and shortages. For example, the power company does not have the generating capacity to meet the demand of all its customers, and blackouts or brownouts are frequent. In the case of the telephone company, customers may have to wait years to receive a connection.

One solution to this problem has been to privatize new facilities but not existing facilities. The objective is to bring in private financing

115

of new capacity because the loss-making state-owned company cannot finance it. The phrases frequently used to describe this type of privatization are *private participation in infrastructure* or, in the case of power, *independent power projects*. The government or international development institutions such as the World Bank may support this type of privatization with guarantees.

I am concerned that this is pseudo privatization. It does not involve the private sector in any meaningful way except as a source of financing. As discussed in Chapter 2, this is the least important contribution of the private sector. Instead, it delays more fundamental reforms of these utilities, including the privatization of existing facilities. It is a clever way for governments to engage in *off-balance sheet financing* of new capacity while still keeping most of the utility in state ownership.

As an example, consider the power sector in a hypothetical but typical poor country. The state-owned power company is badly managed. It has high costs because of overstaffing and low revenue because power prices are kept artificially low. Moreover, many customers refuse to pay even these low prices, but they are still supplied power which results in large accounts receivable for the company, or they simply steal the power through illegal connections (in the euphemistic jargon of the industry, nontechnical losses are high). The company is suffering financial losses and cannot raise capital to build new capacity without either a guarantee from the government or some other credit-worthy party such as the World Bank. As a result, blackouts and load shedding are frequent.

The government has five options to deal with this capacity shortage. The *first option* is for the government to privatize the power company or, at least, that part of it that distributes power to the final consumer, which is where most of the inefficiency and bad management occurs. A commonly used strategy is to divide the power company into three—a distribution company, a transmission company, and a generation company. If the distribution company becomes well managed and profitable, it can afford to pay for power from new generation plants, and thus private investors would be willing to build such plants. The government, however, desperately wants to avoid this option because it requires the politically unpopular action of raising prices to cost recovery levels, halting theft, and laying off members of the politically powerful labor union in the power sector.

The *second option* is for the government to issue its own debt to finance new generation capacity. However, this would further hurt the credit rating of the government, which is already deeply in debt, and would violate agreements with the International Monetary Fund that require the government to keep its budget deficit in check.

The *third option* is for the government to ask the World Bank (or the Asian Development Bank, the African Development Bank, the Inter-American Development Bank, etc.) to provide a loan so that the state-owned power company can build new capacity. However, the World Bank has said that it will no longer lend to the power sector because the government is not implementing reforms that would improve its efficiency, for example, raising the power price to cost-recovery levels. Providing loans will just encourage the government to put off needed reforms.

The *fourth option* is for the government to engage in creative off-balance sheet financing that may escape the scrutiny of the IMF by encouraging an independent power producer to build the capacity. The government signs a purchase power agreement with the sponsors of a proposed new private power project. The agreement guarantees that the state-owned power company or the government itself will buy the new power at an agreed price. Given the certainty provided by the purchase power agreement, the sponsors may then be able to raise the private capital needed to build the power plant.[15]

This purchase power agreement is like a leasing agreement sometimes used by private companies to keep debt off their balance sheets. A private firm will sign a long-term lease to use equipment owned by specialized leasing companies instead of taking out a bank loan to purchase the equipment. The company would have to show the bank loan as a liability on its balance sheet but may not have to show the lease, depending on the accounting rules.

This fourth option, however, often turns out to be impractical because lenders know that the power company probably cannot honor the purchase power agreement. The risk is high that it will not have the revenue needed to pay for the power. Lenders also doubt whether the government will honor the agreement if the power company cannot. For example, the government of Pakistan reneged on a number of these agreements using the excuse that the investors had bribed previous government officials to sign these agreements.

The *fifth option* is for the government to ask the World Bank to guarantee the purchase power agreement. If the state-owned power company and the government do not honor the agreement, the World Bank guarantees that it will compensate the lenders. Thus, even if lenders doubt that the government will honor the agreement, the project can proceed because of the World Bank guarantee. The World Bank and similar international development institutions have provided this type of guarantee for projects in poor countries.

The sad outcome is that the World Bank guarantee has actually helped the government to avoid the difficult reforms needed to make the power sector financially viable. The guarantee does facilitate the involvement of the private sector in building new generation capacity, but this is relatively unimportant. The major inefficiencies in the sector are in distribution and not in generation. Private owners may be able to build and operate power plants slightly better than the state-owned company, but the private sector could make the most important contribution by improving the management of the distribution system. This, however, is delayed because the World Bank guarantee allowed the government to contract with private investors to build new generation capacity and thus temporarily reduce blackouts and load shedding.

In this case, it is hard to see why the World Bank refuses to provide a loan to the state-owned power company to build a power plant but will guarantee its purchase power agreement with a private company. The end result of both kinds of World Bank support is that they allow the government to avoid politically unpopular reforms of the power sector.

One explanation of why this type of guarantee is promoted by the World Bank and similar institutions is that it is one of the few ways that the World Bank can directly support private-sector investment instead of making loans to governments. According to its Web site, "World Bank guarantees have played a significant role in catalyzing private capital flows to several large infrastructure projects in developing countries."[16] Though perhaps well intentioned, such guarantees often reduce meaningful private-sector participation in infrastructure because they delay the much more important privatization of existing state-owned utilities. For example, the World Bank provided guarantees for two power generation projects in Pakistan in the early 1990s after the government promised to undertake reforms to improve the financial solvency of the sector such as privatization. Ten years later, these reforms are just now beginning. The World Bank provided a guarantee for a power project in Bangladesh that was completed in 2001 even though little reform of the sector has taken place.

The Exception That Proves the Rule

Though the huge privatization programs in the transition economies were frequently unable to use the best-practice method for reasons I discuss below, the success of the programs was greater when they could do so. The transition economies are those former communist countries in Central and Eastern Europe and Asia. Though many enterprises have been privatized in these countries, only a few of the larger ones were privatized following the best practice, namely, a sale to the highest bidder in a competitive auction with no restrictions on the bidders. (This best-practice method, however, was commonly used in the privatization of small enterprises, for example, shops and stores.) Most large enterprises were sold through voucher privatization, management-employee buyouts, or some combination of the two. Some of the more valuable enterprises, such as those producing natural resources, were also transferred in nontransparent ways and on favorable terms to relatives of politicians, their supporters, and cronies.

On the one hand, the special circumstances that existed in these countries made it impossible to use the best-practice method of privatization in many cases, and thus I do not criticize these countries for adopting other methods. In my view, a second-best method of privatization is better than no privatization. On the other hand, where it was feasible to use methods that approximated the best practice, the post-privatization performance of these enterprises was better than when other methods were used. Thus, the transition economies are the exception that proves the rule.

The best-practice method was not feasible in many cases because of the huge number of enterprises that needed to be privatized, the lack of domestic investors with capital to purchase them, and the lack of interest by foreign investors. In these countries, almost 100 percent of economic activity was carried out by state-owned enterprises. The private sector was small or nonexistent.

119

As a result, private wealth was small, and almost no one had the financial assets to buy state-owned enterprises.[17] In some countries, foreign investors were interested in purchasing some of the enterprises but had no interest in the vast majority. Even if the best-practice method was tried, privatizing so many enterprises would take a long time and the fear was that the performance of these enterprises would continue to deteriorate under state ownership and the assets would be stolen by the managers and workers.[18] Giving the enterprises away either to the general public by using vouchers or to the managers and workers seemed like the only feasible option in most cases.

In contrast, state-owned enterprises in most other poor countries rarely account for more than 15 percent of economic activity. The substantial wealth and financial assets of domestic private investors are substantial, which allows them to purchase state-owned enterprises. Foreign investors are also likely to be interested in many cases.

Some transition countries were able to privatize some of their enterprises using methods similar to the best practice described earlier, notably, Poland, Hungary, and Estonia. The empirical evidence suggests that the firms in these countries that were sold to a small number of outside investors, in particular, foreign investors, performed better than those privatized through vouchers or management-employee buyouts. No matter what method was used, however, privatized firms almost always performed better than firms remaining in state ownership though sometimes not by much.

Conclusion

The best-practice method of privatization described above (sell 100 percent of the company to the highest cash bidder with no restrictions on who can bid) is simple, straightforward, and transparent. In most cases, it will best achieve the main objectives of privatization, namely, improving the productivity and profitability of state-owned enterprises plus maximizing government revenue from the sale. Other complicated methods of privatization that attempt to achieve a variety of economic and social objectives are of questionable merit even in countries with well-developed government institutions. These methods are particularly suspect in countries with weak institutions.

There is always the possibility that special circumstances may justify deviating from the best-practice method of privatization. Before adopting other methods, however, governments should clearly specify what these special circumstances are. Expert advisers (for example, those from investment banks, consulting firms, and international development institutions) should do more to help poor countries identify the valid objectives and select the best method of privatization, including evaluating special circumstances if any exist. Completing transactions is not the only measure of success in a privatization program. Sometimes the objectives of privatization are considered to be an internal government issue and outside the scope of expert advice. Also, there seems to be the view that any objective or method that appeals to the government is acceptable if the result is privatization in one form or another.

This is not to say that experts or international development institutions should never support a method of privatization that deviates from the best practice described here. In most areas of economic development, countries often adopt less than ideal programs because of political constraints or other special circumstances, and a second-best privatization program may be better than no privatization at all. However, we should always keep in mind what the best practice is and encourage governments at every opportunity to adopt that method.

5. Banks: Better Off without Them

Government interventions that supposedly improve the function-ing of the financial system have probably been the single biggest obstacle to economic growth in poor countries. Because of these interventions, banks, in particular, have performed so badly that most poor countries would probably have been better off if none had ever been established.

Many financial experts will react in horror to this idea and argue that a modern economy cannot function without banks. I agree that good performing banks are a major force for economic growth, but badly performing banks are a major obstacle. The choice in many countries, however, is not between good banks and no banks but between bad banks and no banks. Given this latter choice, the no-bank option has considerable merit. Banks that squander or steal the savings of the public are worse than no banks at all even though the public will have to find other ways to invest their savings.

These same experts will argue that banks in poor countries can perform better by improving their supervision and regulation fol-lowing the example of rich countries. What is needed are better laws, more technical assistance, and training to improve supervision and regulatory capacity.

Actually, government supervision and regulation of banks in rich countries is at best a mixed success as evidenced by the many large-scale bank failures and banking crises in such countries as the United States, United Kingdom, Germany, France, and now Japan. Given the weak government institutions in most poor countries relative to the rich countries, is it realistic to expect that their bank supervision and regulation will result in good banks in the foreseeable future?

I am not actually arguing in favor of the no-bank option, but I do believe that radically different approaches to bank regulation and supervision are needed in poor countries compared with what is usually done in rich countries. The next chapter discusses bank regulation. Rather than assuming that government institutions can be improved in poor countries, government interventions in financial markets should be designed to suit the limited capacity of these institutions. One consequence is that banks may play a smaller role in the economy than they do now but at least they will perform this role better.

The Textbook Model

The activities and functions of banks can be described in two different ways. The first is the conventional or textbook model of how banks should function. The second is how they actually function in most poor countries and some rich countries.

The textbook model is quite attractive and appealing if only banks actually worked that way in poor countries. The primary function of banks is to be *financial intermediaries* in the process of saving and investment.[1] One of the oldest theories of economic growth emphasizes the importance of a high level of savings (in other words refraining from current consumption) and using those savings to make investments in real capital (factories, equipment, housing, infrastructure, etc.). This increase in real capital will increase productive capacity, allow the economy to grow, and increase incomes. The problem is that those who save and have money to invest are often not the same people who have ideas for good investment projects that would contribute to the growth of the economy if only they could be financed. For example, saving may be done by ordinary citizens, but investment is done by large companies.

The textbook model of a bank is that it *intermediates* between savers and investors. It collects the savings of many individuals and then uses this money to make loans to investors such as companies. The bank can finance a much larger project than an individual saver could finance. The bank examines the merits of the investment project to ensure that it will be profitable, and it monitors the borrower to make certain that the project is performing as planned and the loan is repaid. The cost to many small savers, each trying to evaluate and monitor this project, would be high. Because the bank can finance projects over a wide area, savings in one region can be used in another region where the investments are likely to be more productive and profitable.

Also, banks can transform the short-term nature of many deposits into long-term loans needed by a business. The bank can promise that it will return to the depositor his or her money at any time upon demand (hence the term *demand deposits*). However, because the bank knows that only a small fraction of depositors will ask for their money back at any one time, the bank can make a long-term loan to a business that does not have to be repaid for some years.

If banks perform these functions well, the end result is that savings will be channeled to investments with a higher return. This result is good for savers because they receive a higher return on their bank deposits than they could earn on their own and good for the country because the national savings is invested in the most productive way. In the jargon of economics, the *marginal productivity of investment* will be higher as a result of banks acting as intermediaries between savers and investors.

Pyramid Schemes

The second and more realistic model of how banks function in most poor countries is that they are really pyramid or Ponzi schemes. Pyramid schemes are one of the oldest and still common forms of financial fraud perpetrated by confidence men (conmen, for short). The term "confidence man" refers to the fact that the organizer must gain the confidence of investors before the scheme can work. Carlos Ponzi was a famous conman in Boston who defrauded a large number of people in 1920 using a pyramid scheme.

Private pyramid schemes are bad enough but are much more damaging when the government backs them. Sadly, this is the case for bank pyramid schemes in most poor countries. The schemes involving the banks are actually carried out by state-owned banks, or the government guarantees or insures the deposits in private banks.

How does a pyramid scheme work? The organizer or conman promises investors a high rate of return on their money invested in the scheme, for example, 20 percent per month. In other words, investors can double their money in less than a year. The conman says that he can pay such a high rate of return because he has found some extraordinarily profitable investment opportunities and only needs capital to make the investments. Naturally, these fantastic investment opportunities do not exist.

Initially, only a few of the most gullible investors believe his story and give him money. The conman, however, does pay the promised 20 percent monthly rate of return. The first round of investors then tell their friends about this great opportunity and they in turn rush to invest in what seems to be a sure way to get rich quickly. The conman continues to honor his promise and pays the later rounds of investors the promised rate of return. This in turn attracts even more investors. The amount of money invested with the conman grows and grows seemingly without limit, the conman continues to pay the promised rate of return, and it appears that investors in the scheme will become rich.

How is the conman able to continue to pay such high rates of return? What is the trick? Will it ever stop? Will everyone become rich? The simple trick is that the conman is paying the high rate of return to investors out of the money they gave him rather than from the profits from any investments he made. In brief, money from new investors is used to pay the promised high rate of return to the early investors.

How long can the conman keep this scheme going? It can continue as long as the total amount of money given to him is growing by at least the promised rate of return. The conman can keep any money in excess of this amount.

For example, suppose that he promises a 20 percent per month rate of return. Investors give him $1 million in the first month of the scheme. New investors in each succeeding month give him an amount equal to 25 percent of the total given to him in all previous months (i.e., $250,000 in month two, $312,500 in month three, and so on). Some simple arithmetic will show that at the end of just three years, the total given to him will amount to about $2.5 billion. He will have returned about $2 billion to the investors as their promised monthly return, but he will still have $500 million in surplus that he can keep for himself.

If the account books of the conman could be examined, it would show that the scheme is *liquid* but *insolvent*. It is liquid because the amount of money coming in from new investors exceeds the amount going out to the old. However, it is insolvent because the value of the assets held by the scheme is much less than the value of the liabilities (the money invested in the scheme) because the cash inflow has not been used to make valuable investments.

At this point, the conman would be wise to buy a plane ticket to a country without an extradition treaty and take the $500 million surplus with him because the scheme must soon crash and expose his fraud. The scheme will crash when its rate of growth declines to less than the promised rate of return and thus it becomes illiquid as well as insolvent and can no longer make the promised payments to investors. Because the amount of financial capital in the world is finite, eventually new money invested in the scheme must decline. The higher the promised rate of return, the sooner it will crash.[2] The reason why pyramid schemes continue to attract investors is because many people do not realize the power of compound growth rates. After just a few rounds of investing when the promised rate of return is high, the total amount invested would be enormous and unsustainable.

Liquid but Insolvent

Unfortunately, the banking systems in most poor countries more closely resemble a pyramid scheme than they do the ideal textbook model of financial intermediation. The reason is that the owners or managers of the banks have squandered or stolen a large part of the money deposited in the banks. This is true both when the owner is private and when the owner is the state. In fact the state is the biggest offender because a majority or more of banks in poor countries have been and continue to be state owned.[3]

You might ask, if pyramid schemes must crash eventually, why don't bank pyramid schemes also crash? As I discuss below, they do frequently crash but not as often as one might at first think. The reason bank pyramid schemes can continue for a long time is that their deposits are almost always implicitly or explicitly guaranteed by the state. Can you imagine how a conman would jump for joy if he could tell potential investors in his pyramid scheme that the government guarantees their investments?

If the government guarantees bank deposits, the bank pyramid scheme can offer much lower interest rates and still attract depositors. This means that the growth rate of deposits necessary to keep the scheme going can also be lower. As a result, the day of reckoning when the scheme crashes can be postponed a long time, even decades or more.

Like other pyramid schemes, a bank pyramid scheme can continue without crashing as long as the bank is liquid even though it is insolvent. It will crash only when it becomes illiquid, which may be a long time after it becomes insolvent.

A bank is liquid as long as its cash inflow exceeds outflow. The cash inflow is the net increase in deposits plus the income, if any, earned on the bank's investments such as loans. The cash outflow is the interest paid on deposits. However, suppose that all or most of the loans are bad. In other words, the borrowers are in default and not repaying the loans and not paying interest to the bank. In the euphemistic jargon of banks, these loans are classified as nonperforming. Thus, the only cash inflow is from the growth of deposits. If the level of interest rates in the country is not high, say 5 to 10 percent per year, it is still quite possible for the bank to be liquid even when all of its loans are nonperforming. The growth rate of net deposits must only exceed the interest rate paid on deposits. If a large proportion of any interest payments are redeposited with the bank, then it is almost certain the bank will remain liquid.

Thus, the bank can remain liquid and postpone the inevitable crash for a long time even though the bank has no income from its loans or other investments. Customers of the bank never guess that something is seriously wrong with the bank because they continue to receive their interest payments and those who wish to withdraw their deposits are allowed to do so.

The bank, however, is insolvent. Insolvency means that the true value of the bank's assets, mainly loans, is less than the value of its liabilities, mainly deposits. This is what one would expect in a pyramid scheme. The bank owners or managers have stolen or squandered most of the deposits. However, because new deposits continue to come in, the bank may still be liquid and can continue without crashing.

A bank pyramid scheme may crash when depositors become suspicious that the bank is insolvent and start withdrawing their deposits. The bank then becomes illiquid as well. It may also become illiquid and crash due to a downturn in the economy or macroeconomic shock that causes the flow of new deposits to be reduced. Historically, macroeconomic shocks often occur at the same time as a banking crisis caused by the collapse of bank pyramid schemes. Typically, the shock caused the banking crisis by exposing the underlying pyramid scheme and not the other way around. The subsequent banking crisis, however, may worsen the impact of the macroeconomic shock.

Moral Hazard

Economists and financial experts rarely describe bank failures as the result of a pyramid or Ponzi scheme. Instead they describe them as a problem of *moral hazard* resulting from government guarantees or deposit insurance. Moral hazard is a common problem with all insurance. It means that the insured will be less likely to take steps to protect whatever he has insured because he knows that the insurance will protect him against loss. For example, if I have house insurance, I may do less to protect my house against fire because I know that the insurance will compensate me for any loss due to fire.

In the case of banking, moral hazard is a problem because a government guarantee of deposits or deposit insurance means that depositors have a reduced incentive to assess the quality and management of banks. As a result, the interest rate that banks have to pay on deposits does not reflect the riskiness of the loans or other investments made by the bank. Bank managers can then make high-return but high-risk loans or other investments without fear of having to pay higher interest rates on deposits. The bank owners can capture the greater profit resulting from the spread between the low interest rates paid on deposits guaranteed by the government and the high interest rates earned on risky investments.

This incentive for banks to make high-risk and high-return investments is part of the story in some cases. The conventional descriptions of the moral hazard problems in banking assume that owners and managers are basically honest, but their behavior is distorted by the incentives created by government deposit insurance.

I am more concerned when bank owners and managers are dishonest. The concept of moral hazard does not capture the full richness of the variety of ways that dishonest bank owners and managers have often stolen or squandered the deposits entrusted to them. The concept of a pyramid scheme rather than moral hazard is a better way to characterize what has happened in most poor countries.[4]

Loans to State-Owned Enterprises

I am not suggesting that the government officials and politicians who founded state-owned banks intended them to become pyramid schemes. Given the prevailing economic beliefs of the day, the founders no doubt believed that the state-owned banks would contribute to economic development. A variety of circumstances, however, turned these banks into pyramid schemes in which the deposits were used to make bad loans or, in some cases, were simply stolen by corrupt politicians, bank managers, or government officials.

In the early days of Nehruvian socialism that existed in most poor countries, the government intended that the state-owned banks would gather the savings of the population and invest it in those industries specified by government planners, usually state-owned enterprises. The banks did not follow the textbook model of a financial intermediary because they were not evaluating or selecting the most productive and profitable investments. The banks were simply following orders from the government planners. A common concept was that banks were merely the *servants of the real sector* and should make loans when and where they were told to do so.

Thus, the solvency of the state-owned banks became closely tied to the profitability of state-owned enterprises. Except for a few cases when these enterprises were protected from competition and could charge high prices (for example, international telephone calls), these enterprises were unprofitable and often could not repay the loans from the state-owned banks.

Even when it was clear that the state-owned enterprises could not repay their loans, the state-owned banks continued to lend them money under political pressure. The state-owned enterprises often needed the money simply to cover current operating expenses, primarily the high salaries of their large workforces. The managers and labor unions would pressure the government to keep the money flowing from the banks or else face the political backlash of large numbers of unpaid or unemployed workers. Such lending was euphemistically described as *policy-based lending* because lending was determined by government policies, for example, keeping bankrupt state-owned enterprises functioning, rather than by an objective assessment of the merit of the investments to be made by the enterprises using the bank loans.

State-owned utilities such as the power and telephone companies are some of the worst examples. Not only were they badly managed and had an excess of overpaid union workers, they were also often forced to keep prices at below cost-recovery levels, in other words, to subsidize prices. As noted earlier, this was justified on the grounds that it was helping the poor even though the poorest people in the country typically did not have power or telephone service. The middle- and upper-class users of these services would oppose any attempt to increase prices, making it impossible for the utility to operate without a continuous infusion of new bank loans.

Bank and Enterprise Restructuring

Many poor countries now face the complicated mess of many bankrupt state-owned enterprises and insolvent state-owned banks. Trying to sort this out is an economic and political nightmare. Politicians in any country would be loath to take the unpopular actions necessary to untangle this mess.

The government must close or, at the least, privatize the state-owned enterprises, often resulting in large layoffs of workers and increases in subsidized prices. The government must also explicitly recognize that the banks are insolvent. Unless the government intervenes to bail out the banks, depositors will lose their money, causing a major political backlash.

Governments typically step in and replace the bad loans of the state-owned banks with government securities so that depositors do not suffer, in other words, *recapitalize* the banks. Though depositors are protected, taxpayers end up having to pay for the collapsed pyramid scheme because the government must eventually pay the interest and principal on these securities from tax revenues. In effect, the bad loans made by the banks become liabilities of the government. If the depositors and taxpayers are largely the same people, the cost to them will be about the same regardless of whether the banks default on their deposits or the government recapitalizes the banks and raises taxes to pay for it.

After the government bails out the banks, they are solvent again and can make new loans. Unfortunately, this procedure often leads to another round of bad loans, and the banks once more become a pyramid scheme.

The easiest thing for the current generation of politicians to do is to just keep the pyramid scheme going for a while longer and force the state-owned banks to continue to finance the losses of the state-owned enterprises. Government deposit guarantees or insurance is used to assure the depositors that their money is safe and thus avoid a liquidity crisis. Politicians are reluctant to ruin their political careers by taking the unpopular steps needed to bring the scheme to a stop. They justify their inaction by arguing that it was not they but the previous generation of politicians who created the mess anyway. Instead, the current politicians pass the problem on to the next generation, preferably from the opposition party.

For example, the volume of bad loans held by the state-owned banks in China is probably the largest of any in a poor country. It is difficult to tell for certain because government officials have an incentive to hide the problem.[5] The following description in *The Economist* magazine of the problems faced by Chinese state-owned banks is typical of many poor countries, though China seems more willing to deal with these problems than some others.

> [U]nder guidance from central and local political barons, the big [Chinese] banks continue to lend to weak state enterprises—perhaps not as much as they used to, but still far too much. The bad loans this generates are the system's Achilles heel. For several years, the government denied the scale of the problem and pooh-poohed unofficial estimates that put bad loans at 40% or more of the total. But recently a franker assessment by the banks themselves, using international standards of measurement, has brought official figures closer and closer to those earlier unofficial estimates. A best guess by Nicholas Lardy of the Brookings Institution, one of the earliest to draw attention to the problems of China's banks, now puts bad loans in the system at around $500 billion, or over 50% of the total. . . . If China's insolvent state banks are to be nursed back to health—and any suggestion that they might not be would lead to a run on deposits and a full-blown banking crisis that would send China into turmoil—the government will have to pick up the tab. The cost of cleaning up the banking system needs to be added to the government's already considerable pile of liabilities. But instead of facing up to this, says Mr. Lardy, the government shuffles debt around as though it were constructing a Ponzi scheme.[6]

Loans to the Private Sector

State-owned banks also make loans to the private sector often with the same disastrous consequences as their loans to state-owned enterprises. One of the worst cases is agriculture. Governments often require state-owned banks to lend to farmers primarily for working capital, in other words, covering their costs until their crop is sold. It is argued that unless farmers receive these loans, they will not be able to plant their crops, thus raising the fear of food shortages and even famine. The problem is that governments often require state-owned banks to make these loans at low, subsidized interest rates. Even worse, governments periodically may require these banks to forgive the loans and not require repayment. This requirement is usually imposed just before an election.

Crony capitalism exists to some extent in most poor countries. In the past, it was often disguised using the then fashionable concepts of economic planning. Loans from state-owned banks would be made to those private industries that the government's economic planners judged to have the greatest economic potential and thus would contribute most to the growth of the country.

Even if the planners could correctly identify these growth industries, which is doubtful, the government still had to choose which lucky private investors would receive these loans. There was an overwhelming temptation to give the loans to supporters of the party in power, powerful families, and the friends and relatives of the important politicians and government officials.

For example, Pakistan's industrial development policies created a private investment boom in the late 1980s and early 1990s financed by loans from the state-owned banks.[7] These loans were made available to the powerful and politically well-connected investors on noncommercial terms for investment in cotton spinning, sugar mills, and cement. The government had decided that these were the industries with the greatest potential, and thus incentives should be given for private companies to invest in them. (One may very well ask that if these are the industries with the greatest potential, why is it necessary for the government to create special incentives to invest in those industries.)

In the case of cotton, the government kept raw cotton prices below international market levels, and state-owned banks supplied abundant cheap loans to construct spinning mills that transformed raw cotton into thread. As a result, almost anyone could make huge profits by investing in a spinning mill. Politicians, government officials, important businesspeople, and rich landowners became the owners of spinning mills. Through overinvoicing for investment costs, borrowers could convince banks to lend almost all of the investment needed to start a mill and thus contribute little of their own equity. It is reported that some owners actually borrowed more than the investment cost and pocketed some of the loans. These borrowers probably never intended to pay back the loans.

Managing a spinning mill is easy, and absentee owners might visit their mills only once or twice a year. There was little interest in investing in the more complicated and demanding upstream industries such as weaving or garment making. Thus, the value added in the textile industry remains small.

The investment boom turned into a bust when the bad loans of the state-owned banks increased. They became illiquid in 1994 and had no more to lend. In the case of cotton, the government allowed prices for raw cotton to rise to international levels; and a number of poor crops reduced the supply.

As a result, many industrialists who had borrowed from the banks during the boom period now refuse to repay these loans, claiming that their industries are sick. A Pakistani businessman told me that there are sick industries but there are no sick industrialists. He believes that these industrialists have the money to pay and should be required to pay, but this is difficult because they are powerful and politically well connected and the legal system is weak.

Are Private Banks the Solution?

Do only state-owned banks engage in pyramid schemes? Perhaps the easy solution to this problem is to privatize state-owned banks and allow new private banks to start up operations. Though the main theme of this book is the development of the private sector and that private companies will perform better than state-owned companies, I have to admit that private banks are just as likely to become a pyramid scheme if their deposits are guaranteed or insured by the state.

All private banks in all countries make some bad loans. A bank that never makes a bad loan is badly managed because it is too cautious and is passing up good lending opportunities. The problem is how to determine when a bank has made too many bad loans and why. In some cases, excessive bad loans may just be the result of honest but incompetent management. Managers and owners could not accurately judge the profitability of the borrowers and their ability to repay the loans. Sometimes unexpected shocks to the economy or poor macroeconomic policies beyond the control of bank managers can cause many loans to become bad simultaneously, for example, a fall in export prices, war, or recession.

In other cases, however, bad loans may be a deliberate attempt by bank owners or managers to steal money from the bank, in other words, a pyramid scheme. This can be done in many ways. One way described earlier as a problem of moral hazard is to make high-return but high-risk investments. A second way is for the bank to pay high dividends to the owners using the cash flow provided by new deposits rather than any profits resulting from lending. In this way, the bank is *decapitalized*.

A third way is for the bank to lend money to the owners of the bank or their friends and relatives (so-called connected or related lending) on favorable terms. A recent study of private banks in Mexico found that connected lending amounts to 20 percent of all commercial loans. Such loans have interest rates 4 percentage points lower than other loans and are 33 percent more likely to default.[8]

Naturally, the dishonest managers and owners will claim that the bad loans are the result of bad luck, poor judgment, or economic circumstances beyond their control. It is often difficult for even the best investigators and police to prove otherwise.

The Example of the United States

The best description I have seen of how privately owned banks can become pyramid schemes is in an adventure novel dealing with the savings and loan banking crisis in the United States.[9] During the period 1984-91, more than 1,700 savings and loan banks and 1,300 other banks failed. According to one estimate, the cost of making depositors whole was $180 billion, equivalent to 3 percent of the gross domestic product.[10] The description in this novel is far more interesting and understandable than any academic report on the crisis that I have seen.

In the novel, the hero (a woman) protects people who cannot protect themselves. She is asked for help by a former executive of a savings and loan bank (also a woman). The executive embezzled millions of dollars from a failed savings and loan bank. She needs help because the Mafia has discovered her wealth and is trying to take it from her. She cannot turn to the police for help because they will ask where she got the money.

The following excerpt describes how she stole the money from the failed bank. Though this description is fiction, it makes many of the same points that experts have made about this banking crisis.[11] In particular, note how deposits quickly moved to whatever bank was paying the highest interest rate because depositors believed that all deposits of $100,000 or less were essentially riskless thanks to government insurance (guarantee). The only concern of the depositors was to find the bank offering the highest interest rate.

Also note how even an honest banker could be tempted to avoid liquidity problems by attracting new deposits (in other words, begin a pyramid scheme) and how he could hide bad loans by rolling them over into a new loan (sometimes referred to as *evergreening*). The following excerpt also describes the slowness of bank examiners to uncover the problems of the bank and the inability of the legal authorities to prosecute and convict more than just a small fraction of the criminals who stole money from the banks:

> What did you have to do with savings and loans?
>
> I started working in one right out of college. When I got there, the regulators still knew all the players and all the rules were fifty years old. The money coming in was all from local people with passbooks, and the money going out was for mortgages on local one-family houses. . . . One day the rules change, so each savings and loan sets its own rates. The next day, deposit brokers start taking money from everywhere in the world, breaking it down into hundred-thousand-dollar chips and depositing the chips in whatever institution anywhere in the country had the highest interest that day. So if Bubba and Billy's Bank in Kinkajou, Texas, gives an extra quarter point, suddenly it's got millions of dollars being deposited. . . . And it didn't matter if the money was in the Bank of America or the Bank of Corncob, Iowa, because it was all insured.
>
> How did this create an opportunity for you?
>
> Forget about me for a minute. A few other things had to change first. Glockenspiel City Savings is suddenly a happening thing.
>
> What's Glockenspiel City Savings?
>
> You know, the little storefront with a million in assets built up over twenty years. One day they offer a nice rate on their CDs; the next week they've got four hundred million in deposits. That happened a hell of a lot more often than you'd think. There are little pitfalls, though. They're offering, say, nine percent. That means they've got to turn maybe ten, even twelve to make a profit. There's very little in Glockenspiel City that you can invest in that pays ten percent, and nothing

at all that you can invest four hundred million in. So you've got to invest it the way you got it, in the great wide world outside Glockenspiel City. . . .

Glockenspiel Savings is run by a guy named Cyrus Curbstone. . . . One day Cyrus wakes up and finds himself on another planet. He's got to pay nine percent and charge twelve. His million-dollar bank suddenly has four hundred million in deposits. He can't invest it fast enough in the usual way to make the forty or fifty million he needs to turn a profit. In walks a nice person: maybe me. Maybe I've been referred to him by a deposit broker who's been putting lots of those hundred-thousand-dollar chips in the bank. . . . Anyway, I'm a developer, or the general partner in a limited partnership. I've got a piece of land that's been appraised for twenty million, I want to develop it as a resort, and I need a loan of ten million to finance it.

Is the land real?

Sure. That doesn't mean I own it, or that it's worth anything like twenty million. . . .

Well, the day after Cyrus Curbstone starts getting these brokered deposits, he becomes a motivated lender. He's got four hundred million to lend out. If he makes ten percent, that's forty million a year. He pays his depositors nine percent, or thirty-six million, pays his overhead, and he's got maybe two million left in profit. He's part owner, or at least a big stockholder. The others are local people, friends of his. He wants that profit. But if he lets the deposits sit in the vault, he's losing three million a month. . . .

So you got a loan. What then?

Big Deals, Inc., got a loan. Big Deals spent it: building expenses, salaries, et cetera. But Big Deals neglected to pay the interest.

What did Cyrus do about it?

I'll skip a few phone calls, meetings, and threats. Usually that went on for months. At some point Cyrus sees that he's got a problem. He can do several things. One is to foreclose on the land. . . . Another is to accept my excuses and roll over the loan into a new one that includes the interest I owe him. Now it's a new loan for eleven million. Some of these banks carried loans like that for five years.

What for?

Because Cyrus hasn't lost any money until he reports the loan as nonperforming. If he makes a new loan, he not only hasn't lost the ten million, he can put out another million as an asset. This satisfies the regulators, if any should ever get around to Cyrus with all the work they've got. It keeps the bank looking healthy, so Cyrus has breathing space.

Why does he need such expensive breathing space?

Because he didn't make the forty million he needed to turn a profit. If he was a very quick learner, he made maybe thirty-five million: eight and three-quarters percent. He's still got to pay nine percent to the depositors, so he's maybe a million in the hole at the end of the first year. . . . He's on a treadmill that's going faster and faster. . . . As I said, he's not stupid. He knows that he looks great on paper as long as he's moving fast. But if somebody takes a photograph—that is, stops the action and studies it—his bank is insolvent. So now he's interested in keeping the system in motion.

So you got big loans and walked away with the money.

That was my specialty. There were other people who made a lot of headlines by building screwy empires—lending themselves money to build ghost communities in the desert and paying themselves and their families fifty million in salaries for doing it. But what I'm trying to tell you is that it was all going on a long time, and the ones you've read about weren't the only ones who did it. They weren't even the only ones who got caught. They were just the ones who got convicted. They were very unlucky.

Why unlucky?

It meant that one of these overworked low-level federal accountants had to get around to looking at all the loan papers, spot yours, notice there was something really wrong with the loan, ask questions, get the wrong answers, and convince his supervisor to do something about your loan instead of about somebody else's. Even then the procedures were amazing. That stuff we've all heard about the cold-eyed bank examiners popping in at dawn and padlocking everything is a myth. It never happened that way. Not once. . . . It was like being chased by a glacier. You could live a whole life without seeing it get any closer. It was coming, sure. But there was so much time to get out of the way.

And some waited too long?

Only a few. About a thousand people actually got to the point where they went to trial. This meant that their savings and loans were so out of control that the government put them at the top of the list for closure. They had to be losing millions a day for that. Then a couple of agents had to figure you were so obviously guilty that it was worth spending four years of their lives preparing the case. A U.S. attorney had to be sure the case was a slam dunk, so it wouldn't ruin her won-lost record. . . .

How did that work out?

Not so great. In order to convict, they had to take the judge and jury through all these loan papers, land-flips, asset appraisals, and files. The average person can barely follow his own taxes. All this paper was written up to fool qualified accountants. The paper made most of these guys look like victims. For all I know plenty of them were. About a third got off, and of the others only about half got convicted of anything that carried jail time. The average sentence was three years.[12]

The Example of Chile

This novel describes a private bank pyramid scheme in a rich country. There are not many examples of such schemes in poor countries because state-owned banks dominate most banking systems in those countries. Most of the pyramid schemes in poor countries are operated by state-owned rather than privately owned banks.

One of the few examples from a poor country of a private bank pyramid scheme is Chile from 1975 through 1982.[13] The government privatized a number of banks in 1975, but could not reach a decision about whether or how they should be regulated. Initially, the government seemed to favor an unregulated system without government guarantees or insurance for bank deposits. In other words, the public would have to evaluate the financial condition of a bank before making a deposit and could expect no help from the government if they chose wrong.

When some banks failed shortly after privatization, the government recapitalized them and thus protected the depositors from any loss. This protection led the public to believe that the government was implicitly guaranteeing bank deposits. In 1977, the government introduced an explicit guarantee for small depositors.

Once a government has taken the step of guaranteeing deposits, the public has little incentive to evaluate the financial condition of the banks or to make deposits only in sound banks. At this point, the government must step in and attempt to regulate the banks to ensure that they are well managed. If not, the government will have to make huge payouts to compensate depositors for the pyramid schemes that are likely to arise.

Unfortunately, the government of Chile did not introduce effective regulation after it had begun to guarantee deposits. Regulations were introduced restricting bank-lending practices, but only 10 inadequately trained and inexperienced bank inspectors were available to enforce these regulations for about 40 banks.

Though there is some debate as to when the bank pyramid scheme began, it continued until about 1982. For the previous five years, bank loans were growing at an annual rate of 43 percent. The former state-owned banks were privatized by selling them to local business groups. These groups then borrowed heavily from the banks. This is an example of *connected lending* in which a bank makes loans to one of its owners. The bank managers had little incentive to question the ability of their owners to repay the loans. As with other pyramid schemes, such a high growth rate was unsustainable, and the Chilean scheme crashed.

Because the government had guaranteed deposits, it had no choice but to bail out the banks and cover the bad loans. The fiscal cost borne by taxpayers was more than 40 percent of the gross national product.

The Example of Mozambique

The privatization of the state-owned Austral Bank in Mozambique provides an even more tragic example of the risk of looting and theft by private owners of banks. The government sold a 60 percent stake in the state-owned Austral Bank in 1997 to a consortium consisting of a Malaysian bank and local investors. According to news reports, the local investors were prominent members of the ruling political party. They did not pay cash for their shares but were allowed to pay in the future using the bank's dividends.

By 2001, the bank had collapsed under the weight of its bad loans. The private owners refused to provide additional capital and returned their shares to the government. The central bank appointed Antonio Siba-Siba Macuacua, a dynamic young economist, to be the new chairman. He launched an investigation into the activities of the previous bank management and attempted to collect some of the bad loans, many of which were reportedly made to individuals and businesses with political connections or to the Mozambique owners of the bank. On August 11, Siba-Siba was pushed down the stairwell of the bank's headquarters from the 14th floor and killed. His murderers have not been caught.

Later in the year, the bank was privatized a second time by the sale of 80 percent of its shares to the Amalgamated Banks of South

Africa for $10 million. It is unclear the extent to which the government had to take over the bad loans of the bank to restore its financial solvency before it could be privatized. Though bank deposits are not formally guaranteed by the government, it is widely accepted that the government will not allow depositors to suffer because of the mismanagement of the bank.

Bank Crises

Although I have described how banks can become pyramid schemes and gave a few examples (the United States, Chile, and Mozambique), what evidence is there that they are in fact a serious problem in many countries instead of just a theoretical possibility? The most compelling evidence is the large number of banking crises that have occurred around the world in both rich and poor countries

According to one inventory (Table 5-1), there have been 168 banking crises involving bank insolvencies of differing severity around the world since 1976 or about 6 per year. More than two-thirds of poor countries experienced such a crisis.

The number of crises is greater than the number of countries because many countries had multiple crises. For example, Argentina holds the record with four. Kenya and the Democratic Republic of the Congo have had three. Bolivia, Brazil, Mexico, Russia, Czech Republic, Chile, Estonia, Ghana, Guinea, Nigeria, Indonesia, Malaysia, and Costa Rica have had two.

Surprisingly, the same proportion of the large, rich OECD countries have also had at least one banking crisis during this period. Great Britain has had two. The fact that so many rich countries have had large-scale bank failures indicates that the conventional system of bank regulation and supervision even in rich countries has serious weaknesses. If these countries cannot successfully implement such a system, is it plausible that poor countries can do so given their weaker governmental institutions and political systems? In spite of this dismal record of failure to adequately supervise banks in both rich and poor countries, most banking experts continue to support the current system. A better alternative at least for poor countries will be discussed in the next chapter.

Perhaps I am being extreme in attributing all of these banking crises to crashed pyramid schemes. Are there other plausible causes

141

Table 5-1
BANKING CRISES (1976–2002)

	Number of Banking Crises	Number of Countries with Crises	Total Number of Countries	Countries with Crises (percent)
Low & Medium Income Countries[1]				
East Asia and Pacific	14	11	22	50
Europe and Central Asia[2]	28	23	29	79
Latin America and Caribbean	32	18	33	55
Middle East and North Africa	9	8	16	50
South Asia	4	4	8	50
Sub-Saharan Africa	53	41	48	85
Subtotal	140	105	156	67
High Income OECD Countries[1]	18	16	24	67
Other High Income Countries[1]	10	6	28	21
TOTAL	168	127	208	61

[1] World Bank classification of regions and income levels.
[2] Includes Slovenia.
SOURCE: Gerard Caprio and Daniela Klingebiel, "Episodes of Systemic and Borderline Financial Crises," World Bank, January 2003. Available on the World Wide Web (http://wbln0018.worldbank.org/html/FinancialSectorWeb.nsf/Search General?openform&Banking+Systems&Statistics).

of banking crises? Other causes might include an unexpected macro-economic shock that causes a larger percentage of bank loans to go bad or a banking panic in which depositors rush to take money out of banks that are otherwise sound and well managed (called *systemic risk,* which is discussed in the next chapter). To determine whether any other possible causes are important requires a detailed examination of the hundreds of banking crises that have occurred.

One study that examined 29 banking crises, including most of the important ones, concludes that: "... the primary causes of bank insolvency are considered to be deficient management, faulty supervision and regulation, government intervention, or some degree of connected or politically motivated lending...."[14] This sounds to me like these crises were caused in large part by pyramid schemes.

Cost of Bank Pyramid Schemes

The cost to the government and the economy of these bank failures and crises has been substantial. As noted, the government has typically had to step in and replace the bad loans of the failed banks with government securities so that the banks would not default on their deposits and other liabilities. At least for the time being, the banks are then solvent and depositors are protected.

One study has measured the cost to the governments and ultimately the taxpayer of these bank failures.[15] For bank crises in 40 countries, the cost to the government on average was about 13 percent of the annual gross domestic product for each crisis. The cost was much higher in some countries. The governments of Argentina and, as noted previously, Chile had to spend as much as 40 to 55 percent of GDP to bail out their banks in the early 1980s. The recent crisis in East Asia may also cost the governments there as much as 50 percent of GDP.

According to that study, the total cost for crises to date in poor countries is shocking—in excess of $1 trillion. To give some idea of the importance of this amount, it equals almost 17 years' worth of foreign aid (official development assistance) at current rates to these countries provided by the rich countries.[16] Bad banks in poor countries have squandered an amount of money equal to many years of economic aid from the rich countries.

What scares me is that this estimate may be just a fraction of the true amount wasted by bank pyramid schemes in poor countries. There is little reason to believe that these schemes have been stopped. By their nature, the extent of current pyramid schemes is hidden. With the backing of the government in the form of explicit or implicit deposit guarantees, they can continue without crashing for many years.

Everyone has an incentive to hide the true extent of the problem. If it is a pyramid scheme run by state-owned banks to finance state-owned enterprises (the most common situation) or finance businesses owned by cronies of the nation's leader, the government is not going to admit that there is a problem. Even honest and well-intentioned politicians who want to clean up the mess will be reluctant to reveal the full extent of the problem until they have a plan and resources to do something about it. If the size of the problem is revealed, the pyramid scheme is likely to collapse immediately when worried depositors withdraw their money.

If it is a private bank pyramid scheme, the owners and managers will do their best to hide the extent of bad loans from whatever bank regulatory agencies might exist. As we saw in the U.S. example, one way of hiding what is going on is to roll over a bad loan into a new loan so that the old loan does not have to be declared in default or nonperforming. All I can say is that I have worked in a number of poor countries, and in every one, there is concern about the extent of bad loans in the banking system.

The IMF As Bank Regulator

One might expect that the International Monetary Fund (IMF) or the World Bank knows the full extent of the bad loan problems in poor countries and whether pyramid schemes are prevalent. There has been some movement toward making the IMF an international bank regulatory agency. Because the IMF has been asked to bail out countries that experienced major banking crises (for example, the recent crisis in East Asian countries), the IMF now attempts to assess more thoroughly the state of the financial system in poor and even some rich countries. It is hoped that this advanced warning system will enable the IMF and the World Bank to help countries at risk to improve their financial system before a crisis occurs.[17]

This new function of the IMF is not surprising because it follows a common pattern in poor countries. As we saw in Chile, once a government or any other institution such as the IMF guarantees the deposits or other liabilities of banks, it has no choice but to step in and begin to regulate the banks to protect itself from bank pyramid schemes and from having to pay for huge bank losses. Though the financial help that the IMF provides countries in crisis is rarely described as guaranteeing the liabilities (deposits) of the banking system, it usually has that effect. One expert concludes, "While [IMF] assistance is often couched as 'liquidity' assistance to resolve 'balance of payments' problems, in fact assistance is designed to absorb the losses of insolvent banks and their borrowers in developing economies, and to insulate international lenders from the losses that they would otherwise suffer."[18]

Like many bank regulatory agencies in poor countries, the IMF may not be very effective in this new role. The key feature of this new role is that the IMF along with the World Bank will carry out Financial Sector Assessments in countries around the world. Knowledgeable staff in these organizations have told me that the IMF and the World Bank have only modest resources to prepare each assessment. A team from these two organizations usually spends only two weeks or so in each country.

More important, the IMF and World Bank team typically does not independently assess the quality of the loans of the banking system and relies primarily on information provided by the regulatory authorities in the country. Thus, it is quite possible that the banks are misleading the regulatory authorities as to their true financial picture or the regulatory authorities are misleading the IMF.

Recently in the case of Japan, the IMF decided to make an exception and not rely entirely on information provided by bank regulatory authorities. The IMF requested that it be allowed to examine in more detail the financial situation of Japanese banks. Japan has the second largest economy in the world, and the extent of the bad loans in its banking system may be the largest ever recorded in absolute terms. Estimates range between $335 billion and $2 trillion.

Not surprisingly, the bank regulatory authority (the Financial Services Agency) refused the IMF's request, giving the feeble excuse that it does not have enough manpower to assist IMF staff. After a spate of bad publicity over this decision suggesting that Japan was trying to hide the extent of bank insolvencies, the minister for financial services announced that the Financial Services Agency would cooperate though the details would be negotiated with the IMF.[19]

Even though the IMF emphasizes that countries should be more transparent and disclose more financial information, the IMF itself does not make these financial assessments public. Thus, no one outside of the IMF or the World Bank can use the information in these assessments such as it may be to determine the full extent of the bad loan problems in countries around the world. If a bank pyramid scheme is operating in a country (in other words, the banks have large amounts of bad loans), the IMF also has an incentive not to disclose this even if it knows the extent of the problem. The IMF does not want to be accused of causing the pyramid scheme to crash. Instead it intends to help the country privately "... to increase the effectiveness of efforts to promote sound financial systems."[20]

Off–Balance Sheet Financing

The IMF has sometimes been effective in imposing discipline on government spending in poor countries but generally not on the lending of state-owned banks. The IMF provides various forms of financial assistance to most poor countries (Stand-By Arrangements, Extended Fund Facility Arrangement, Supplemental Reserve Facility, and so forth). Before providing this assistance, the IMF examines the government's tax revenues and expenditures to ensure that the budget deficit and thus government borrowing are not excessive. The IMF may require the government to reduce the deficit as a condition of providing the financial assistance.

This discipline creates an incentive for a government to use state-owned banks to finance activities that it cannot finance through the budget, such as providing money to state-owned enterprises or cronies of the president. However, the government implicitly or explicitly guarantees the deposits of state-owned banks. Thus, if borrowers do not repay the loans provided by the state-owned banks, the loans become a liability (debt) of the government. These bad loans, however, are often not counted in the official debt of the government. This is also called "off–balance sheet financing" because the bad loans are not officially recorded as liabilities on the balance sheet of the government.

In part because of oversight of the IMF and because information about government's expenditures and taxes is more readily available to the public, corrupt or incompetent politicians and officials are somewhat constrained in their ability to misuse government revenues though there are major exceptions. However, because there is often little oversight of lending by state-owned banks, they face few constraints on their ability to misuse the money provided by depositors. As a result, the large amount of bad loans found in state-owned banks and the frequency of banking crises should not be surprising.

As an example of how difficult it is to change the views of politicians concerning the management of state-owned banks, one country under pressure from the World Bank had agreed to bring in an executive from a large international bank to become the chief executive of the largest state-owned bank. The government asked him to restructure the bank and ensure that it was managed on commercial principals in preparation for privatization. In a personal interview, his main complaint was that the prime minister kept calling him requesting that the bank make a loan to a particular company or individual. When the executive refused, the prime minister became upset and threatened to fire him. The prime minister did not seem to understand that such loans were inconsistent with the objectives given to the executive.

Impact on Growth

Though the textbook model says that banks use the public's savings to finance the most productive new investments, the sad reality is that banks in many poor countries and even some rich countries have squandered a large proportion of these savings. The exact amount of the misused savings is unclear because no one knows the full extent of bad loans held by banks.

Though I cannot conclusively prove it, I suspect that the misuse of the public's savings by state-owned banks is a major cause of the low rate of growth in many poor countries. Only a few studies are available that attempt to connect dysfunctional banking systems with low rates of economic growth.

The most recent study shows that a high level of state ownership of banks is associated with a lower rate of economic growth.[21] According to this study of banking systems in 92 countries, governments on average in 1970 owned 59 percent of the equity of the 10 largest banks. This percentage has declined somewhat because of bank privatization but was still 42 percent in 1995. This study found that countries with a high level of state ownership in 1970 are associated with subsequent lower economic growth and, in particular, lower growth of economic productivity. The slow growth of productivity suggests that state-owned banks did not channel the national

147

savings to the most productive investments—in other words, they were failures as financial intermediaries.

This study does not prove that private banks always perform better than state-owned banks. Privatization of state-owned banks is not a panacea that will solve all the problems of the banking system. As noted previously, private banks are also likely to become pyramid schemes if their deposits are implicitly or explicitly guaranteed by the state.

Government Must Get Out of Banking

Governments in poor countries must get out of the commercial banking business. The high hopes of 50 years ago that state-owned banks would mobilize the public's savings and channel it to the most productive new investments have turned out to be a cruel joke. State-owned banks must be privatized or shut down. Leaving ownership of the banking system in the hands of politicians creates temptations that most cannot resist. When the famous American bank robber Billy Sutton was asked why he robbed banks, he responded, "That's where the money is." Too many politicians view state-owned banks in the same light.

Privatization will be politically difficult because a bank cannot be privatized until it is restored to solvency. Politicians do not want to admit the full extent of the pyramid scheme that they have been running for years and do not want to face the budgetary costs of paying the depositors in these banks. Powerful business groups with connections to the ruling politicians may also oppose privatization because they will lose access to bank loans on preferential terms (for example, repayment is not required). The labor unions representing bank employees will oppose privatization because they know that it will undoubtedly mean reducing staff and laying off workers from relatively high paying jobs.

Assuming, however, that the government can be removed from the banking business, the important question remains as to how a private banking system should be structured and regulated. How can the same governments that have so mismanaged state-owned banks do a better job of regulating private banks so that state pyramid schemes are not replaced by private pyramid schemes?

6. Bank Regulation: Depositors Beware

A common problem in all markets is how to ensure that consumers have adequate information about the quality of the products and services they are buying. If they don't, they may be victimized by paying high prices for low-quality products and services or even products that are harmful and dangerous. In the jargon of the economist, this is called *asymmetric information* because the seller of the product or service has more information about its quality than the buyer.

Inadequate information is certainly a problem in the markets for financial securities. In addition to bank deposits, financial securities include common stock of a company, mutual fund shares, bonds, contributions to a pension plan, and insurance policies. An investor needs to make a judgment about the likely return on his investment and the risk of that investment.

Two types of government regulation have been used to protect consumers who may have inadequate information about the quality of products and services, including financial securities. The first is *minimum quality regulation*. The second is *information disclosure regulation*. I believe that poor countries (and perhaps rich countries) have made a mistake by adopting minimum quality regulation for banks rather than information disclosure regulation. Let me describe and give examples of these two types of regulation.

Two Types of Regulation

In the first type of regulation, minimum quality regulation, the government takes on the responsibility of assessing the quality of goods and services and requires the supplier to sell only those that meet the government's minimum quality standards. There are many examples of this first type of regulation. In the United States, the country I am most familiar with, the government requires all automobiles to meet minimum safety standards (seat belts, air bags, etc.). The manufacturers of pharmaceutical drugs have to demonstrate to

149

the government that their drugs are both safe and effective before they can be sold. Doctors, lawyers, and accountants (but not economists) have to pass various tests and other requirements before they are allowed to practice.

In the second type of regulation, information disclosure regulation, the government requires suppliers to disclose information about the quality of their product or service, but does not prohibit them from selling low-quality products and services. As long as the supplier discloses the information required by the government, he is free to sell a product or service of any quality.

Examples of this second type of regulation in the United States include required ingredient and nutrition labeling on food products, fuel efficiency labeling on automobiles and appliances, disclosure of possible adverse side effects of drugs, and "truth in lending" regulations that require lenders to provide in easily understood terms the interest and terms of loans before the borrower can agree to a loan. For some products and services, both types of regulation are used together, for example, minimum quality standards for drugs combined with disclosure of possible harmful side effects.

The rationale for quality regulation is that the cost of thousands of consumers attempting individually to measure the quality of a complex product or service would be great. Government regulators and inspectors can determine the quality for all consumers and prohibit the sale of those products and services that fail to meet a minimum standard. Quality regulation certainly makes sense when the use of a low-quality product or service could actually cause death or severe injury (for example, drugs or automobiles). If a consumer guessed wrong about quality, he might not have a second chance.

A weakness of quality regulation is that consumers may still have to spend a great deal of effort or money to determine the quality of even those products and services that meet the minimum standard set by the government. This type of regulation does not guarantee that all brands or sources of a particular regulated product or service are of high quality. It only provides some assurance that the product or service meets a minimum standard. Consumers who want to buy a product or service that exceeds this minimum standard must still obtain information about the quality of the product and service and attempt to distinguish between low-quality and high-quality suppliers. For example, just because the government gives a doctor a license to practice is no guarantee that he is a highly skilled doctor or the best available to treat a particular illness. Smart consumers still have to evaluate the doctor's capabilities.[1]

In contrast, the rationale for disclosure regulation is that it will lower the costs for consumers to obtain information. Disclosure regulation enables consumers to judge for themselves the quality of products and services and to decide which level of quality to buy.

Current Bank Regulation

In the financial securities markets both types of regulation are used. Quality regulation is typically used for bank deposits while disclosure regulation is used for the sale of stocks and bonds.

In brief, the quality regulation of banks usually consists of various restrictions on the business activities of the bank with the objective that the amount of bad loans incurred by the bank will never rise to a level such that the bank cannot pay its liabilities (mainly deposits). For example, the regulators may restrict the amount of lending to insiders (connected lending), purchases of securities such as common stock whose value may fluctuate greatly, the ratio of a loan to the value of the security or collateral provided by the borrower such as real estate or common stock, and the amount of lending to a single borrower or industry.

Despite these restrictions, some loans or other investments will go bad even in the best managed banks. To protect depositors or other creditors against excessive loan losses, the owners of the bank are required to have equity capital invested in the bank that increases with the perceived riskiness of the bank's loans and other investments (referred to as *capital adequacy*). The idea is that any failed loans or other investments will be borne by the owners of the bank through a reduction in their equity capital rather than by the depositors or other creditors.

If the capital adequacy of the bank falls below the required levels, the regulator will require the bank to take corrective action to increase the amount of capital. If the bank is unable to increase its capital adequacy, the regulator may shut down the bank before its financial situation deteriorates further and use the assets (loans and investments) to pay off the liabilities (deposits). If the regulator has been diligent and prompt, the value of the assets will be at least equal to the value of the liabilities though the owners may lose their entire equity capital. In this way, it is hoped that government regulation will ensure that deposits in the banking system are high quality, in other words, low risk.

Securities Regulation

The second type of regulation typically used for the sale of securities such as stocks and bonds makes no attempt to regulate the quality of the security, in other words, its riskiness. The only regulation is that the seller of the security must honestly disclose enough information about the security so that investors can reasonably decide for themselves the degree of risk involved in purchasing the security. The United States pioneered this form of securities regulation in the Securities Act of 1933, sometimes referred to as the "truth in securities" law.

Using the United States as a typical example, the role of the regulatory agency (Securities and Exchange Commission or SEC) is primarily to ensure that the information disclosure is adequate and will not allow the security to be sold until it is adequate. The disclosure typically takes the form of a prospectus that contains financial statements, a business plan for how the proceeds of the securities sale will be used, and a description of the risks associated with the investment. Someone, for example, is free to sell shares in a company that is planning to raise pineapples in Antarctica as long as the seller discloses this important fact and the risks involved.

If disclosure of important facts is incomplete or inaccurate, almost everyone involved in the sale of the securities may be liable to pay the losses of investors resulting from the sale. These include directors and officers of the company selling the securities and investment bankers that facilitated the sale. Investors can bring a claim in the courts for damages resulting from the sale. Furthermore, the government can bring criminal charges resulting in fines or imprisonment against those who make false or misleading statements in the prospectus.

A key feature of disclosure regulation is that the regulatory agency makes no promise about the quality of the security, in other words, its riskiness. In fact, the prospectus must make no claim that the regulatory agency guarantees the accuracy of the information in the

152

prospectus or has determined that the securities are safe investments.

Though information disclosure regulation is typically used for the sale of securities, it could be used for bank deposits instead of the quality regulation that is now used almost everywhere. Bank deposits are not fundamentally different from other financial securities such as common stock or bonds. Before making a deposit, a bank customer would be given a prospectus describing the financial situation of the bank, including the various risks involved, and the customer would have to decide for himself whether the promised rate of interest will compensate him for the riskiness of the investment. The customer could also rely on the opinion of bank industry analysts who may be better able to evaluate the financial situation of the bank. As with securities, no government agency would evaluate the riskiness of making a deposit with the bank or guarantee that the bank will be able to pay the promised interest or return the deposit when requested by the depositor.

Enforcement

Obviously, more important than the details or specifics of the regulations is the ability of the regulatory authorities to enforce them. The most sophisticated regulations are meaningless if they are ignored either by banks or by sellers of securities. I am pessimistic about the ability of many poor countries to adequately enforce either type of regulation.

In regard to quality regulation, bank examiners who are supposed to enforce the regulations are often corrupt, underpaid, poorly trained, and few in number. Furthermore, the banks can often bring political pressure on the regulatory agency not to enforce its regulations. For example, even in the United States with its relatively honest and competent judicial and political system, Charles Keating, who controlled a savings and loan bank, was successful in arranging for five U.S. senators to pressure the regulatory authorities to stop their investigation of his bank. The end result was that his bank pyramid scheme continued for another two years and eventually cost the U.S. government $2.6 billion to compensate depositors. It was probably the largest single bank failure in U.S. history. Though Keating was initially convicted of various crimes, his conviction was overturned; and he was set free after serving four and a half years.

The five senators and the regulatory authorities suffered no civil or criminal penalties.

In regard to disclosure regulation, enforcement is often split between the regulatory agency and the courts. Investors who have been misled by false or misleading disclosure can bring suit in the courts for damages against the sellers of securities. Such court cases, however, are complicated and involve difficult issues of law, accounting, and finance. Only a few judges in poor countries have the training and experience to handle such cases.

In spite of my pessimism about enforcement of either type of regulation, I still favor applying disclosure regulation to banks instead of quality regulation. The basic reason is that the harm caused by failed quality regulation is likely to be much greater than that caused by failed disclosure regulation. Even if my pessimism is not justified and the government can effectively implement either type of regulation, I see no reason to think that quality regulation is better than disclosure regulation.

Deposit Insurance

My fear is that if a country introduces quality regulation for private banks, it will come under irresistible pressure to also provide guarantees or insurance for bank deposits. If quality regulation is weak, the ideal conditions are then in place for private bank pyramid schemes to operate. Depositors and other creditors of the bank know that they are protected against a bank failure and thus do little to monitor or supervise the financial situation of the bank. This will continue the past pattern of numerous and widespread bank failures and banking crises in poor countries and the misallocation of the public's savings.

I use the terms government guarantee and deposit insurance interchangeably. Though they may differ in form, the substance is usually the same. Instead of a government guarantee, the government may go through the motions of creating a state-owned or managed insurance scheme, and banks are required to make premium payments to a fund. This fund is then used to pay off the depositors in failed banks. In almost all cases, however, the government stands behind the insurance scheme and will supplement the fund if the insurance premiums prove to have been inadequate.

154

Though it is theoretically possible to have quality regulation without some form of government guarantees (insurance) of deposits, this is unlikely for three reasons. First of all, the public can justifiably claim that it relied on the government's promise that it was adequately regulating the banks and made deposits in the banks on that basis. If bank regulation was inadequate, there will be strong public pressure to compensate depositors for this government failure.

Second, the argument that depositors should be compensated for the failure of bank regulation is reinforced by the secrecy surrounding most regulation of banks. In particular, regulators usually do not disclose the results of their examinations of a bank's financial health. If they detect a problem, for example, undercapitalization, they may require the bank to take corrective action. However, they usually do not tell the general public that the risk of making deposits in that bank has increased. The ignorant public continues to make deposits relying on government assurances that the bank is financially sound.

This practice is quite different from the quality regulation used for other products and services. If the regulators find that quality has dropped, they immediately announce this information so that the public can stop using that product or service, and they may ban its sale. If the regulator for pharmaceutical drugs, for example, discovers that a drug currently being sold has harmful side effects, it would be unthinkable for the regulator not to inform the public and let consumers continue to buy an unsafe product. For example, criminal charges were brought against French health officials who knew that blood supplied for transfusions had probably been contaminated with the AIDS virus but allowed the blood to be used without informing the public. Yet this practice of not informing the public seems to be routine for bank regulators.

There may be good reasons why regulators keep the results of bank examinations secret. For example, it might avoid the closing of a bank that could be saved after management takes corrective actions or reduces the risk of panic withdrawals that could spread to other banks. The only way, however, that secrecy can be justified to depositors is if the government also guarantees deposits and other liabilities of the banks so that the public is not harmed by the failure of the government to disclose the results of bank examinations. If I made a deposit in a bank after the government had secretly determined it was high risk and then the bank subsequently failed, I would be enraged that my government, which is supposed to protect me, did not provide me this information about the financial health of the bank. I would demand that the government compensate me when the bank failed.

Third, powerful special-interest groups will pressure the government to introduce some form of government guarantees or deposit insurance, another example of *rent-seeking behavior*. Historically, the major supporters of deposit insurance are parts of the banking industry itself rather than the general public concerned about the safety of their deposits. A cynic might suppose that the banking industry wants deposit insurance so that it can more easily carry out pyramid schemes. Though this might be part of the reason in some cases, the usual situation is that one segment of the industry wants deposit insurance so that it can better compete against another segment of the industry.

Because such insurance makes all deposits equal in risk, higher risk banks will support insurance or government guarantees because they can then compete more effectively against lower risk banks. Otherwise they might not be able to attract deposits at all or only by paying higher interest rates to compensate for the higher risk.

The introduction of deposit insurance in the United States, the first country to have such insurance, is a good example of this type of rent seeking on the part of the banking industry. In spite of the many bank failures during the Great Depression, the president, bank regulatory agencies, and larger banks resisted any proposal for nationwide deposit insurance based in part on the poor experience with previous insurance schemes operating in individual states. Powerful members of Congress, however, under the influence of the many small banks, blocked any banking legislation unless it included deposit insurance.[2] The result was that the Banking Act of 1933 introduced nationwide deposit insurance.

Thus, instead of a scheme to protect small depositors, deposit insurance was primarily designed to protect small banks that are competing with large banks. The Independent Bankers Association, which represented small banks, was quite clear about the purpose of deposit insurance, stating that it is ". . . a powerful instrument in the perpetuation of independent banking. It has put the small bank on a par with the large bank in the eyes of the average depositor."[3]

This pressure by small community banks for deposit insurance continues today. Small banks now want to increase the limit on deposit insurance from the longstanding $100,000 per person. According to one newspaper account, "[a]lmost every congressman and senator has a few small community banks with headquarters in his or her district. While regulators and big banks oppose an increase in coverage limits, saying it would boost costs and weaken market discipline on lending, community banks say raising coverage is essential to their competing against the giant bank conglomerates."[4]

Small banks were a powerful political force in 1933 because of terrible government regulation that created thousands of small, high-risk banks. Federal and state regulation prohibited a bank in one state from doing business in another. In other words, nationwide branch banking was not allowed. Even worse, many states did not allow a bank to have branches even within the state. This prohibition continued until the early 1980s when these restrictions began to break down.[5]

Other countries were slow to follow the example of the United States in creating deposit insurance, probably with good reason. Other countries did not begin to adopt explicit deposit insurance schemes until almost 30 years later. Subsequently, deposit insurance has spread to about 33 poor countries and 25 rich countries. It is the official policy of the European Union and it is recommended by the International Monetary Fund.

Various reasons are given as to why deposit insurance is a good policy. For example, it provides a "safety net" for small, unsophisticated savers or creates more stability in the banking system by reducing "systemic risk." I suspect, however, that a closer examination of the political forces in favor of deposit insurance will show that, like in the United States, certain segments of the banking industry are the major supporters of deposit insurance for their own self-interest. For example, as economic integration increases within the European Union, banks in one country would be at a competitive disadvantage if that country did not have deposit insurance while other countries did.

In a poor country, local domestic banks are concerned about competition from international banks that may begin to operate in their country. They recognize that if given a choice between local banks and branches of large international banks with good reputations, depositors will choose the international banks. Deposit insurance makes the local banks equal to the international banks in terms of risk.

Also, many poor countries have a mixed system of state-owned and privately owned banks. The public generally believes that the government guarantees deposits in the state-owned banks even though a formal deposit insurance scheme does not exist. Thus, private banks pressure the government to give them the same treatment and to explicitly guarantee or insure the deposits of all banks.

Systemic Risk

Other than helping some segments of the banking industry to avoid competition, the one possibly valid argument for deposit insurance is that it will reduce *systemic risk* and thus reduce large-scale bank failures and banking crises. Systemic risk supposedly results because banks use short-term deposits to make long-term loans. Thus, a bank faces the risk that, for some reason, a high percentage of its depositors will simultaneously want their money back—called a *run* on the bank—and the bank will not have the money to pay them until the bank's loans are repaid or other assets can be sold.

The essence of systemic risk is that a single bank failure may cause the general public to lose confidence in other banks even though they are well managed and solvent. This loss of confidence is also referred to as *contagion* because a sick bank infects a healthy bank. Out of ignorance and panic, the public will rush to withdraw their deposits from even healthy banks, thereby causing widespread bank failures and a banking crisis. In effect, solvent banks can become illiquid. Thus, deposit insurance is needed to give the public confidence in its banks.

This idea gained widespread acceptance because of the large number of bank failures during the Great Depression in the United States. A popular belief was that depositors were rushing to take their money out of their local small-town banks because of a false rumor that the bank might fail even though the honest but beleaguered owner knew that the bank was well managed, solvent, and could repay the depositors if only he had time to raise the necessary cash.

Though a theoretical possibility, this phenomenon seems rare.[6] Proponents of deposit insurance talk about this possibility at length but rarely give examples. Most banking crises occur because there are good reasons to believe that many banks are insolvent. Depositors are not being irrational when they rush to withdraw their deposits. This rush was certainly the case in the United States in the Great Depression when ultimately about 9,000 insolvent banks failed.[7] Most of these failures were small rural banks whose prosperity depended on their loans to the agriculture sector that suffered the most during the economic downturn.[8] In contrast, only one bank failed in Canada during this period because its banks were typically large, operated over the entire country, and made loans to all types of businesses.

Even if this phenomenon is a serious problem, there seem to be other ways to deal with it rather than a government guarantee for all deposits. Central banks were supposedly established in most countries to deal with this problem. If an otherwise healthy bank is having a liquidity problem due to a failure of public confidence in the bank, the central bank is supposed to make a loan to the bank or buy some of its assets to tide it over until the bank can raise the necessary cash to pay its depositors.[9] Another way to deal with this problem is for banks to more closely match the term of their deposits with the term of their loans. In other words, deposits that could be withdrawn without any notice would only be invested in short-term, liquid securities. Only deposits that could not be withdrawn for a specific period (sometimes called time deposits) would be used to make long-term loans.

Whether or not deposit insurance reduces or increases the likelihood of widespread bank failures or banking crises is in the end an empirical question. If, on the one hand, systemic risk is a serious problem rather than just a theoretical possibility, then deposit insurance would reduce the likelihood of banking crises. If, on the other hand, most banking crises are the result of crashed pyramid schemes, then deposit insurance will increase the likelihood of banking crises.

I know of only one study that has attempted to measure the impact of deposit insurance on the stability of banking systems. After analyzing empirical evidence for a large number of countries, the study concludes that ". . . explicit deposit insurance tends to be detrimental to bank stability, the more so where bank interest rates have been deregulated and where the institutional environment is weak."[10] I interpret this to mean that when weak bank regulation

159

is unable to stop bank pyramid schemes, deposit insurance will increase the likelihood of such schemes and thus widespread bank failures and crises. Unfortunately, this situation is likely to apply to many if not most poor countries and even to some rich countries.

Concern about the problems created by deposit insurance, especially in poor countries, seems to be growing. The World Bank recently published a major report on institutions that support a market economy. Concerning deposit insurance, the report states it was designed to reduce financial fragility but has been "identified as the greatest source of fragility."[11] Furthermore, the report suggests that deposit insurance may not be desirable unless "complementary institutions" such as effective bank regulation have been developed. Though stated in polite terms, this report implies that deposit insurance or government guarantees coupled with ineffective quality regulation is a disaster waiting to happen.

The World Bank report goes on to discuss how governments might deal with the problems created by deposit insurance. Not surprisingly, the report talks about the need to improve bank regulation and supervision, which is the usual response of banking experts. The report does go on to discuss other measures to encourage private individuals and institutions to monitor the performance of banks and thus supplement the efforts of the government regulators. These measures include requiring the owners of banks to have more capital at risk, limiting the coverage of deposit insurance so that larger depositors and other creditors are not covered, and including subordinated debt on the balance sheet of banks.

I am convinced, however, that the only way to encourage private monitoring of banks is to eliminate deposit insurance entirely. Moreover, the only way to eliminate deposit insurance is to eliminate quality regulation of banks. As discussed earlier, as long as the government purports to regulate the risk of bank deposits and does so secretly, the political pressure to guarantee all bank deposits and most other bank creditors as well will be irresistible.

For example, the United States supposedly limits deposit insurance to deposits under $100,000, and large depositors or other creditors may suffer a loss if a bank fails. Presumably this limitation gives larger depositors and creditors an incentive to monitor the financial health of banks and supplement government regulation.

In practice, however, the United States instead of closing a failed bank has often merged a failed bank with a healthy bank and then provided funds to make certain the combined bank is healthy (called the *purchase and assumption method*). The end result is that all creditors and depositors are protected and not just those with deposit insurance. This method is frequently used in other countries as well.

Information Disclosure Regulation Is Best

Instead of quality regulation, disclosure regulation should be used for banks just as it is used for other securities in most countries. Its main advantage is the clear message that it sends to depositors and other bank creditors. The government is saying that it will help depositors and other creditors to obtain information about the financial health of a bank, but they must decide for themselves whether the bank is financially sound and whether a deposit in that bank is high or low risk. Even more important, by requiring banks to disclose information, the government makes no promise that a bank is financially sound and certainly does not guarantee deposits placed with that bank. Bank deposits are treated like any other financial investment, and investors are entirely responsible for their own investment decisions, in other words, depositor beware.

To have any chance of producing a sound, prudently managed banking system, this method of regulation should be supplemented by the privatization of state-owned banks. Because state-owned banks have an implicit government guarantee, the government is compelled to guarantee deposits in private banks as well.

Also the government must allow the free and unrestricted entry by new banks, in particular, foreign banks. Information disclosure regulation may very well result in a *flight to quality*. The public may shun former state-owned banks and domestic private banks when they are not protected by government guarantees or insurance and will instead turn to branches of reputable foreign banks. This action might result in most banks being foreign owned, but at least the banking system will be well managed. The public's savings will not be squandered in pyramid schemes organized by domestic banks and guaranteed by the government.

Various theoretical arguments have been made as to why it might be desirable for the government to limit competition in banking, for example, to disallow unrestricted entry of new banks.[12] Though I can't deny that these arguments have some validity, I doubt whether

161

governments and bank regulatory agencies in poor countries will be able to determine when a new entry is in the public interest or not.

More likely, the regulators will come under the influence of the existing banks that will argue strongly that more competition is bad. I have never heard a private company argue that more competition was good. They will use the theoretical arguments of economists to promote their own self-interest. In addition, they will undoubtedly raise the hoary arguments that foreign ownership of such an important and strategic sector of the economy is somehow bad. They will prey on the nationalistic and xenophobic fears of the public and the politicians to keep out foreign banks.

Free entry into banking is not a perfect policy and does have some risks. However, it is a better policy than allowing government officials and regulators to decide when entry is in the public interest. Though perhaps well intentioned, this government intervention to supposedly improve the functioning of the banking sector will probably end up harming it.

Even those who favor bank privatization sometimes support the idea of keeping one state-owned bank operating that would act as a safety net for small depositors. This bank would be like a postal savings bank or state savings bank. The key features of this bank are that it would only invest in government securities, and its deposits would be the only ones guaranteed by the state. Such a bank is referred to as a *narrow bank* because its investments or loans are strictly limited.

My concern about such a bank is that it will come under political pressure to make loans to the private sector. Unless it is certain that this would not happen, such a bank is a bad idea. Powerful members of the business community will argue that they are handicapped by an inability to obtain financing for their new investments from private banks. If the government wants to spur private-sector development and increase the rate of economic growth, the state savings bank should be allowed to loan to the private sector. If this happens, this bank is likely to become another pyramid scheme in which politicians allow their relatives, cronies, or supporters to obtain loans from the bank that are then rarely repaid.

The New Zealand Example

To my knowledge, only one country has adopted information disclosure regulation for banks—New Zealand. This country has never had deposit insurance. This method of regulation seems to have worked well since it was introduced in the beginning of 1996.

The fact that information disclosure regulation has worked for New Zealand, however, is not conclusive proof that it will work in poor countries because New Zealand has a relatively strong political and legal system. As mentioned earlier, the main enforcement mechanism is private lawsuits in the courts. Though no such lawsuits concerning banks have arisen in New Zealand, its courts are capable of handling such complex cases. Courts in poor countries may not be.

As an example of information disclosure regulation for banks, New Zealand requires each bank to disclose financial and other information every three months to anyone requesting it and to post summaries of the information at each bank office.[13] This information includes

- income and balance sheet,
- names of the bank directors and any possible conflicts of interest,
- asset quality and provisioning for bad loans,
- number of large exposures as measured relative to the bank's equity,
- related party exposures as measured relative to the bank's equity,
- sectoral exposures,
- capital adequacy, including off–balance sheet items,
- market risk exposures, and
- credit rating, if any.

These disclosure statements must be audited and certified by the bank's directors as being not false or misleading. If the directors permit a false or misleading disclosure statement, penalties include fines and imprisonment. Moreover, directors have unlimited personal liability for claims brought by creditors who lost money based on false or misleading statements. If a bank's capital adequacy ratios fall below certain limits, the bank must provide the central bank (Reserve Bank of New Zealand) a plan to restore its capital and to publish this plan at the first practical opportunity. In contrast to quality regulation of banks used in other countries where the weak financial health of a bank is kept secret by the regulatory authorities, this information must be publicly disclosed in New Zealand.

Instead of a government regulatory agency monitoring the financial health of a bank, New Zealand hopes that this information disclosure will allow private parties to do a better job of monitoring the bank. Banks provide the same information to both the government and the public at the same time.

The most important of these private monitors are owners, directors, and managers of the bank who have a legal responsibility to disclose accurate information or face various criminal and civil penalties. Second are the auditors of the financial statements and credit rating agencies. Third, other banks that are creditors or *counter parties* to the bank will find this information useful in deciding to do business with the bank. Finally, financial sector analysts and the depositors themselves should be able to make reliable judgments about the soundness of the bank.

It is not easy to show empirically that private monitoring of banks will be effective because most countries have either state-owned banks whose deposits are implicitly guaranteed or private banks whose deposits are protected by government insurance schemes. As a result, depositors and creditors have a reduced incentive to monitor bank performance.

One study, however, has examined this issue.[14] Even in countries with government guarantees of deposits and little disclosure of financial information about banks, depositors do monitor the financial health of private banks to some extent and identify those that are high risk. This study shows that in Argentina, Chile, and Mexico depositors punish banks for risky investments by withdrawing their deposits. This corrective action suggests that in the absence of government guarantees and with more information disclosure by banks, private monitoring might be effective in regulating bank behavior.

Some experts have dismissed this approach to regulation in New Zealand as not relevant for poor countries because almost all of the banks in this country are branches of large, reputable foreign banks. It is claimed that New Zealand is simply relying (*free riding*) on the relatively good regulatory systems in the home countries of these banks.

Though there is some truth in this argument, most poor countries should be thankful if their entire banking system is composed of high-quality foreign-owned banks. Locally owned banks whether private or state owned have proven to be a disaster for most poor countries. Taking a free ride on the good regulation in rich countries is likely to be a much better option than relying on weak domestic regulation. This is why I favor unrestricted entry by foreign banks and hope that good foreign banks will be willing to enter poor countries.

Bad Banks Are Worse than No Banks

If information disclosure regulation is applied to banks in poor countries, two possible outcomes are possible. Both are likely to be better than conventional quality regulation coupled with government guarantees or insurance.

The first possible outcome is that information disclosure regulation is effective in poor countries. To be effective, this regulation should be coupled with the privatization of state-owned banks and unrestricted entry by new banks both domestic and foreign. The government should not guarantee or insure the deposits of any bank.

Because of greater information disclosure and lack of deposit insurance, increased private monitoring may spur banks to be well managed and healthy and not create pyramid schemes. If domestic banks do not perform well and depositors suffer losses in these banks, there may be a flight to quality in which most depositors turn to branches of reputable foreign banks. Again, this is a good outcome because there is little reason to prefer domestic banks to foreign banks.

Because banks are honestly run and well managed, the public is willing to entrust a large share of their savings to the banks. Banks are good financial intermediaries and channel these savings to the most productive investments. In other words, the banking system behaves according to the textbook model and is a major engine for economic growth.

Though I can hope that this new regulatory regime will be effective, I am not highly optimistic. The legal system may not be strong enough to impose sanctions on bank directors and managers who do not disclose adequate information, auditing companies that are supposed to verify the accuracy of financial statements are known to be corrupt and unreliable in many poor countries, and credit rating agencies may not exist. Politicians may continue to interfere in the lending decisions of private banks. Foreign banks may have little interest in entering small, poor countries or may only serve a few large international companies with local operations even if they do enter.

Thus, the second and worst possible outcome is that the public has little faith that banks are well managed. After some banks fail and depositors lose their money because deposits are not guaranteed or insured, the public largely refuses to deposit their savings with the banks. The banking sector shrinks and plays only a small role in the intermediation of savings. Only larger, more sophisticated companies or rich individuals may make deposits with banks because they can better monitor their performance.

I am not happy with this second outcome and would prefer that banks actually follow the textbook model. However, it is a better outcome than the widespread pyramid schemes and banking crises that are likely to result with conventional quality regulation coupled with government deposit guarantees and insurance. If, because of weak institutions in the country, information disclosure regulation does not result in honest, well-managed banks, I doubt that quality regulation will be effective either. If anything, I would bet that thousands of bank customers and creditors will do a better job of monitoring bank performance if they know that their deposits are not guaranteed than will a few underpaid, undertrained, and under-motivated bank examiners who are subject to political pressure and bribes.

The Importance of Banks Is Exaggerated

A reduced role for banks in poor countries is not as harmful to economic development as one might imagine. Even in rich countries today with mostly well-managed and honest banks, their importance in financial intermediation is often exaggerated. Their importance in the past was even less, and yet these economies grew rapidly. This exaggeration of the importance of banks leads some to suggest that bad banks are better than no banks at all. The public should be encouraged to make deposits in banks, for example, by introducing deposit insurance, even though the probability of their savings being squandered is high.

To emphasize the importance of banks, some argue that banks are the largest source of outside financing for private businesses. This is true. Even in rich countries, other sources such as the sale

Figure 6-1
CORPORATE FINANCING FROM INTERNAL SOURCES

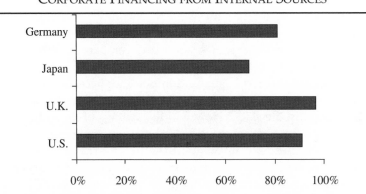

SOURCE: Jenny Corbett and Tim Jenkinson, "The Financing of Industry, 1970-1989: An International Comparison," Discussion Paper Series No. 948, Centre for Economic Policy Research, 1994.

of corporate bonds or the sale of equity (common stock) are much less important.

This argument is misleading, however, because *outside* financing from all sources, including banks, is small relative to *inside* financing. A fact of life in all countries is that the biggest source of financing for private companies is their retained earnings or internal cash flow from operations and not bank loans or any other source of outside financing.

In the four largest rich countries (see Figure 6-1) with presumably the most advanced banking systems, corporations generate between 69 and 97 percent of their financing from internal sources, primarily retained profits and depreciation allowances. In other words, corporate savings and not the savings of individuals is the primary source of finance for corporate investments. The balance comes from a mixture of bank loans, the sale of equity and bonds, and trade credit.

Thus, the key for companies in poor countries, just like in rich countries, to obtain financing for new investments is to be efficient, well-managed, and profitable. In this way they can finance new investments mostly from the cash flow generated by old investments. The companies that are the best managed and profitable automatically obtain most of the financing they need to expand and grow.

167

Companies that are not profitable are denied funds for expansion. I am concerned that government policies intended to increase the size and importance of banks and to encourage them to finance more corporate investments will mean that loans are provided not to the best private companies but to the companies with political influence and connections.

If banks are reduced in size and importance because they cannot be trusted, what other channels of financial intermediation are available to take up the slack? How will the savings of individuals and companies be transferred to those that have good investment projects but lack the funds to implement them? The transactions costs incurred by savers and investors of using other channels of financial intermediation will be higher compared with those of a well-functioning banking system, but the savings will still reach investors and will be used to make productive investments. This outcome is certainly better than dishonest or poorly managed banks that steal or waste the public's savings, and thus these savings are never used to make productive investments.

A variety of other channels of financial intermediation exist besides banks. As mentioned, the internal savings of companies is the largest source of financing for corporate investment. Formal financial intermediation is not needed when a company's cash flow is reinvested in the same company.

However, a company may have profits or cash flow that cannot be profitably reinvested in itself but could be profitably invested by another company in another line of business. Connected business groups are a way of transferring surplus capital from one line of business to another. Such business groups are common in poor countries. For example, in 1980 (the latest date for which comprehensive data are available), the 20 largest business groups in India were estimated to account for more than two-thirds of total private-sector industrial assets.[15] Because there are often ownership links between companies in the group, the group may have access to better information about the merits of specific investment projects in each company than would outside investors or lenders and thus do a better job of allocating capital to the most profitable investments.

Another way that companies provide financing to each other is through what is called trade credit or vendor financing. In this case, the seller of a product or service does not require buyers to pay immediately but allows them to pay with a delay. In effect, the selling company is making a loan to the buying company. Even in economies with relatively well-developed banking systems, the amount of such financing is huge. In the United States, for example, the amount of such credit exceeds the total amount of business lending by banks.[16]

In regard to small businesses, financing is often obtained from family and friends. Even well-managed banks have difficulty lending to small businesses. I heard one bank manager say that only three types of people lend money to small businesses—family, friends, and fools. A large share of the savings of ordinary individuals may be invested in the small businesses started by themselves, relatives, or their friends. Reducing the size of the banking system and thus the amount of the public's savings wasted in loans to large companies, particularly state-owned companies, may increase the flow of savings to small businesses.

Many small informal financial institutions, sometimes referred to as *rotating savings and credit institutions*, exist in which a limited number of people pool their savings to make loans often to each other, and these can be an important source of financing for farmers and small businesses. Because these institutions are small and closely monitored by the participants, the risk of pyramid schemes is small. Studies suggest that the informal financial sector may be larger than the formal one in some African countries. For example, almost everyone in Cameroon belongs to at least one of these institutions.[17] Such institutions played a major role in the development of the knitted garment industry in Tripur, India. The Gounder community, a caste traditionally engaged in agriculture that had substantial savings, used these institutions to provide loans to entrepreneurs who could not obtain loans from the state-owned banking monopoly.[18]

Similarly, a large share of the savings of farmers will probably be directly invested in improving or expanding their farms or to provide working capital (in other words, paying for seed and fertilizer until the crop can be harvested and sold). Though investment in manufacturing is often emphasized, the biggest industry in most poor countries is still agriculture.

Ordinary people may invest in real estate. A large share of the nation's savings is needed for housing. In the United States, for example, housing accounts for about 30 percent of total private fixed investment. The other 70 percent is business structures and plant and equipment. Though it would be desirable if banks provided mortgages to people to buy homes, this is a fairly recent innovation even in rich countries. Historically, people had to use their own savings or the savings of relatives to build a home.

One approach is to build a home in stages as savings are available. In many poor countries, the first floor of a home is completed and occupied, but concrete columns extend upward so that a second or third floor can be added later when enough savings have been accumulated. For individuals with more savings, investing in small apartment buildings is a possibility. Even in a rich country like Germany, a large share of the people live in small, private apartment buildings with six or so units. The owner and investor lives in one of the units and rents out the remainder.

Rich individuals may make equity investments in companies and take an active role in their management. Carnegie Steel, for example, was the largest U.S. enterprise when it was created in 1889 and was a partnership formed by a number of rich individuals. In the 19th century, investment bankers such as J. P. Morgan brought together rich individuals in the United States to finance a new company. The involvement of J. P. Morgan was like a certificate of quality that the company would be well managed.

As a final example of how badly banks in poor countries have performed and yet how private business is able to find other sources of finance, consider the case of China. According to *The Economist* magazine,

> It is the banking system that collects up the bulk of China's great pool of domestic savings, equivalent to nearly 40% of GDP. Sadly, the banks misallocate the savings on an even grander scale than the stock markets. The four big state-owned banks that dominate the system direct four-fifths of their lending to state-owned enterprises, which destroy value more often than they create it. The vibrant private and export sectors—which have created perhaps 40m new jobs in the past five years, as many as the state sector has shed—are left largely to fend for themselves. They rely on retained earnings and foreign direct investment, or else on informal sources of credit.[19]

Conclusion

The best strategy for poor countries is to quickly privatize or shut down state-owned banks; allow free entry of private banks, in particular, foreign banks; introduce information disclosure regulation following the example of New Zealand; and, above all, *not* introduce government guarantees or deposit insurance.

The worst possible outcome of this strategy is that disclosure regulation proves to be ineffective. Initially, bank failures are common. Consequently, the public refuses to make deposits in domestic banks, and foreign banks are not interested in entering the market. As a result, the size and importance of the banking sector are reduced.

In such an outcome, however, banks have been proven to be poor financial intermediaries, and it is best that the public not entrust their savings to these institutions. Other channels of financial intermediation will have to be used instead. This course is still better than what is likely to happen if quality regulation coupled with deposit insurance is introduced. In this case, the banking system may be large, but the risk is high that a large proportion of the nation's savings will be stolen or squandered in bank pyramid schemes.

In contrast, the best possible outcome of this strategy is that disclosure regulation will force domestic banks to be well managed, or, if not, reputable foreign banks are willing to enter the market. A large share of the nation's savings will be entrusted to the banks because they don't cheat their depositors. They are good financial intermediaries and use the nation's savings to finance the most productive investments, which leads to higher rates of growth and reduced poverty.

7. Bankruptcy: Swift and Certain Liquidation

All countries must establish procedures for dealing with private companies that become insolvent (bankrupt) and cannot pay their creditors. Rich countries often provide for three options when a company is insolvent. Though the terminology and specifics vary from country to country, these options are

1. a private restructuring of the company negotiated between the company and its creditors,
2. a government or court-managed restructuring, or
3. liquidation.

Unfortunately, poor countries are often encouraged to provide the same three options.

Because of weak government and legal institutions, it is a mistake for governments (or the courts) in poor countries to become involved in the restructuring of bankrupt companies except to provide for swift liquidation if private restructuring fails. Frequently, government restructuring of bankrupt companies amounts to their nationalization. Given the poor performance of governments in managing state-owned enterprises, they should not be encouraged to take over the management of bankrupt private companies.

As has been the case for state-owned enterprises, governments or the courts in most poor countries are likely to do a poor job of restructuring bankrupt enterprises because of incompetence, corruption, pressure from special-interest groups, and political interference. In rich countries, governments have tried to shield government management of bankrupt companies from political pressure by giving responsibility to special bankruptcy courts and trained administrators and trustees. I doubt whether this has been entirely successful in rich countries and believe that it will not be successful in most poor countries because of weak institutions.

Supporters of government or court restructuring argue that this is necessary to reduce the possibility that a viable company that could be saved is instead forced into liquidation, and thus the company ceases operations and its assets are sold. In contrast, I am concerned that government restructuring will instead result in a different but even more serious problem. It will permit unviable companies to continue to operate and waste resources that could better be used by other companies. The nation's resources will be trapped in zombie companies with no economic future that are kept alive by the government.

Private restructurings negotiated between the insolvent company and its creditors are likely to be more effective and efficient than government restructurings. If a company is viable, then it is in the interest of both the company and its creditors to restructure the company rather than to liquidate it. Private restructurings are the most common form even in rich countries that permit government or court restructuring. By not allowing companies the option of choosing a government restructuring, the effectiveness of private restructurings will be enhanced even more. If a company cannot negotiate a private restructuring with its creditors, the only alternative should be swift and certain liquidation.

Unfortunately, there is little research on whether the option of government restructuring is desirable in poor countries. As with other government interventions, many experts simply recommend that poor countries follow the models established in the United States or the European Community that provide for the option of government restructuring. In the United States, for example, Chapter 11 of the bankruptcy laws provides for court-managed restructuring while Chapter 7 provides for liquidation.

The Need for Restructuring

Even the best managed private companies sometimes encounter financial difficulties because of unexpected events beyond their control and are unable to meet their obligations to creditors. Creditors may include banks that have made loans to the company, bondholders if the company has sold bonds to the public, suppliers who have provided raw materials and other inputs but have not been paid (referred to as trade creditors), workers with unpaid wages or pensions, and the government if the company owes taxes.

If a company cannot meet its contractual and legal obligations to its creditors, it must either be restructured so that it can continue to operate or else be forced into liquidation and cease to operate. Other terms for restructuring commonly used include reorganization, rehabilitation, workouts, turnarounds, administration, concordato, and composition. Regardless of what it is called, its only objective should be to ensure that viable companies or parts of companies continue to operate and the others cease to function, in other words, maximize economic efficiency. Unfortunately, as with many government interventions in the private sector, other objectives are often introduced such as saving jobs under pressure from labor unions or protecting company owners and executives who are cronies of powerful politicians.

Whether to Restructure or Liquidate

To maximize economic efficiency and thus economic growth, a bankrupt company should continue to operate after restructuring if its *going-concern value* exceeds its *liquidation value.* If not, the company should be liquidated, cease operations, and sell its assets to others who can make better use of them. Though this principal is easy to state, it is difficult to implement in practice. As shorthand, I use the term *viable* to describe a company whose going-concern value exceeds its liquidation value and *unviable* or *not viable* if not.[1]

In technical terms, the going-concern value is the *present discounted value* of the future operating cash flow of the company using a discount rate equal to the cost of capital. Operating cash flow is the difference between future revenues and operating costs such as taxes, wages, materials, and investments in new plant and equipment. Interest or repayment of existing debt is not included.

The going-concern value is difficult to estimate with a high degree of certainty. Its estimation requires that a business plan or operational restructuring plan for the company be prepared that is likely to maximize future cash flow if implemented. Such a plan may call for reducing costs (for example, firing surplus workers), selling unneeded assets, producing different or higher quality products or services, investing in more efficient plant and equipment, entering new markets, merging with another company, and so forth.

Even the most experienced businesspeople may disagree about the best business plan for the company. This should not be surprising. If it were easy to develop a successful business plan, making a profit in business would be easy, and no firm would become insolvent. Given how difficult this task is, one should doubt whether governments (even including specialized bankruptcy courts or trained administrators) have the capability to determine the optimum restructuring plan that will maximize the company's going-concern value. If governments could do this effectively, they would do a better job of managing their state-owned enterprises.

The liquidation value of the company is somewhat easier to estimate but is still difficult. In this case, one must estimate the likely revenue from selling the company's assets (land, buildings, vehicles, inventories, plant and equipment, etc.) to other businesses. Though the company knows what it paid for these assets, the value of these used assets to another firm is uncertain until they are actually sold.

If the going-concern value exceeds the liquidation value, the assets of the company will make the largest contribution to the economy if they continue to be used by the company in its ongoing operations. Also, the company will be able to repay a higher percentage though probably not all of its existing debt compared with liquidation. If, however, the going-concern value is less than the liquidation value, the assets will make a larger contribution to the economy and allow a higher percentage of its existing debts to be repaid if the assets are sold to another business through the liquidation of the company.

If the company's creditors conclude that the going-concern value is less than the liquidation value (i.e., not viable), they will force the company to liquidate. This outcome will provide the maximum return to the creditors and to the economy as a whole. If the option of government restructuring exists, the risk is that the government (including a bankruptcy court) will intervene and keep the company alive even though it is worth more dead than alive.

Who Should Decide?

Who should determine whether the going-concern value of an insolvent company exceeds the liquidation value? Even in those countries that permit the option of government restructuring, most often the decision is made through negotiations between the company and its creditors outside of the formal, legal bankruptcy process (sometimes called an out-of-court restructuring).

Exact numbers are difficult to obtain because these negotiations are private and do not have to be reported. It is estimated, however, that more than 90 percent of insolvent companies in the United States first try to deal with their financial problems through private negotiations with their creditors. If the company is unhappy with the restructuring plan demanded by the creditors or the creditors insist on liquidation, the company has the option of entering the government's bankruptcy process, which includes the option of government restructuring (Chapter 11) that the company hopes will be more favorable to the owners and managers.[2] Another study found that approximately 50 percent of U.S. public firms that experienced financial distress in the 1980s successfully dealt with their problems through negotiations with their creditors.[3] Even those that argue for a government restructuring option admit that most restructurings take place through private negotiations.[4]

The difficult but important question is whether adding the option of a government restructuring improves or worsens the overall bankruptcy process. It is improved if this option reduces the chances that a viable company is liquidated. The process is worsened if this option increases the chances that an unviable company continues to operate. In rich countries with good government and legal institutions, the option of government restructuring may lead to a more efficient outcome, though I have my doubts even in those countries.

I am convinced, however, that including this option in most poor countries would worsen the outcome by permitting unviable companies to continue to operate. Supporters of this option, however, would argue that it reduces the possibility that a viable company would be forced into liquidation because of the difficulties encountered in the private negotiations between the company and its creditors. As discussed below, there are some theoretical arguments as to why these private negotiations may be biased in favor of liquidation though I think they have little importance in practice.

Little empirical research on this question has been done. Ideally, one would like to compare a country with just the two options of private restructuring and liquidation with a similar country that also has the third option of government or court restructuring. Another possibility would be to compare the outcomes of the bankruptcy process in the same country but over two different periods. In the first period, only the private negotiation and liquidation options are available. In the second, all three options are available. Unfortunately, in spite of little empirical evidence, many experts and international development institutions support the option of a government or court-managed restructuring in poor countries simply because it is what the rich countries do.

Shareholders and Creditors: A Partnership

Bankruptcy procedures are often characterized as being either debtor friendly or creditor friendly. For example, the United States is said to be debtor friendly while the United Kingdom is creditor friendly. Unfortunately, this comparison gives the impression that the interests of debtors and creditors are in conflict and that one has to choose whether to be on the side of one or the other. The government or the courts must be involved to make certain that each side is not taking unfair advantage of the other and to balance and protect the rights and interests of both. Because of these conflicting interests, the assumption seems to be that a negotiated solution between the parties is not likely.

This characterization might have some validity for personal bankruptcies, but not for corporate bankruptcies. In personal bankruptcies, there is a moral question of how much the individual should be made to suffer to satisfy the claims of his creditors. There is a clear conflict between the interests of the bankrupt individual and those of his creditors. In ancient times, a bankrupt individual could be sold into slavery to satisfy his creditors. More recently, he could be thrown into debtor's prison. Today, the main issue is how much of the debtor's existing assets and future income he will be allowed to keep and how much must be used to satisfy his debts. I agree that the law and the courts are needed to define a fair balance between the individual debtor and his creditors.

A bankrupt corporation is different. The arrangement between the shareholders and the creditors is more like a partnership than an adversarial situation that requires the courts to intervene. Certainly, there are differences in the interests of the two groups and the potential for conflict exists, but both have a strong incentive to maximize the value of the company. Both have provided capital to the company (though in different forms and under different conditions), and any return on that capital has to come from the revenues of the company, including the revenue from liquidation as a last resort.

There is usually a clear agreement between the owners of a corporation and its creditors about how the revenues of the company should be used, including in the event of liquidation. Inherent in the nature of a limited liability company and in contrast to a personal bankruptcy, shareholders may only lose the amount of their equity investment in the company regardless of the debts of the company. Shareholders cannot be forced to sell other property or use income from other sources to pay the debts of the company. Shareholders may earn large profits if the company is successful, but there is an automatic lower limit to how much they can lose if the company is not profitable, namely, the value of their equity investment.

In contrast, creditors have first claim to any revenue of the company to satisfy their loans before any dividends are paid to the shareholders. In the event of liquidation, the revenue from the sale of assets will be used first to pay the creditors before any is distributed to owners (shareholders). In exchange, creditors earn a fixed rate of interest on their loans to reflect the lower risk of this type of investment, and their interest income does not increase even if the company becomes hugely profitable.

If a company is in financial difficulty, both the shareholders and the creditors have an incentive to work together to maximize the value of the company. This partnership allows them to earn a higher return on their investments whether it is equity or debt. The popular notion that creditors only want to liquidate a bankrupt company even if the going-concern value is greater than the liquidation value is a myth.

Assume, for example, that the likely revenues of the company will not be large enough to pay all of its debts, and thus the company is insolvent. However, the going-concern value is greater than the liquidation value. Next, assume that if the creditors and the company cannot reach a voluntary restructuring agreement, the only option is liquidation. In other words, there is no option of government or court intervention to restructure the company. In this case, there is a strong incentive for the shareholders and the creditors to reach an agreement that continues the operations of the company because this gives both groups the opportunity for a greater return than liquidation.

This is not to say that there will be no disagreements about how the future revenue of the company will be split between the shareholders and the creditors. All of the parties are likely to know how they will fare if the company is liquidated. Each party will insist on a split of future revenue that is no less than what that party would receive in liquidation. All of the parties will try to bargain for a larger share, but they know that if they cannot reach an agreement, all will suffer if the company is liquidated. This negotiation is like a fable in which two sworn enemies are given a pot of gold. They are told that they must agree on a split of the gold. If they cannot agree, the gold will be taken away from them and both will suffer. In this case, they are likely to reach an agreement.[5]

Private Restructuring Is Best

The bargaining between the company and its creditors may be difficult and the final agreement complex, but they have more information, expertise, and incentives to develop a restructuring plan than would the government or the courts. If one party refuses to cooperate or is unreasonable, the other can threaten to force the company into liquidation.

The biggest disagreement is likely to be about the business plan that will result in the highest going-concern value. On the one hand, the shareholders are likely to prefer a high-return but high-risk plan because they benefit when profits are high, leaving a large residual to pay dividends after paying the fixed interest due to the creditors. On the other hand, the creditors do not benefit from high profits and are likely to argue for a lower return but safer business plan that gives greater assurance that revenue will at least be adequate to pay the agreed interest and principal of the company's debt.

In addition to negotiating an operating plan, the two parties will have to negotiate a new agreement concerning the split of the future revenues of the company. In effect, they must agree on a new implicit partnership. This agreement is sometimes called a financial restructuring.

The options for the financial restructuring are many. If the financial problems are not large, a creditor, for example, a bank, may agree to a limited moratorium on interest and principal repayments of its loans until the company is again solvent. The unpaid interest will be added to the outstanding loan to be repaid later after the company has returned to profitability. In more extreme cases, the creditors may agree to write down (reduce) the amount of the debts owed by the company to levels that the company can repay. Another option is a debt-equity swap in which the creditors become shareholders in exchange for reducing their debt claims. If new investment is necessary to implement the agreed-on business plan (for example, modern equipment must be purchased), the creditors may even provide additional loans.

One issue for the creditors to consider is how to maintain an incentive for the shareholders and managers to prudently manage the company. As noted earlier, the company has an incentive to undertake a risky business plan that offers the potential for a high return but also a high probability of failure if the financial restructuring leaves almost nothing for the shareholders. To avoid this outcome, the creditors may have to agree to a financial restructuring that leaves the shareholders with a higher value of their equity than they might receive under liquidation. By giving the shareholders a greater stake in the future of the company, the company may be better managed. Alternatively, the creditors can insist on more closely monitoring the performance of the company. Monitoring can be done by receiving frequent and detailed operating and financial reports, placing covenants concerning how the company will be managed in any agreements for loans, or by having a representative of the creditors sit on the board of directors.

Restructuring Experts

An operational and financial restructuring plan negotiated between the creditors and the company is not a rare event. It is a frequent and routine part of the activities of well-managed banks. Banks know that some of their corporate borrowers will have financial difficulties. Some banks have created workout departments whose staff are experienced and trained to deal with problem loans and to work with the borrower to maximize the value of the company so that more of the bank's loans can be repaid.

Some banks seem to specialize in helping troubled companies (for a fee of course). The J. P. Morgan Chase bank in the United States has a special restructuring group whose business is booming at the moment because of the economic downturn.[6] It helps not only those companies that have borrowed from the bank but also companies that have borrowed from other banks or have other types of debt. If a company can show promise of eventually being profitable, the bank can help to restructure its debt or obtain new financing. Before agreeing to help a troubled company, however, the bank has to determine that the company has a viable business plan.

Some consulting companies specialize in helping both the banks and the companies in *turning around* companies in financial difficulty. In the United States, this type of consulting is well established. There is even a trade association of consulting firms and other specialists who work in the field called the Turnaround Management Association that has about 4,000 members.[7] It sponsors a periodical, *The Journal of Corporate Renewal,* and the Association of Certified Turnaround Professionals.

I attended a seminar in which one of these consulting companies explained how private restructurings are carried out.[8] The consulting company may be asked for help either by the insolvent company that wants to present a convincing restructuring plan to its creditors or by a bank that realizes that an important borrower needs help.

The speaker emphasized that restructuring is simple though I believe he was exaggerating for effect. According to the speaker, the first task is to carry out a quick, initial restructuring of the company so that it has a positive operating cash flow (revenues less labor and materials costs). If the company cannot at least cover its operating costs, excluding any interest or repayment of its debt, then it has no going-concern value at all. There will be no cash flow after paying operating expenses to pay any of its debts. The only option is to liquidate the company and sell its assets for whatever they are worth. Even if a positive operating cash flow can be achieved, however, this is not a guarantee that the going-concern value is greater than the liquidation value, and negotiations with creditors may still result in deciding that liquidation is best.

The consultant said that achieving a positive operating cash flow was usually easy. All the company has to do is to keep laying off more and more of its headquarters staff until revenues exceed operating costs. The consultant said that there is always surplus staff in the headquarters who can be let go without harming the profitability of the company at least in the short run. Laying off production workers is usually a bad idea because they will be needed in the factory to manufacture the products that the company must sell to be viable.

Also, it may be necessary to fire the chief executive officer or managing director and the chief financial officer. Because they created the current situation in the company, the lenders may want to see a change in top management before agreeing to a financial and operational restructuring. Once the company has a positive operating cash flow and new managers committed to restructuring are in place, then the company has a good chance of negotiating a restructuring with its lenders.

It might be argued that such institutions as workout units in banks or consulting firms that specialize in helping companies in financial difficulty do not exist in many poor countries. Thus, the government or the courts need to step in and help the creditors with the restructuring of insolvent companies. The problem is that governments or the courts in these countries are even less capable of managing a restructuring and are likely to be captured by special-interest groups. If the creditors (primarily banks) are privately owned, they have a strong profit motive to obtain the expertise necessary to negotiate a restructuring of insolvent companies. Though their expertise may lag behind what is found in financial institutions in rich countries, they will still do a better job than the government, including specialized bankruptcy courts.

Much of the debate about bankruptcy in poor countries seems to focus on the design of bankruptcy laws and is dominated by lawyers. Numerous studies can be found comparing the merits of bankruptcy laws in the United States, Europe, and other rich countries. The implicit assumption in these studies seems to be that bankruptcy courts will deal with all insolvent companies. Little attention is given to the fact that most financial restructurings even in rich countries take place outside of the courts or how bankruptcy laws may hinder or help these private restructurings.

I am convinced that allowing government or court restructuring in addition to liquidation will hinder private restructurings. In many cases, the insolvent company will see this option as a way of escaping from the harsh restructuring plan demanded by its creditors, hoping that the government or the courts will be more lenient. This option will be particularly attractive if the creditors have concluded that the company is not viable and should be liquidated.

Private Banks Are Essential

The most important obstacle to a private restructuring is whether the creditors, in particular, banks, are badly managed. This is likely if the banks are still state-owned or, if privately owned, under the control and influence of the government. Such banks are not likely to have the skills or incentives necessary to negotiate a successful restructuring of insolvent companies. This situation is made even worse if the insolvent companies are also state-owned.

In such cases, it will probably make little difference if the government or the banks negotiate the restructuring. Either type of restructuring will be controlled by the government to achieve political objectives rather than the normal commercial objectives of maximizing company value or economic efficiency. The only relevant bankruptcy options are government restructuring or liquidation.

Thus, the recommendation here that poor countries should only permit either private restructuring or liquidation does not make sense unless the banking sector is first reformed, primarily by privatizing state-owned banks and allowing free entry of foreign banks as discussed earlier. Once the banking sector has been successfully reformed, it is then desirable to eliminate the option of government or court restructuring of insolvent companies.

Secured Creditors

Other obstacles to private restructurings are often mentioned, but their importance is exaggerated or could be overcome. One such obstacle is that some of the creditors may have made secured loans backed by liens, pledges, or other types of claims on the assets of the company (real estate, equipment, vehicles, etc.). These assets are referred to as *collateral* for the loans. If the company is not able to service these loans, the secured creditor has the option of taking possession of the collateral as payment for its loan.

It is often argued that these secured creditors will not be interested in restructuring the company and will only want to take possession as soon as possible of the collateral that has been pledged to them as security for repayment of their loans. If the secured creditors take these assets, the company probably cannot function, and a private restructuring that enables the company to continue to operate is impossible. Supporters of the government restructuring option often mention that it enables the courts to stop secured creditors from taking possession of the company's assets until a decision has been made whether or not the company should continue to operate or be liquidated.

The fact that so many private restructurings take place even though many loans are secured by liens on the company's assets suggests that this is not a serious problem. Though such lenders have this added security, they will still favor a restructuring if the company is economically viable and will not snatch away their collateral at the first sign the company is in financial trouble. They will only insist on claiming their collateral if the company is not viable. Whether or not the secured creditors agree with the proposed restructuring is an almost foolproof test of whether the company is viable and should be restructured or whether it should be liquidated.

The reason is simple and rests on the definition of a viable company. Recall that a company is viable if its future cash flow is worth more than the liquidation value of its assets. If the company is viable, it should be able to convince its secured creditors that it will earn the necessary cash flow to make payments to them that at least equal (in present value terms) the value of those assets pledged to them as collateral. As long as the company does nothing to erode the value of the pledged assets, the secured creditors have every reason to permit the company to implement its restructuring plan. This plan will give them a return at least as great as claiming their collateral. They can still take possession of the collateral in the future if the plan is not successful.

Another incentive for the secured lenders not to claim their collateral is that most would rather not become the owners of used physical assets such as buildings, land, or vehicles. They then incur the costs and risks of trying to maintain and dispose of these assets. The value of these assets in the resale market is uncertain. If there is a reasonable chance that the restructured company can provide them with a return at least equal to the resale value of these assets, they will not want to take possession.

Naturally, the secured creditors have a strong incentive to claim their collateral if the company is not viable. If it is unlikely that the company can achieve a cash flow that is worth at least as much as the value of the assets pledged to secured creditors, then the going-concern value is clearly less than the liquidation value. If the secured creditors cannot be convinced to participate in a private restructuring, the company is most likely not viable and should be liquidated.

Those who argue that secured creditors will be an obstacle to a private restructuring are saying, in effect, that the company should be restructured even if it is not viable. This bias in favor of restructuring over liquidation is frequently seen in many of the comments and analyses of bankruptcy. In much of the discussion of bankruptcy, restructuring is always the best option and should always be attempted even if it is clear that a company is not viable. If secured creditors object to restructuring an unviable company, proponents of government restructuring argue that the government or bankruptcy courts should override their objections and legal rights.

Coordination, Collective Action, and Holdouts

Another obstacle to a private restructuring may arise when there are many creditors of an insolvent company. If there were only a single creditor, I do not think that a convincing argument could be made for the government restructuring option. There is little reason to think that the single creditor and the company could not negotiate a private restructuring if the company is viable. If there are many creditors, however, economists and lawyers have identified a number of problems that may make it difficult, if not impossible, for them to collectively negotiate with the company on a restructuring. As a result, many argue that in this case the courts or some other governmental body should determine the best restructuring plan and then impose it upon the multiple creditors and the company.

Though these problems exist to some degree, I believe that their importance is exaggerated; and there are solutions short of allowing the government or the courts to determine the restructuring plan. In the end, any weaknesses of the private restructuring option must be compared with what I believe are the vastly greater weaknesses of the government restructuring option.

Even if these problems exist in rich countries, they are less severe in poor countries because their companies usually have fewer creditors than companies in rich countries. A large company in the United States or Europe may have loans from a number of different banks, may have sold bonds or other debt instruments to many investors, and have hundreds of trade creditors who supply raw materials and other inputs. The fact that even in rich countries private restructurings are the most common way of dealing with corporate insolvency suggests that a large number of creditors is not an insurmountable problem in most cases.

Three problems may arise when the number of creditors is large. First, the difficulty, time, and cost of simply organizing negotiations between a large number of creditors and the company may be prohibitively high. Second, some creditors may refuse to accept a reasonable and fair restructuring and *hold out* for special treatment that unfairly benefits them. By threatening to block the negotiations, a single creditor may hope to gain at the expense of the others. Third, creditors have an incentive to rush to the courthouse to make the first claim against the company for nonpayment and obtain a lien on a particular company asset in satisfaction of their claim. The reason is that the courts typically grant such claims on a first-come, first-served basis.

Instead of hundreds of creditors who must participate in the private restructuring, a typical company in a poor country may only have a few creditors that matter, namely, banks that have loaned it money. Banks still dominate the financial markets in most poor countries. It is conceivable that one of these banks may hold out in the negotiations in the hope of a better deal or rush to the courts to place a lien on company assets to the detriment of the other banks. However, the number of banks in such a country is not large, and they will probably have to work together to negotiate the restructuring of other companies in the future. A bank cannot afford to gain a reputation as being unreasonable or uncooperative with other banks because it will only cause similar behavior by the other banks in future negotiations. Also, most of the assets of a company may already be pledged to the secured lenders. Thus, there is little point in any creditor rushing to the courts to place a lien on the company's assets.

Concerning the many trade creditors who demand payment, the major lenders such as banks and the company may simply have to agree that the company will satisfy the claims of the trade creditors in full as part of the private restructuring. If the company wishes to continue to operate, it cannot afford to alienate its suppliers who then may refuse to grant credit in the future and will only deliver after receipt of payment. Also, trade creditors may be reluctant to force a company into liquidation because they are then losing a market for their own goods and services.

Corporate financing through the sale of corporate bonds or other debt instruments is still rare in most poor countries because debt markets are not well developed. Even if they have been sold, just a few large institutions may hold them, and thus including them in the negotiations on restructuring would be feasible. If the government restructuring option is not allowed, all creditors, including holders of company debt, have an incentive to participate because otherwise the company might be forced into liquidation, which would be a worse outcome for all creditors, assuming that the company is viable.

In rich countries, clever strategies have been developed to convince bondholders to agree voluntarily to a restructuring that could also be used in poor countries when this type of financing becomes more common. One strategy is to offer bondholders a new security in exchange for the old. The new security has a lower value but is given higher payment priority or preference in the event of default. The bondholder will have to choose between a new lower-return but lower-risk security versus the old higher-return but higher-risk security. Since the risk of liquidation is significant as evidenced by the attempt to restructure the debt of the company, bondholders are likely to accept the less risky new security in exchange for the old. Those who do not accept the new security run the risk that, in the event of default, they will not be paid anything while those who accept the new security will be paid at least something.

A similar problem may arise if the company has many owners who must agree on a restructuring. Depending on the company law in the country and the corporate charter or bylaws, all of the shareholders or at least a majority may have to agree on certain features of the restructuring. Most likely this situation would occur if the restructuring involves a debt-equity swap in which the creditors accept shares in the company in exchange for all or part of their loans to the company. The original shareholders may have to agree to such a swap. If the company is widely held with many small shareholders, obtaining their agreement may be difficult.

This is less likely to be a problem in poor countries than in the rich. As discussed earlier, most companies are closely held or family owned with only a few shareholders. Obtaining their agreement may not be a problem. In those few companies that have many shareholders, one option is to negotiate a restructuring that does not involve a debt-equity swap and thus does not require shareholder agreement. Also, the company law could be changed to permit debt-equity swaps in the event of bankruptcy without the approval of all shareholders.

Prepacks and Cramdowns

Let us assume, however, that there are such a large number of creditors that negotiating a restructuring proves to be impossible even though the company is viable. For example, it was simply not feasible to include all of the many small trade creditors or bondholders in the negotiations. The few large creditors such as banks have been able to agree with the company on a restructuring plan but are thwarted by the inability to obtain agreement from the many small creditors. These small creditors may not disagree with the plan—it is just impractical to obtain their consent. Is there anything that can be done to facilitate a private restructuring short of adopting the option of government or court restructuring?

Two concepts have been used in the United States that may deal with this problem—*prepacks and cramdowns*. Prepack is short for a prepackaged restructuring plan that some, but not all, of the creditors and the company have negotiated and then submitted to the bankruptcy court for approval. Cramdown describes how the court can accept a restructuring plan even though it is not approved by all of the creditors and then force the holdouts to accept it if the court believes that it is fair to all of the creditors.[9]

If a large percentage of the creditors and the company have negotiated a restructuring plan (prepack), this plan could be presented to the bankruptcy court for approval even though some creditors have not agreed. For example, the plan could be submitted to the court if two-thirds of the creditors measured by the value of their claims and more than one-half of the creditors by number have agreed to the plan. The minority of creditors who have not approved the plan would have to abide by the plan if approved by the court (cramdown).

Strict limitations on the discretion of the court in approving or rejecting this plan should be put in place to prevent the court from modifying the plan or substituting its own plan for that agreed on by the creditors and the company. This limited option of a prepack should not become a slippery slope leading to government or court restructuring of the company.

189

The court should only have the option of approving or rejecting the plan—not modifying the plan. Both the company and the specified percentage of creditors must agree to the plan before it can be submitted. Neither the company nor the creditors may submit a plan that is not approved by the other. This approval avoids the possibility that the company may use this option to avoid accepting a tough restructuring plan insisted on by the creditors and instead turn to the court in the hope that it will be more lenient.

The only legal basis for the court to reject the plan should be that it is unfair to the minority of creditors who have not agreed to it. Other considerations such as impact on employment should not be allowed. Strict time limits should be imposed so that the court must reach a decision quickly. If the court rejects the plan, the company and the creditors would be in the same position as they were before the plan was submitted. They would have to decide whether to prepare another plan or force the company into liquidation.

Government Restructuring

Allowing the option of government or court restructuring of an insolvent company would be a serious mistake in most poor countries because special-interest groups will probably capture this process. The likely outcome is that unviable companies will be allowed to continue to operate even though it is detrimental to the creditors and the economy in general.

Other than the company's secured creditors, every special-interest group or stakeholder has an incentive to keep the company operating and avoid liquidation even if the company is not viable. The return to the shareholders, for example, from liquidation is likely to be small or nonexistent. Government restructuring that reduced the company's debt would give them a second chance to make the company profitable. They have little to lose from a government restructuring and may gain from it. If they are supporters of the party in power or cronies of the president or prime minister, they may have the ability to influence the government or court restructuring in their favor.

Unsecured creditors may have an incentive similar to the shareholders'. In liquidation, the secured creditors may take possession of most of the company's assets leaving the unsecured creditors with little or nothing. Thus, the option of government restructuring gives the unsecured creditors the chance that the company may some day be able to pay at least part of their loans.

The workers and their unions will always pressure the government or the courts to restructure the company instead of liquidating it. This pressure will preserve their jobs and the positions of the union leaders even though the cost to the nation may be high. Local governments for those areas in which the company has its operations will be concerned about losing tax revenues if the company goes out of business.

The managers of the company may have their own reasons to keep the company alive independent from those of the shareholders. Restructuring will often allow them to keep their high-paying jobs and control over the company. If they know that liquidation is still inevitable because the company cannot achieve even a positive operating cash flow, they may loot the company of its remaining valuable assets and enrich themselves.

One study argues that the major beneficiaries of government restructuring (Chapter 11) in the United States are the professional managers of the company.[10] Both the owners (shareholders) and creditors suffer. After the adoption of the Bankruptcy Reform Act of 1978, managers of companies found it easier to use the government restructuring option. Also the managers were allowed to stay in charge of the company under the supervision of the bankruptcy court during restructuring. One consequence was that the number of companies taking advantage of the government restructuring option (Chapter 11) rose dramatically. In the 10 years after 1978, the number of companies using this option increased more than sevenfold.

More important, however, was that the value received by both the shareholders and the creditors after the government restructuring dropped substantially for bankruptcies initiated after 1978 compared with earlier ones. The authors of the study conclude that the professional managers were using the government restructuring option to enrich themselves to the detriment of both the owners and the creditors of the company.[11]

To be fair to supporters of the government restructuring option, this result in the United States may be caused by allowing managers to remain in charge after entering bankruptcy proceedings. Other countries appoint receivers, administrators, or trustees to manage a company undergoing government restructuring in an attempt to avoid this problem. I am concerned, however, that even they will be pressured by special-interest groups and politicians to adopt other objectives besides economic efficiency, such as preserving jobs.

Restructuring Intermediary

Some countries have adopted an option that is part way between a purely private restructuring and a government or court restructuring. This involves the use of an existing or new government body to assist and facilitate a private restructuring between the company and its creditors—a *restructuring intermediary*.[12] This option has been used in countries with a severe banking crisis and many insolvent companies, and thus the bankruptcy system was simply not capable of handling so many cases.

The first use of such an intermediary seems to have been in the United Kingdom to deal with widespread bank insolvencies in the early 1990s. This intermediary option has been referred to as the London Approach or the London Rules. In response to the East Asian banking crisis in the late 1990s, a number of countries in that region followed the example of the United Kingdom and created similar intermediaries.

Such intermediaries may serve a useful purpose if the creditors or insolvent companies have little experience with negotiating a restructuring. They can advise and assist the parties in the same way as the specialized consulting firms do in the United States.

A risk of establishing such intermediaries, however, is they may have the power to direct or control the negotiations. They decide, instead of the company and its creditors, what the restructuring plan will be. The more power they have, the more this option is similar to the government or court restructuring option with all of this option's weaknesses.

In the United Kingdom, the intermediary was the Bank of England. It tried to limit its role to being an honest broker and not attempt to control the negotiations or influence the outcome other than to help and encourage the parties to reach an agreement if they could. The Bank of England recognized that because it was also the regulatory authority for banks, it might appear that it was using that authority to influence the negotiations. To reduce that appearance, the department of the bank facilitating the negotiations was separated from the banking supervision department. Even then it was always uncertain whether a suggestion from the Bank of England should be interpreted as an order. This is like that old joke about the military officer speaking to his assembled troops: "Men, I need three soldiers to step forward and volunteer for a dangerous assignment. Jones, Smith, and Cooper, step forward."

In contrast to the United Kingdom, the East Asian countries were more willing to give their intermediaries explicit legal authority to direct the negotiations. For example, in Korea, the intermediary can modify the restructuring plan, if necessary, and fine a creditor who fails to comply with the plan.

In conclusion, I see some merit in government attempts to train banks or provide technical assistance on how to restructure insolvent companies. It is dangerous, however, to give a government agency authority to direct or control the negotiations.

Impact on Financial Markets

Bankruptcy laws and other government policies that keep unviable companies alive raise the cost of capital for all companies. The creditors almost always bear the increased cost of keeping such a company alive. They then must recover this higher cost by charging higher interest rates. In the case of banks, this means that the spread between the rates they charge on loans and the rates they pay to depositors must increase to cover this cost. Alternatively, creditors may attempt to reduce this cost by only lending to companies in which the probability of insolvency is small, in other words, toughen the standards they use in making loans. The end result is that companies who wish to borrow may either be charged higher interest rates or be refused credit if they do not meet the tougher lending standards.

In the case of insolvency, creditors will almost always bear some costs. The definition of insolvency is that the company cannot repay all of its debts. An important issue is how bankruptcy procedures can be designed to minimize that cost and thus the interest rates paid by businesses on their debts. As argued earlier, the option of government or court restructuring will frequently allow unviable companies to continue to operate. Though they may still be able to pay some of their debts if their operating cash flow is positive, they could have paid more if they were liquidated.

Even worse, they may never be able to achieve even a positive operating cash flow. They will need additional infusions of credit just to keep operating. Under court restructuring in many countries, the courts may permit the company to borrow even more to finance this negative cash flow. Since no sensible creditor, for example, a bank, would make a loan to such a company, the court must create a special inducement for the bank to lend the money. Typically, the court may give the new lender first priority for being repaid even above the existing creditors. For example, in the United States, such financing is called *debtor in possession financing*. (I won't attempt to explain the origin of this term.) The end result is that earlier creditors will find that the future repayment of their loans will be reduced even more when this company is eventually liquidated.

Lessons from Rich Countries

Over the last couple of decades, a number of rich countries have revised their bankruptcy laws to emphasize the option of government or court restructuring and to reduce the likelihood that a company will be liquidated. The United States, as noted, revised its laws in 1978, the United Kingdom in 1986, France in 1985 and again in 1994, and Germany in 1999.

Some argue this trend should be followed by poor countries. If the rich countries believe that government or court restructuring should be given greater emphasis, then poor countries would be wise to follow their example. This argument would have some merit if poor countries had political, government, and legal institutions that were as developed as those in the United States, United Kingdom, France, and Germany.

I am also not convinced that emphasizing government restructuring even in rich countries is a good idea. All of these revisions in the law were largely motivated by political pressure to save existing jobs. Little recognition seems to be given to the fact that transferring assets from unviable to viable companies through liquidation is likely to create more jobs in the long run than are lost in the short run. The French law is the most blatant in this regard. Its revised law has three objectives—maintain the firm in operation, preserve employment, and, lastly, enforce credit contracts.

Instead, the interesting fact to me about these relatively recent changes in bankruptcy laws in rich countries is how well these economies functioned in the past when the option of government or court restructuring was not emphasized. Failure to use the option of government restructuring did not seem to impose huge costs or inefficiencies on their economies. As with many other government policies and institutions, poor countries may be wise to adopt the bankruptcy procedures that existed in rich countries in the past rather than today.

Consider the experience of Germany. From 1877, when the previous German bankruptcy law was enacted, to 1999, when the new law became effective, bankruptcy procedures in that country almost always resulted in the liquidation of a company that could not negotiate a restructuring with its creditors. Though court restructuring (Vergleich) was technically permitted, various constraints meant that only a small fraction of companies entering the court bankruptcy process used this option.[13]

As in other countries, this fact was used as evidence of why the previous law was defective. It must mean that many viable firms were being forced into liquidation. Another complaint was that most of the physical assets of German companies were pledged to lenders, typically banks. It was argued that these secured lenders preferred simply to take possession of their security, thus forcing the company into liquidation instead of attempting to restructure the company and keep it operating. One consequence was that unsecured creditors usually received little or nothing from the liquidation.

To quote one expert on the political motivation for changing the law, "Politically, the early understanding of insolvency proceedings was that this process eliminated weak enterprises, but this view was quickly overtaken. The development of the labor market and increased economic independence demand the revival of weak enterprises rather than their liquidation to satisfy creditors. . . ."[14]

Though I have not been able to find any studies on the importance of private restructurings in Germany during the period before the new law, I suspect they were the usual way of dealing with insolvent firms. Germany is noted for having had a financial system dominated by a few large banks and the close relationship between banks and companies. Companies received most of their outside financing from bank loans rather than from selling securities such as bonds. The banks were also frequently major shareholders of companies or they controlled large blocks of shares through proxy voting arrangements, for example, Deutsche Bank was the dominant shareholder in Daimler Benz.

For all of the reasons discussed, I find it hard to believe that the banks would have an incentive to force a company into liquidation when it was viable and could pay off a larger portion of its loans if it continued to operate. Why should banks force a company into liquidation when this reduces their own profitability? Because each company probably only had a few important creditors, namely, banks, negotiating a restructuring was not greatly hindered by the problems mentioned that may arise when a company has many creditors. The fact that banks were also shareholders gave them an extra incentive to negotiate a restructuring. I suspect that only the worst performing companies were forced into liquidation because the banks could find no way to save them.

The financial systems in poor countries are likely to be bank-based as in Germany until markets for other securities such as bonds are more developed as in the United Kingdom and the United States. If the former bankruptcy law in Germany worked reasonably well for 120 years, then poor countries would do well to examine it as a model for their own bank-based financial systems rather than the recent laws enacted in many rich countries. Further research on bankruptcy in Germany under the previous law would be a valuable contribution to the debate on which bankruptcy system is best for poor countries.

Lessons from Poor Countries

Far more research seems to have been done on the effectiveness of bankruptcy procedures in rich countries than in poor countries. The few that I have found concerning poor countries have emphasized the length, cost, and inefficiency of government or court-managed procedures. Unfortunately, many seem to draw the wrong conclusions from this experience.

India is one of the worst examples. A study of its procedures concluded, ". . . firms that should have been liquidated were maintained as going concerns, often with vast injections of new, subsidized financial resources."[15] The major reason seems to be that all stakeholders, including creditors, labor, and state and federal governments, must approve any restructuring plan. As discussed, this creates a strong bias in favor of restructuring insolvent firms, even those that should be liquidated.

In Russia, the first bankruptcy law enacted in 1992 was completely ineffective. A second law was enacted in 1998 following the latest models from rich countries. In addition to liquidation, it included the option of court-managed restructuring (referred to as *external management)* out of concern that creditors might force viable companies into liquidation.

Though the law may be good from a legal point of view, its implementation has been poor. Local government officials, in particular the governor of the province, often pressure the bankruptcy court to restructure rather than liquidate large, important companies even though they are not viable.[16] Only small enterprises are liquidated. As a result, the creditors of these large companies suffer. Since the important creditors are often the federal government because of unpaid taxes or banks and suppliers from outside the province, the governor and the local bankruptcy courts give little weight to their interests.

As the Russian example indicates, there is a tendency among some experts on bankruptcy to focus on drafting the perfect law according to the standards of rich countries with little regard for whether the poor country has the capability to implement the law. Little attention is given to drafting a law that the country can implement. As another example, a report by the Legal Department of the International Monetary Fund lays out broad principals for a sophisticated bankruptcy procedure that includes the option of government or court restructuring following the example of bankruptcy laws in rich countries. It barely mentions, however, that poor countries may not have the necessary institutions to implement such procedures. Its only recommendation in this regard is that judges in bankruptcy courts should have "... adequate training in commercial and financial matters."[17]

Government or court-managed restructuring may be even more likely to place the interest of owners and managers ahead of creditors if the creditors are foreign. According to an article in the *Wall Street Journal,* some foreign analysts believe that the recent restructuring plan approved for a large, bankrupt Thai company whose creditors are largely Japanese ". . . is driven as much by Thai politics as by legal considerations. Since he took office, [Prime Minister] Thaskin's brand of economic nationalism has included various measures that favor borrowers over creditors and local businesses over foreign ones."[18] According to the Japanese creditors, the restructuring plan would unfairly benefit one creditor of this family-controlled company, namely, the brother of the company's founder. Under the plan, the other creditors would only receive 20 percent of what they are owed. They would rather liquidate the company than help restructure it under current family management. This case is likely to discourage future foreign investment and lending, but this may not concern the prime minister who, according to the article, believes that Thailand should rely less on foreign investment for economic development and more on its own resources. This restructuring plan was approved under a new bankruptcy law enacted after the 1997 financial crisis under pressure from the International Monetary Fund.

In a World Bank report on Bulgaria, the authors note that the bankruptcy law is being revised to fix certain weaknesses but conclude that "[b]ankruptcy and liquidation provide a classic case in which the most significant weaknesses are not in the law but rather in the way it is implemented."[19] The report, however, only briefly mentions how to improve the institutions that implement the law. This is like designing such a complicated car that no one can drive it and then blaming the drivers for being inadequate.

In an unpublished World Bank report, the authors complained that the bankruptcy procedures in the country under study had two major weaknesses. First, the government and the courts did a poor job of implementing the existing liquidation procedures that resulted in long delays, reduced the value of the company's assets, and thus lessened the return to both the owners and the creditors. Second, and even more important, the existing laws did not provide for court-managed restructuring in addition to liquidation. The authors noted with approval that the government was planning on changing the law to allow for this option. My question is, if the government cannot implement relatively simple liquidations of unviable companies, why do the authors expect it to be capable of implementing complex procedures to restructure companies?

A detailed World Bank report on Latin America points to many weaknesses in the current bankruptcy systems, including corruption, a bias in favor of debtors over creditors, a bias in favor of labor claimants and preserving jobs, corruption, and weak court judges.[20] The report then goes on to make broad recommendations for reform. The report, however, seems to favor the concept that "social costs" of liquidation should be taken into account, including job losses and "other disruptions of economic relations" in addition to maximizing economic efficiency. The report says that the creditors will not take into account these social costs, and thus some form of government or court restructuring is needed. The report seems to be an invitation for special-interest groups to argue that the social costs of liquidation are high and that the courts should keep unviable companies alive.

Creative Destruction

The famous economist Joseph Schumpeter argued that: "Creative Destruction is the essential fact about capitalism . . . ."[21] In a dynamic, growing economy, some firms and even entire industries will shrink and die but will be replaced by new firms and industries. This reality requires that capital and labor move from the declining to the growing firms and industries.

Too often, the objective of government or court restructuring of insolvent firms is to halt this process and to freeze the current structure of the economy. Under the banner of saving existing jobs, government restructuring is likely to slow the process of moving assets and workers from unviable to viable companies and thus creating new jobs.

Unfortunately, many powerful special-interest groups (shareholders, managers, and workers in these companies) believe they will benefit by keeping unviable companies alive and preserving existing jobs. No one is available to speak on behalf of the new industries and companies yet to be created that can make better use of the resources and workers trapped in these unviable companies.

8. Competition: Government Is the Problem, Not the Solution

The major economic argument for a private market economy is that competitive pressure will ensure that private firms are well managed and efficient and will sell high-quality products and services at reasonable prices. If competitive pressure is weak, there is little reason to prefer a private market economy over government planning and state-owned enterprises. Reducing barriers to competition is one of the most important policies that the government of a poor country can implement to increase economic growth and thus reduce poverty.

Barriers to competition can be created either by the government or by private firms. Government barriers include legal monopolies, high tariffs, and limits on entry of new firms, both domestic and foreign. Private barriers include price-fixing agreements, mergers to reduce the number of competitors, and abusing monopoly power.

In most poor countries and even in some rich countries, government barriers are far more important than private barriers. Government barriers are backed by the force of law and cannot easily be overcome. In contrast, there is a strong profit motive for firms to circumvent private barriers. If private barriers result in high profits, private firms have an incentive to enter the market. This incentive increases competition and eventually eliminates the high profits.

Thus, the focus of government attempts to increase competition should be to eliminate those government laws, institutions, and policies that are barriers to competition. This is difficult, however, because various special-interest groups benefit from these barriers, especially private and state-owned firms and their labor unions, and they pressure the government not to change them. Instead, it is often politically more acceptable to focus on the less important private barriers to competition. Naturally, businesspeople hate competition because it reduces their profits and makes their lives difficult. Increased competition may be good for the economy as a whole, but it is not good for a particular business. It creates a strong incentive for the business community and labor unions to pressure government to reduce competition, most often by instituting policies that restrict entry.

The power of a labor union to force a company to increase wages is enhanced if the company does not face competition. India is an example of a poor country in which greater competition in the early 1990s reduced the power of unions. Previously, government licensing and protection from foreign competition allowed many firms to earn high profits. It reduced their incentives to minimize labor costs. Liberalization of the economy introduced greater competition that encouraged firms to circumvent labor-market regulations and resist union pressure. One consequence is that strikes by unions declined.[1]

Many argue that the way to deal with private barriers to competition is to pass a law that prohibits private activities that are anticompetitive and to create a competition agency that will enforce the law. International development institutions and foreign experts on competition often encourage the creation of a competition law and agency.

The problem with creating a competition agency, however, is that economists have yet to establish clear principles or guidelines for determining when private activities are barriers to competition. Thus, the private activities prohibited by these laws are poorly defined thereby leaving the competition agency and the courts broad discretion to determine when a private activity reduces competition. Even worse, many of the laws require the competition agency to pursue other social or political objectives in addition to increasing competition.

Consequently, the competition agency typically has sweeping powers and wide discretion to intervene in the economy to promote unclear and often conflicting objectives. Because of the weak government and legal institutions in most poor countries, giving a government agency this relatively unconstrained power is dangerous. A likely outcome is that the competition agency will itself become a barrier to competition.

Measuring Competition

It is not easy to measure the extent of competition in a particular market. At one end of the spectrum is what economists refer to as *perfect* or *atomistic competition*. In this case, there are so many sellers of the same product or service that no single seller has any influence on the price he receives. Sellers must accept whatever the current market price is. The usual examples of this type of market are agricultural products, for example, wheat sold by thousands of farmers at the price set by supply and demand at an impersonal commodity exchange in a distant city.

At the other end of the spectrum is a *monopolist* who is the only seller of a particular product or service. Even then, the monopolist's ability to set a high price is constrained because consumers may switch to a substitute or may decide simply to do without if the price is too high. When the number of sellers is somewhere between these extremes (less than many but more than one), the extent of competition is unclear, open to dispute, and experts frequently disagree.

Perhaps more important than the current number of sellers is the ease or difficulty with which new producers can enter the market and begin selling the product or service. If competition among the few existing sellers is weak and they are able to charge high prices, the resulting high profits will attract new sellers to the market, increase supply, and force down prices. Even though there may be only one or two sellers currently of a particular product or service, they will be constrained in their ability to set high prices because of the threat of entry by other sellers.[2]

Entry into a particular market in which competition is weak can come about in two ways. First, existing producers in another market (for example, a market located in another part of the country or in another country) may begin to sell their product in the uncompetitive market. Second, investors may start up a new business in that market to sell the product or service. Thus barriers to entry involve either keeping out products manufactured in other markets or stopping new firms from beginning production of the product or service.

Impact on Growth

I would like to focus on two of the harmful impacts caused by lack of competition.[3] First, the high prices and thus high profits earned by private firms in uncompetitive markets will probably worsen the distribution of income. These markets hurt the poor but benefit the rich. Private firms are typically owned by relatively rich individuals who enjoy the high profits earned in these markets. Yet the poor buy the high-priced products and services sold by firms in uncompetitive markets. Increasing competition is one sure way to help the poor in most poor countries.

Second, lack of competition results in businesses that are inefficient and backward and slows the rate of economic growth. Protecting firms in poor countries from competition may mean that these economies may never develop and grow. In theory, competition is not necessary to encourage a private firm to be as efficient as possible. Even if it is a monopoly and faces no competition, the profit motive should still encourage a firm to do everything possible to be more efficient and reduce costs. Every dollar reduction in costs results in a dollar increase in profits to the owners of the firm. Though the firm may already be making huge profits because it faces little competition, it could make even more if it reduced costs or developed better products and services that consumers would pay more for.

In practice, however, owners and managers of firms are like everyone else and may become satisfied with the current high profits in an uncompetitive market even though profits could be increased. They see little reason to work hard to increase efficiency and thus increase profits even more. This attitude is particularly prevalent if the owners have weak control over the managers. Since the managers often do not benefit substantially from higher profits, they are less inclined to work hard to increase them just for the benefit of the absentee owners.

In contrast, increased competition threatens to reduce profits as more efficient and better managed firms offer lower prices or higher quality products. If competitive pressures are strong, firms may see their profits disappear and they may be forced into bankruptcy if they do not become as efficient as their competitors. Owners may lose their entire investment in the firm, and the managers may lose their jobs. These are powerful incentives for owners and managers to improve their companies. The carrot of higher profits may not motivate owners and managers nearly as much as the stick of reduced profits, bankruptcy, and job losses caused by increased competition.

Country Examples

A number of sophisticated statistical studies show that increased competition results in greater business efficiency and productivity growth. I won't attempt to summarize these studies here, but would instead like to give some examples from both rich and poor countries.[4]

I believe that the high level of economic development in my own country, the United States, is due in large part to its being a huge common market for more than 200 years. The U.S. Constitution prohibits the 50 states from interfering in or regulating commerce between the states. Thus, a business in any one state can freely sell its products or services in another state. Similarly, a business in any one state may have to face competition from other businesses located anywhere in the country.

In recent decades, the United States has also reduced or eliminated most barriers to foreign firms selling their products or starting up operations that compete with domestic firms in the United States. Foreign competition has been a major incentive for U.S. firms to improve. One only has to compare the quality of U.S. automobiles produced before 1970 when Japanese firms began to sell in the United States with those produced in recent years.

The one glaring exception is the U.S. banking industry. Until recently, banks in one state could not do business in another state or even in another community in some cases. This restriction resulted in a noncompetitive, fragmented, and inefficient industry whose weaknesses contributed to, if not caused, the Great Depression (see Chapter 3).

Similarly, a motive for creating the European Common Market after the Second World War was to increase competitive pressures by allowing firms in any one country in Europe to do business in any other on equal terms. Increased competitive pressure is also a major benefit of other free trade agreements such as the North American Free Trade Agreement (NAFTA) that creates a free trade area covering the United States, Canada, and Mexico.

Other large countries with a federal system of government have not followed the example of the United States or the European Union and have suffered as a result. In China, for example, economic planning was mostly carried out at the provincial level. Thus, the economy in each province was largely self-sufficient, and little trade existed between provinces. Each province would have a steel mill, an automobile factory, a machine tool industry, and so forth, resulting in many small, inefficient firms each enjoying a monopoly in its province. Provincial officials discouraged "imports" from other provinces as well as foreign countries because they hurt the local companies and threatened jobs. This practice has begun to change in recent years, however. Agreements that China made to join the World Trade Organization mean that many of these barriers to competition from firms in other provinces as well as from other countries will have to be eliminated.[5]

The McKinsey Global Institute (affiliated with the well-known business consulting firm McKinsey and Company) recently carried out detailed analyses of the economies of Japan, Russia, and India to determine the obstacles to faster economic growth. In all three, lack of competitive pressure was the most important.

In regard to Japan, some of its industries lead the world in productivity and efficiency (for example, automobiles and electronics), but others lag behind. The major difference is that the backward industries face little competitive pressure to improve. According to McKinsey, productivity in the Japanese retail sector is 50 percent of that in the United States, productivity in the domestic food processing sector is 39 percent, and productivity in residential construction is 45 percent.[6] In these industries, lack of competition has meant that small, inefficient firms dominate. For various reasons, larger, more efficient firms have not been allowed to enter the market.

In regard to India, the McKinsey analysis describes numerous barriers to competition and concludes:

> The lack of competition in India industry is the main reason for the poor operational performance of Indian companies and hence for the low labour and capital productivity.... In the absence of strong competition, managers can afford to ignore significant operational issues under their control (such as excess workers, poor OFT and inadequate equipment) and are able to earn high profits despite these inefficiencies.[7]

In regard to Russia, McKinsey examined 10 representative sectors and found that productivity levels averaged less than 20 percent of U.S. levels.[8] Again the major reason was that barriers to competition allowed inefficient, loss-making companies to continue to operate and prevented more modern and efficient companies from entering the market.

One barrier was government subsidies to the inefficient companies, which could then compete with more efficient companies that did not receive such subsidies. Another barrier was that inefficient firms would persuade local government officials to create regulatory and other obstacles to new firms entering their markets. As is often the justification for bad government policies, these barriers were intended to prevent the inefficient companies from shutting down and firing workers.

Surprisingly, increasing competition in poor countries seems to be given a low priority by international development institutions such as the World Bank. World Bank analyses of the business environment describe many obstacles faced by private businesses, for example, government corruption, a poor financial system, high taxes, restrictive labor laws, and poor infrastructure. These are major obstacles to private firms that want to become more efficient and productive. However, what is even more important is the lack of competitive pressure on firms to be more efficient and productive. Firms could overcome many of these obstacles if they had the incentive to do so. The only detailed studies of the competitive environment in poor countries that I have been able to find have been carried out by the private McKinsey Global Institute described above rather than any of the international development institutions.

Part of the reason why the World Bank does not give lack of competition a high priority may be the methodology it uses to evaluate the business environment or what the World Bank refers to as the investment climate. The World Bank has a large program to systematically survey businesspeople in poor countries and ask them to describe the barriers or obstacles they face in operating their business.[9] Naturally, they have a long litany of complaints about the lack of financing, high taxes, bad roads, and so forth. However, it is unlikely that a businessman will complain about lack of competition from other firms. If a businessman is asked why his firm is inefficient and backward, he is going to blame someone else rather than admit that he faces little competitive pressure and can still be profitable without improving his firm's performance.

Government Monopolies

Experience in most poor countries suggests that government barriers to competition are the most important. The existing businesses and their labor unions exert powerful pressure on the government to create barriers or at least to not remove those that already exist. Many of the existing barriers grew out of the previous model of economic development that emphasized government planning, state-owned enterprises, and domestic production instead of imports (the strategy of import substitution).

Now most governments say that they want to adopt a new approach to economic development that emphasizes private firms operating in competitive markets free from government control. However, it is often politically difficult for governments to remove the barriers to competition created under the old economic system. Any major change will usually harm one or more interest groups that benefited under the old system even though most of the citizens would benefit from the change. Those interest groups have an incentive to resist change.

If a firm faces competition that threatens to reduce its profits, it will often pressure the government to create a barrier to competition. What type of barrier might a firm ask for? The simplest and most effective barrier is for the government to declare the firm a monopoly and prohibit by law any other domestic or foreign firm from providing the same product or service.

This barrier is common in the important energy and infrastructure sectors in poor countries. Most of the firms in these sectors that enjoy monopoly status are state owned, but the same status has sometimes been extended to firms even after privatization. The fact that these are state-owned companies means that any monopoly profits will accrue to the government and thus presumably benefit all citizens. However, the monopoly granted to these firms has reduced their incentives to be efficient and well managed. The end result is that instead of earning monopoly profits, they often incur losses in spite of the lack of competition.

The usual justification for granting a monopoly to firms in these sectors is that they are required to achieve costly but important social objectives. Thus, they cannot compete with other firms that do not have such social objectives. The most common social objective is that these monopolies must cross-subsidize one class of customers at the expense of others. The firm charges certain customers high prices that are above the cost of production so that the firm can then charge other customers low prices that are below the cost of production.

Naturally, if competitors were allowed to supply the same product or service, they would immediately target the customers now forced to pay high prices. The former monopoly would be left with the money-losing, low-priced customers. To justify keeping their monopoly, existing firms in these sectors derogatorily refer to this likely strategy of new competitors as "cherry picking" or "cream skimming" and imply that they would somehow harm the country.

To give some examples of cross-subsidization, the monopoly telephone company in many countries charges high prices for international calls, domestic long-distance calls, and business phone service that are above the cost of supplying those services. The company charges low prices for residential phone service and local calls. International calls are often the most overpriced and thus the most profitable because the technology for making these calls using satellites and fiber-optic cables has improved dramatically in recent years. The existing telephone company may agree to competition for other types of service but will hold on to its monopoly on international calls as long as possible because these calls are so profitable. Governments may agree because most international calls are made by businesses, and thus high prices for these calls have little direct impact on ordinary citizens and voters.

The monopoly electric power company in many countries often charges the highest prices to industrial and commercial customers to subsidize the prices charged to residential customers. Industrial customers can argue that high power prices are hurting them in their competition with foreign firms, and this limits to some extent the prices that the power company charges them. However, commercial customers (stores and offices) cannot make this argument, and the power company often charges them the highest prices of all. If the power sector were opened up to competition, new suppliers would target the overpriced industrial and commercial customers, leaving the money-losing residential customers to be served by the previous monopoly.

The postal service is another example. In this case, the cross-subsidy is between urban and rural customers. For letter mail, the common practice is for the postal service to charge a single rate for all customers regardless of distance or location (hence the term *postage stamp rate*). The cost of serving urban customers is low because of their geographical density while rural customers may be located far apart. In many countries, mail other than letters (for example, packages or premium express mail) has been opened up to competition from private postal companies. The state-owned postal service, however, still keeps a monopoly on letter mail to subsidize rural customers at the expense of urban customers.

Governments are loath to permit competition in these industries. To do so, they must either eliminate the cross-subsidy or provide the subsidy from the government budget. Neither option is very attractive to politicians. The customers who now enjoy low subsidized prices will argue against eliminating the subsidy. Their usual argument is that these subsidies are helping the poor.

The cruel fact is that these subsidies more likely result in a transfer of income from the poor to the nonpoor and increase inequality rather than reduce it. The high prices for telephone service or power paid by business and industry are passed through to customers in the form of higher prices for all products and services. This transfer hurts both the poor and the nonpoor proportionately. However, the very poor, in particular, those living in rural areas, are often not even connected to the power grid, do not have a phone, and thus receive no benefit from the low subsidized residential prices. The beneficiaries of the cross-subsidy are likely to be the middle or upper classes at the expense of the very poor.

In those countries that have substantial domestic resources of oil and gas, a monopoly state-owned petroleum company is often established to exploit those resources. Though cross-subsidies may be part of the justification for this monopoly, the more important reason is that the government uses it to capture the high profits from producing the oil.[10]

There are other ways of doing it, however, besides creating such a company with all of its inefficiencies and high costs. Methods have been developed for the leasing of natural resources to competing private companies that allow the government to capture the high profits and yet still have the benefits of private management and competition. One example is the system of bonus-bid leasing used by the U.S. government for leasing oil and gas reserves on government land to private firms.[11]

The subsequent problem, however, is to ensure that the government uses this revenue for the proper functions of government. There are too many examples of the government wasting the oil revenue, using it to centralize political and economic power, and enriching a small number of citizens (for example, friends and relatives of the president or king). The majority of the people may actually suffer from the discovery of this oil wealth.

Import Competition

If becoming a legal monopoly is not possible, a strategy for a firm facing competition from foreign producers is to pressure the government to impose high tariffs and other trade barriers against imports. This strategy will be particularly effective if the country is small and has only a few domestic producers of a product. Foreign producers may be the only source of competition that would encourage domestic producers to become more efficient.

Many poor countries have made substantial progress in lowering tariffs and other trade barriers. In previous decades, it was not uncommon to see tariffs of 100 percent or more. Today the average level of tariffs in a poor country is usually below 30 percent with many at 10 percent or less. The average (unweighted) for all poor countries is about 18 percent. The highest tariffs are found in Sub-Saharan Africa, the Middle East, and North Africa.[12]

Though tariffs are much reduced, they still can be a substantial barrier to competition. The end result is those domestic firms that are as efficient as foreign firms can earn large profits. Even worse, domestic firms can be inefficient and backward and still be competitive.

Focusing only on the average level of tariffs can hide other more serious tariff barriers to competition from imports. Since these are unweighted averages, a low tariff on a product that is not produced in the country is given the same weight as a high tariff on a product that is produced in the country. Thus, the tariffs on imports that do compete with domestic producers could be much higher than the average. The maximum tariffs in poor countries can still be as high as 100 percent even though the average level of tariffs is much lower.[13]

Even if tariffs on average are low, substantial protection can still be given to domestic producers by continuing to charge high tariffs on finished products while lowering tariffs on imported raw materials, intermediate goods, and other inputs used by domestic producers. This practice permits the domestic producer to charge high prices for its finished product without fear of losing sales to imports

211

but yet purchase imported inputs at low world prices without paying high tariffs.

Though tariffs may not be high, a country may have a wide variety of nontariff barriers to imports to protect domestic producers. The most obvious are quotas on the amount of a product that can be imported even though tariffs are low on these products. Restrictive licensing is also used to limit imports, most notably, of fuel, minerals, rubber, machines, and precious stones and metals. Another is the difficulty and time involved in taking imports through customs, the cost of which may be substantial. One estimate is that the cost of dealing with complex custom procedures ranges from 7 to 10 percent of the value of the products being imported. In some countries, the cost of delays at the border can raise costs by another 6 percent.[14] Inefficient and high-cost ports and transportation networks can also be barriers.

Health and safety standards can also be a tool for keeping out imports. For example, Japan has been able to protect its high-cost apple industry by claiming that importing cheaper U.S. apples might introduce diseases harming the domestic industry.

The Heritage Foundation has tried to evaluate all of the various tariff and nontariff barriers to imports and to rank countries according to their levels of protectionism (see Figure 8-1). Of the approximately 139 poor countries examined, about 55 percent are ranked as having a high or very high level of protectionism.

Antidumping

One method used by domestic producers to limit competition from foreign producers is to file a complaint under the national antidumping law. As tariffs have been reduced and competition from imports has increased, producers in many countries are using this method more and more. This method started in the rich countries but has now spread to most poor countries, where it is now even more common than in the rich countries.[15]

An antidumping law allows a domestic industry to argue that it is being unfairly injured by a foreign producer. The usual basis for the complaint is that either the foreign producer is selling the product for less than it is selling the product in its own country (in other words, engaging in price discrimination) or is selling the product

Figure 8-1
DEGREE OF TRADE PROTECTIONISM
(PERCENTAGE OF POOR COUNTRIES)

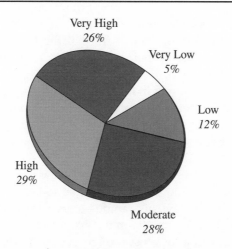

Very High
26%

Very Low
5%

Low
12%

High
29%

Moderate
28%

SOURCE: Gerald P. O'Driscoll Jr., Edwin J. Feulner, and Mary Anastasia O'Grady, "The 2003 Index of Economic Freedom," Heritage Foundation and *Wall Street Journal,* 2002.

at below cost. If the domestic industry can prove its complaint, the foreign producer may be subjected to special tariffs.

A great deal of debate has occurred on how to determine whether the foreign producer is selling below cost or engaging in price discrimination. In most cases, proving either of these allegations is not easy. I believe that valid examples of dumping are rare. In many cases, domestic producers are simply bringing the charge to reduce competition. But whether or not the charge is valid is not the main issue.

Suppose that the charge of dumping is correct. Why should the country importing this product be concerned or take action against the foreign producer? If anything, the foreign producer should be praised—not criticized. For whatever reasons, the foreign producer is supplying the product at a price below that charged by domestic producers, which benefits all consumers of the product. This increases the standard of living in the country and reduces poverty.

I agree that the owners of the firms in the domestic industry may be hurt by this increased competition. The objective of public policy, however, should not be to protect the owners of domestic firms from suffering a reduction in profits. Private businesspeople know they would receive little public sympathy in an antidumping case so instead they emphasize the harm that the foreign producer is causing to their workers. Their workers and labor unions will no doubt support this claim.

Thus, the basic argument in favor of antidumping laws is the one frequently used to justify bad economic policies, namely, saving jobs. As discussed previously, this argument is the basis for bankruptcy procedures that restructure insolvent companies even though they are unlikely to be viable.

The early 19th-century French economist and wit Frederic Bastiat would probably ridicule those who argue today in favor of anti-dumping laws by telling his famous story of the French candle makers. In the story, they petition the government for help because of competition from a low-cost foreign producer. This producer is hurting the profits of the candle makers and destroying high-paying jobs in the industry.

This foreign producer is the sun. The candle-making industry requests the government to require all households to close their shutters during the day so that they will buy more candles. Not only will this help the candle-making industry and increase employment, but it will help many other industries and their workers that supply materials for making candles. In the unlikely event that foreign producers are dumping their products at below cost in my country, I would be thankful for my country's good fortune just as I am thankful for the free light of the sun.

To be fair, there is one possibly valid argument for antidumping laws. It is conceivable that a foreign producer is engaged in *predatory pricing*. Its intention is to charge such low prices that the domestic industry will suffer large financial losses and be destroyed. The foreign producer can then charge high prices because there is no domestic competition.

Such a strategy is unlikely, however, because it would only be successful if there were no producers elsewhere in the world. The foreign producer might be successful in destroying the domestic competition in one particular country, but it would still have to face competition from other producers around the world who would rush in to supply the product. Predatory pricing would only be successful if the foreign producer is the only producer in the whole world except for the domestic industry. The first 1916 antidumping law in the United States required that predatory intent by the foreign producer must be shown. Since this is so implausible, the law was changed so that domestic producers only had to show that the foreign producer was selling at below cost or engaging in price discrimination.

Government Barriers to Entry

Another strategy for a domestic firm that wishes to reduce competition is to have the government create barriers to the entry of a new domestic firm in the same line of business. In this way, the existing firm could charge high prices without attracting new firms into the industry. A new firm could be started either by domestic or foreign investors.

One barrier encountered by both types of investors wishing to start up a new firm is the various government permits or licenses that must be obtained before the new firm can legally begin operations. There are at least three reasons why governments have created a complicated and lengthy process for obtaining these permits and licenses:

- First, the process may be a holdover from the old socialist economic system in which the government believed it must regulate and control the private sector to ensure that it was achieving the government's development objectives. An applicant has to prove that he is qualified to manage the new firm, and that the services or products produced by the firm are needed and fit into the national economic plan.
- Second, complex processes make it easier for corrupt officials to extract bribes before they will issue the necessary permits.[16]
- Third, existing businesses may encourage a lengthy and costly process because they know that it helps to keep out new competitors, especially if they can influence the government not to issue the necessary permit or license.

A recent study describes the procedures required to establish a new firm in 75 countries, including both rich and poor.[17] The length, cost, and complexity of the process are usually greater in poor than in rich countries. Switzerland, Austria, and France are notable exceptions. An entrepreneur in Austria, for example, wishing to start a new business must spend about 5 months to complete 12 separate procedures and pay more than $11,000 in fees. Similarly, an entrepreneur in Bolivia needs to spend almost 3 months to complete 20 procedures and pay $2,696 in fees. In contrast, an entrepreneur in Canada only has to spend 2 days to complete 2 procedures and pay $280 in fees.

Another study describes the various administrative barriers to entry in five African countries (Ghana, Mozambique, Namibia, Tanzania, and Uganda).[18] In addition to the procedures required to obtain a business permit, the study describes the difficulty in obtaining the use of land. Since most developed land in these countries is owned or controlled by the government, the entrepreneur often faces a lengthy and complex procedure to buy or use this land. Similar problems arise in obtaining connections to state-owned utilities such as water, power, and telephones. Additional government permits and approvals are required for firms that wish to invest in certain industries such as fisheries, forestry, and tourism.

The study also examines the additional barriers to entry faced by foreign investors. Though most countries now say they desire and encourage foreign investors, the reality is that they may face even greater barriers to entry than do domestic investors. With one hand, the government promises fiscal and tax incentives to attract foreign investors. With the other hand, the government imposes burdensome requirements on the foreign investors, for example, the requirement to prepare detailed feasibility studies and demonstrate compliance with often vague eligibility criteria. Even after starting operations, foreign investors may face foreign exchange controls or difficulties in bringing in expatriate managers and experts. The study concludes that this whole maze of often duplicative, complex, and nontransparent procedures can mean delays of up to two years in obtaining all of the approvals required.

The Canadian Chamber of Commerce asked its member firms which government barriers they faced in investing in countries around the world. The firms listed a large variety of formal and informal barriers. These include limitations on the industries that foreign firms may invest in, industries under the control of public monopolies, limitations on the legal form of the subsidiaries of the foreign investors, preference for foreign investment in new assets ("greenfield investments") rather than the purchase of existing firms or assets, quotas on the number of foreign firms allowed, requirements that government procurement must only be with domestically owned firms, limitations on the geographic location of investments, and limitations on foreign firm access to domestic sources of finance.[19]

Though the time and cost needed to obtain the necessary permits or other approvals are important barriers to entry, an even greater barrier may arise if the entrepreneur is denied a permit to start a new business without good reason because of pressure exerted by his competitors. Anecdotal evidence suggests that this may be a serious problem, but there is no comprehensive analysis of how many permits are denied or why they are denied.

In some countries, there is evidence that a permit to start a new firm is not given unless there is a demonstrated need for a new supplier of the product or service. If the government judges that the capacity of existing suppliers is adequate to meet demand, then the government may refuse to allow entry by a new firm. I doubt whether the government is capable of judging when new capacity is needed. In any event, why should the government's judgment override that of the private entrepreneur who sees a profitable business opportunity and is willing to invest money pursuing that opportunity? In India, for example, new dairy processing plants must be located a certain distance away from any existing plant. This ensures that each plant has a monopoly over the dairy farmers in the region surrounding the plant.

Governments may ask the existing firms in the industry whether additional capacity is needed and whether a new firm should be allowed to enter. Naturally, it would be rare for the existing firms to conclude that a new competitor is needed. A frequent requirement is that the applicant for a permit to start a business must register with the local chamber of commerce. Also, the application must be announced in the official government newspaper or gazette for a specified period before the permit is granted. I can see no reasonable justification for requiring an entrepreneur to announce his intention to start a new business to all of his potential competitors. This requirement only gives his competitors the opportunity to prepare a defense against the new firm, including pressuring the government not to grant the necessary permits.

Rich countries may have set a precedent for this practice. For example, any new store in France must be approved by a regional board that includes existing storeowners. These boards typically approve only about 40 percent of applications.[20] Just recently in my own community, owners of small dry-cleaning establishments used their political influence to convince local government officials not to allow large, more efficient, and lower-cost establishments to begin operating. Following this example in Kampala, Uganda, the local government councilman for the district in which the new firm will be established must approve the granting of needed permits. The justification is that the councilman needs to ensure that there is no conflict with existing businesses.[21]

Crony Capitalism

Though hard to document, crony capitalism is probably a major barrier to entry. Existing firms with close ties to senior government officials or the ruling party can use their influence to make certain that a new competitor is not welcome in the country. Politicians and government officials may benefit from the high profits of firms that face little competition and will use their influence and power to restrict competition. In many countries, a foreign investor would be foolish to start a business that competes with one owned by a relative or friend of the country's president or prime minister.

One way for a foreign firm to ensure that it will be welcomed is to offer friends and relatives of powerful politicians and officials the opportunity to become investors in the new venture. As shown recently in Indonesia, however, this strategy can backfire if the ruling party changes, and foreign investors are tied to discredited officials and politicians who may now be in jail.

In some countries, including local investors is more than an informal requirement for success. These countries do not allow foreign investors to own more than a certain percentage of a firm in the country, for example, 25 or 49 percent. This forces the foreign investor to share ownership with local investors. I have never seen any reasonable justification for this requirement. It only seems to allow local investors to free ride on the efforts of foreign investors and enjoy high profits with little effort. Just recently, for example, China proudly announced that foreign investors would now be allowed to own up to 49 percent of insurance companies. My question is why should there be any limit at all on foreign ownership of an insurance company? Such limitations seem to be widely accepted with no justification other than appealing to nationalistic pride and the xenophobic belief that local businesses should be owned by citizens of the country instead of by foreigners.

Private Barriers to Competition

If all of the barriers to competition created by the government just described were eliminated, to what extent could private firms create barriers? Are private barriers likely to be a serious problem? I believe that it is difficult for private firms to create long-lasting barriers to competition. If successful, such barriers would allow private firms to enjoy high profits, but such profits attract new competitors and thus increase competition forcing profits down to normal levels. In most cases, private firms will only enjoy monopoly profits for a long time if they are supported by governments that use the force of law to keep out new competitors. Let me give some examples.

Suppose that for whatever reason, a single firm is the only supplier of a product in the country and thus appears to be a monopoly. If this firm charges high prices and enjoys high profits, then consumers can import the product unless the government has created tariff or nontariff barriers to its importation. Without government help, the apparent monopoly firm cannot keep out imports.

Suppose, however, that only one firm produces a service (for example, electricity, retailing, banking, or construction) that cannot be imported because of its physical characteristics.[22] It must be purchased from a domestic supplier. If this firm is earning high profits, then both domestic and foreign investors have an incentive to set up new firms in the country to sell this service. Unless the government puts in place barriers to entry by new firms, the existing firm probably cannot keep them out and thus earn high profits for very long.

Even though a number of firms may now sell the product and service, they may get together to agree on a high price or reduce output to drive up the price, in other words, create a cartel to limit competition. Though there are many examples of firms trying to do this, it is difficult to maintain a cartel without government support. Cartels tend to break down because some members simply cheat on their agreements with the others (there is no honor among thieves). If the members agree on a high price, then each member has an incentive to steal customers away from the others by charging a slightly lower price. The cartel may not be able to detect the cheating because the price discounts are given in secret. Such cheating can cause the cartel to collapse because the members who do not cheat see their sales and profits decline.

Another strategy is for the cartel to limit production by each member to keep prices high. This approach is used by one of the most famous cartels, the Organization of Petroleum Exporting Countries (OPEC). As illustrated by OPEC, there are constant disputes about how much each member should be allowed to produce. Even if the cartel members could agree on a production quota for each member, it would be difficult to enforce without some system to inspect the production facilities of each member. For example, OPEC often complains that one or more of its members are producing more than their agreed-on quota and thus forcing down prices.

Finally, if the cartel is successful in keeping prices high, this will attract either imports if the product can be imported or new entrants who are attracted by the high profits. For example, OPEC is concerned that keeping prices high will result in the exploration and development of new, high-cost oil fields and will force prices down. A cartel is likely to be successful for a long period only if the government uses the force of law to require higher prices or lower levels of output and to keep out imports and new entrants.

Are Competition Laws and Agencies Needed?

If I am correct that private activities that successfully limit competition are rare and not a major problem unless they are supported by the government, then there is little need for the government to enact a competition law and create a competition agency. In spite of my belief, about 90 countries have enacted competition laws and more are being planned. Canada and the United States were the first to do so in 1889 and 1890, respectively. European countries followed this example in the 1950s and some poor countries in the 1990s.

These competition agencies often have broad powers to intervene in the private sector. An agency can stop two or more firms from merging, prohibit firms from engaging in business practices that are viewed as anti-competitive, fine companies, jail executives, and force companies to be broken up.

Creating competition agencies in poor countries is probably a mistake because of their weak government and legal institutions. Instead of promoting competition, two other outcomes are more likely. The first outcome is that they may be just ineffective and have little impact for better or worse. A recent report of the World Bank suggests that competition agencies in poor countries have thus far not been very active.[23] I am concerned that they might become active.

The second outcome is that they intervene in the economy to pursue undesirable objectives instead of increasing competition or they actually become another government barrier to competition. There is substantial precedent for this outcome in the operation of competition agencies in rich countries.

Many economists would argue that the only objective of competition agencies should be to enhance competition. The usual way of determining whether competition is increased is if consumers benefit or economic efficiency is increased. In addition to enhancing competition, politicians, members of parliament, and government officials often believe that other objectives should be considered as well. Because they write and enforce the laws, it is not surprising that competition laws and agencies often emphasize other objectives. One point of view is that ". . . competition policy is based on multiple values that are neither easily quantifiable nor reduced to a single economic objective. These values reflect a society's wishes, culture, history, institutions, and perception of itself, which cannot and should not be ignored in competition law enforcement."[24] What I find troubling about this view is that it would give a government agency authority to intervene in the private sector to pursue broad, unclear, and contradictory objectives. Given the past history of government interventions, should this be encouraged?

Though competition policy today in the United States largely focuses on consumer welfare and economic efficiency, this was not true in the past. A well-respected legal scholar and judge, Robert H. Bork, wrote in 1978: ". . . modern antitrust has so decayed that the policy is no longer intellectually respectable. Some of it is no longer respectable as law; more of it is not respectable as economics;

and I wish to suggest that, because it pretends to one objective while frequently accomplishing its opposite, and because it too often forwards trends dangerous to our form of government and society, a great deal of antitrust is not even respectable as politics."[25] Thanks to the efforts of both economists and lawyers like Justice Bork, competition policy in the United States has since improved.

Competition policy in the European Union has a variety of objectives. Its dominant objective is economic integration of its member nations. Other objectives include enhancing opportunities for small- and medium-sized firms, increasing employment, raising the economic level of worse-off nations, and general concepts of fairness.[26] The competition laws recently enacted in Latin America " . . . target a whole series of social and political objectives, such as the promotion of freedom in industry and commerce, the equitable participation of small- and medium-sized enterprises, and the decentralization of economic power."[27]

Particularly troubling is the notion that a competition agency should promote *fair competition* or *fair trade*. This objective often appears in competition laws, including the title of the law. It is difficult enough to determine when a private action restricts competition without attempting to determine when it is fair. This concept inherently requires the competition agency to make ethical or value judgments that balance the interests of one competitor against another. It can be used to justify almost any intervention in the economy.

When Is a Private Activity Anti-competitive?

Even when the objective of competition policy is limited to increasing consumer welfare or economic efficiency, there is a great deal of disagreement among experts about which private actions are anti-competitive and whether intervention by the competition agency will increase competition. It is hard to precisely define or give clear guidelines to determine when intervention by the competition agency will benefit consumers or increase efficiency. Judging whether something increases competition is like judging fine art. An art expert may not be able to define what great art is, but he claims to know it when he sees it though other experts often disagree. Like art experts, competition experts often disagree.

In the jargon of U.S. competition policy, only a few activities are considered to be *illegal per se*. Most must be judged under the *rule of reason*. Thus, the competition agency must usually evaluate the specific circumstances surrounding each activity to determine whether it is anti-competitive and thus illegal. In some cases, an activity may be judged illegal, but in other cases under different circumstances it may be legal. It is argued that the competition agency must be given broad discretion to determine whether a specific activity is anti-competitive. Granting of such discretion worries me when the governmental and legal systems in many poor countries are weak.

For example, a textbook on competition by two U.S. economists evaluates the theory and empirical research to determine whether clear guidelines exist concerning which activities are anti-competitive. They conclude the following (emphasis added):

- "Some see *mergers* as an important source of efficiency; others emphasize their prominence as an outlet for managerial empire-building instincts whose pursuit degrades, not enhances, efficiency; still others focus on mergers' role in altering market structures and enhancing monopoly power."[28]
- "The *vertical restraints* that . . . sellers attempt to impose on their customers and on those customers' conduct toward buyers even farther downstream are extremely complex, with equally complex economic consequences. Economic efficiency may be increased, reduced, or left essentially unchanged."[29]
- "There are many kinds of *price discrimination*, with such diverse consequences, that simple generalizations about their economic effect are apt to be misleading. Some forms . . . increase the efficiency of resource allocation, others are essentially neutral, while still other types . . . lead to possibly serious inefficiencies."[30]

Concerning *cartels*, most experts do agree that an agreement between producers to set prices or limit output is anti-competitive with almost no exceptions. In the United States, this is the only activity that is illegal per se. In other words, no defense or justification for this activity is assumed to exist, and competition agencies have little discretion in deciding whether it is illegal. The United States is one of the few countries that imposes criminal penalties on corporate executives who participate in cartels. However, the

European Union takes a more lenient position and in some cases may permit a cartel. Justifications for a cartel may include chronic overcapacity in an industry, the need to foster small- and medium-sized firms, and if the impact is sufficiently small (de minimis). Though cartels are generally illegal in Japan, a large number of industries received an exemption in the past and were allowed to form cartels. For example, in 1991, there were 247 active cartels.[31] This practice, however, is disappearing.

Capture of the Competition Agency

Given the multiple objectives of competition law in many countries and the inability to specify clear criteria or guidelines for determining when an activity is anti-competitive, the competition agency usually has wide discretion to intervene in the private sector. But this discretion is likely to be misused and become another barrier to competition. Private firms will view the competition agency as just another weapon in their competitive struggle and will attempt to use it to reduce competition. (In the jargon of economics, the agency may be *captured* by private interests.) Though competition agencies are often established as independent agencies to reduce the chance that they come under political pressure to decide a case one way or another, a firm with political connections may still be able to pressure the agency.

If one firm is aggressively lowering prices, for example, a second firm may complain to the competition agency that the first firm is engaging in illegal price discrimination or predatory pricing. Even if the agency eventually determines that this pricing is not anti-competitive, the cost to the first firm of defending itself may deter it and others from lowering prices in the future. If two firms are planning to merge to reduce costs that would make the combined firm more competitive, a third firm may complain before the competition agency that this merger will reduce the number of firms in the industry and reduce competition. If nothing else, the complaining firm knows that the merger will be delayed until the competition agency makes a decision, which can take years in some countries.

Although most competition agencies in poor countries are not very active, the limited experience of those that are active is not encouraging. Let me give some examples from annual reports of competition agencies and various news reports.

In Indonesia, the competition agency has been investigating a number of complaints of anti-competitive activities. Small retailers complained that the large Indomaret chain of stores engaged in predatory pricing by selling instant noodle products at low prices that the small retailers could not match. A domestic cooperative that produces soybean products has accused a foreign firm of practicing price manipulation to undercut local producers. An oil company, PT Caltex, was accused of unfair practices in its procurement of pipes because small- and medium-sized firms could not participate in the tender. The minimum amount of pipe that the company would agree to purchase from any one vendor was larger than smaller firms could supply. Though these complaints are not yet decided, the disturbing fact is that the competition agency seemed to be taking them seriously and citing them as examples of how it intends to vigorously investigate unfair competition. Note that the objective of the agency is to eliminate unfair competition rather than increase competition.

In Korea, as in Indonesia, the competition agency believes that one of its objectives is to promote small- and medium-sized firms. It attempts to regulate what it calls "unfair subcontracting practices" so that smaller firms have a fair opportunity to participate in the subcontracting carried out by larger firms.

In Argentina, an association of stationers and bookstores filed a complaint that a supermarket chain engaged in predatory pricing by selling writing paper at below cost. In this case, the competition agency wisely dismissed the complaint because the supermarket chain had only a small share of the market for writing paper and was unlikely to achieve a monopoly by this practice. Also, the alleged predatory pricing only occurred for 15 days. The practice of selling an item at below cost (*loss leader*) for a short time to attract customers to a store is a common marketing technique. Though the complaint was eventually dismissed, the supermarket chain still had to incur the expense of defending itself, and this is likely to deter it from lowering prices below its competitors in the future.

In Brazil, one of the most important cases decided by the competition agency was the proposed merger between two beverage companies to create a new larger firm, American Beverages. According to one account, the justice ministry attempted to halt the merger, prodded by Coca-Cola, which owns a stake in a competing company. In response, American Beverages convinced Brazil's president, Fernando Henrique Cardoso, to support the merger, and the competition agency approved the merger a year later. In the end, it appears that the case may not have been determined by an objective analysis of whether the merger reduced or increased competition but by a political battle in which the various firms and their political supporters attempted to use the competition agency to harm competing firms.

Even then, the agency attached questionable conditions to the approval. Though it is common to impose conditions on a merger in rich countries to ensure that competition is protected, one of the conditions seemed to have nothing to do with competition but instead seemed to be designed to protect workers in the industry. Presumably, an important justification for the merger is that it would reduce costs for the combined company and make it more efficient, for example, by reducing labor costs. However, the agency required American Beverages to offer "retraining and repositioning" to any workers who lose their jobs as a result of the merger in the next four years.

A Limited Competition Policy

All in all, giving competition agencies in poor countries unclear objectives combined with broad discretion and authority to intervene in the private sector is probably a mistake. Because government barriers to competition are usually more important, perhaps competition agencies should instead review government policies that hinder competition and argue for their elimination. Competition agencies in some countries have been given this authority. The agencies can become the spokespersons for consumers and the poor who will benefit from greater competition. In most countries, there are powerful special-interest groups allied against increasing competition. In contrast, an increase in competition may only provide a small benefit to an individual consumer though the total benefit to all consumers would be large. Thus, consumers often do not perceive or understand the benefit that they receive from greater competition. Even if they do, they may have a weak voice in government decision-making compared with companies and labor unions.

In some cases, competition agencies have been effective advocates of increased competition by intervening in government decision-making and arguing against government policies that restrict competition. For example, in South Korea, the competition agency says that it was consulted about the competitive impact of 561 laws and regulations in 1999.[32] In the Czech Republic, the competition agency argued in favor of increased competition in the power, gas, post, rail, and telecommunications sectors.[33] In Mexico, the competition agency reviewed the government's plans to issue permits for companies to engage in natural gas distribution and to use the radio spectrum. It also became involved in the government's plans to regulate, restructure, or privatize a number of infrastructure sectors, including airports, liquefied petroleum gas, and electricity.

Though one government agency might not be an effective advocate for eliminating barriers to competiton created by other government agencies, I see little downside risk that giving an agency this advocacy function would actually reduce competition. Thus, there is some merit in creating a government agency that would focus only on government barriers to competition. Such an agency, however, should not be given authority to intervene in private markets for the reasons referred to earlier.

Conclusions

Competitive pressure is probably the single most important force for creating efficient and well-managed private firms that can grow, hire more workers, and thus reduce poverty. In spite of this, the major barriers to competition are various government laws and policies. In most cases, private efforts to limit competition without government support will not be effective and certainly far less important than government barriers. Thus, efforts to increase competition should primarily focus on government barriers.

Many rich and poor countries have enacted competition laws and created competition agencies to eliminate private barriers to competition. Frequently, these agencies are given a variety of unclear and contradictory objectives, only one of which is to enhance competition, and have wide discretion to intervene in the private sector in pursuit of these objectives. Even when they focus on increasing competition, economic theory and empirical research give them little guidance as to when a private activity will reduce or increase competition.

As a result, firms are likely to bring complaints to the agency for the purpose of reducing competition from other firms—not increasing it. Bringing a complaint becomes another weapon in the competitive battle between firms. The end result is that a competition agency may become just another government barrier to competition. This is more likely in poor countries with weak political, government, and legal institutions. On balance, most poor countries would be better off by not enacting a competition law and not creating a competition agency.

9. Conclusions—The Example of New Zealand

In this book, I argue that economic growth is essential for reducing poverty in poor countries. Creating an efficient, dynamic, and growing private business sector is the only way to increase the rate of economic growth. If governments wish to reduce poverty, they need to improve the environment in which private business operates. A good business environment will encourage private companies to be more productive, offer better products and services at lower prices, export more, expand and invest in new capacity, hire more workers, and above all else increase wages and salaries.

The business environment includes all those institutions, policies, laws, and regulations that affect the performance of private firms. Examples are competition laws and policies; the financial system; the legal and regulatory system; tax administration; labor laws; tariffs and customs; the quality of infrastructure such as roads, power, telecommunications, water supply, sewers, and ports; and the health and education of the workforce. To improve the business environment, governments may decide to regulate some activities of private firms because of what economists call market failures. The more important are the result of externalities (for example, pollution) and information asymmetries (for example, inability of consumers to judge the safety or quality of products).

A great deal has been written about government policies in poor countries to improve the business environment and thus encourage private firms to be more productive.[1] The main conclusion of this book is that many government programs, policies, or interventions designed to help the private sector actually impede its development. This result is due to the poor quality of government institutions, the high level of corruption, and the influence of special-interest groups, including the private sector, that manipulate the government for their own benefit. Though politicians and government officials now

229

say that they support an increased role for the private sector, many still favor heavy-handed policies to control business.

Private markets have many weaknesses, but a government's ability to fix them is limited. In spite of this, many experts recommend policies that most governments in poor countries cannot successfully implement. International experts often recommend what they know best, namely, the policies that exist in the rich countries even though those policies are not suitable for poor countries. Economists are inclined to focus on the theoretical failures of private markets (externalities, information asymmetries, etc.) and recommend sophisticated government interventions to fix these failures.

This book recommends policies to improve the business environment that governments in poor countries are more likely to implement successfully. More research, however, needs to be done on policies that are better suited to countries with weak governments. International agencies that provide help to poor countries should be more willing to recommend policies designed for the low quality of the government institutions in those countries. Instead they focus on programs to improve the functioning of these institutions that may not be effective for many years. Both should be done.

Establishing Priorities

Because most governments in poor countries have limited capacity, they need to establish priorities. While the government of a rich country may have the capacity to intervene in the economy in a variety of ways to improve the business environment, the government of a poor country needs to be more selective and choose policies according to two criteria. First, will the policy have a major impact on improving the business environment? Second, is the intervention within the capacity of the government to implement effectively?

It is not easy to determine which government policy will most improve the business environment. A common technique used by governments and international development institutions is to survey businesspeople in poor countries. They are typically asked to identify the biggest constraints or obstacles to the operation of their businesses.[2]

Though such surveys are helpful, they must be interpreted with care. The ideal business environment according to a typical businessman may not be the ideal environment from a national perspective.

A businessman, for example, would prefer weak competition so that he can charge high prices, abundant bank loans at low interest rates to finance his operations, low taxes, and low wages.

The best business environment, however, from the national perspective may be one that businesspeople complain about. Such an environment has intense competition, stingy bankers that rigorously evaluate the company and its investment plans before making loans, strict bankruptcy laws that result in the liquidation of unviable companies, and neutral tax systems that do not distort business decisions or subsidize some activities.

The country studies carried out by the McKinsey Global Institute discussed in Chapter 8 offer a different perspective on the business environment from that found in these surveys of businesspeople.[3] Using their management consulting expertise, McKinsey compared the operations of firms in a poor country with what is considered best practice both by other firms in the country and in other countries. They found that many firms lag far behind best practice and thus are inefficient with low productivity.

When businesspeople are asked why their company's performance is so bad, they are likely to blame the banks for not giving them loans to modernize, high interest rates, high taxes, government corruption, or bad infrastructure such as roads or power supply. They rarely blame their own inadequate management. McKinsey concludes that poor management is often the most serious problem and is frequently caused by lack of competition. In other words, these companies can still be profitable without improving their performance because they face little competition. Owners and managers have little incentive to change.

The Example of New Zealand

To illustrate the conclusions and recommendations of this book, I would like to use the example of New Zealand. The country is about the size of Great Britain but with a population of less than four million. It is located in the South Pacific about 1,200 kilometers from its nearest neighbor, Australia. Historically, it has depended on exports of agricultural products such as wool, lamb, dairy products, and fruits.

Beginning in 1985, New Zealand implemented economic reforms that exceed in scope and depth those in any other rich country.

The economy was transformed from being one of the most heavily regulated and dominated by state-owned enterprises into one of the most liberal and free from government ownership, controls, and interventions. Because I worked for some time at the Treasury of New Zealand during the early part of this reform, I was strongly influenced by the economic theory used by officials and ministers to develop the reforms. It should not be a surprise to the reader that the policies recommended in this book are similar to those adopted by New Zealand though there are important exceptions that I will discuss.

After leaving New Zealand, I proposed that the World Bank study and evaluate these reforms as a possible model for poor countries. The thinking of the World Bank and other experts seemed to be that the example of New Zealand was of limited use to poor countries because New Zealand was a relatively rich country with strong government institutions. As a former British colony, New Zealand had adopted Britain's honest and competent government institutions. Thus, one should not expect poor countries to be able to implement the reforms in New Zealand.

I drew the opposite conclusion. New Zealand had a long experience with state ownership and complicated government policies and interventions designed to improve the business environment, but concluded that these policies had reduced economic growth rather than increased it. In other words, New Zealand's relatively competent and honest government could not make those policies work. The government then privatized many of its state-owned enterprises, eliminated policies designed to control or guide the private sector, and instead relied more on unregulated private markets. If the government in a poor country has the political will to do so, following the example of New Zealand is not difficult because this country's reforms reduce the size and scope of the public sector and thus make it easier for a government with limited capacity to carry out these reduced responsibilities. If these reforms are desirable in a rich country with strong government institutions, they are even more desirable in a poor country with weak institutions.

The breadth and scope of reforms enacted by the Labour Government from 1985 until its defeat in 1990 and to some extent by subsequent governments are large. I won't attempt to describe in detail all of the reforms but will focus on those dealing with the issues discussed in this book.

The Importance of Economic Growth

Much of the current debate about how to help poor countries ignores or downplays the importance of increasing the rate of economic growth and the role of the private sector. For example, the United Nations recently proposed the Millennium Development Goals to guide international assistance to poor countries. Faster economic growth and the role of the private sector in achieving these goals are barely mentioned. Others argue that economic growth only benefits the rich, and the poor are left behind. Yet, recent studies show that economic growth in most countries results in about the same percentage increase in income for both the rich and the poor. The only alternative to faster economic growth is to redistribute income from the rich to the poor. Moreover, government schemes to redistribute income are often unsuccessful, costly to the economy, and help the rich more than the poor.

Though a relatively rich country, New Zealand moved away from a focus on redistributing income to faster economic growth as the best way to raise incomes. New Zealand was an early pioneer in social legislation. Before 1985, there was a widespread expectation that the government would provide cradle-to-grave protection against economic uncertainty. After 1985, however, the government cut various social welfare benefits and better targeted the benefits to the poor.

The major reforms began after the election of the Labour government in 1984, supported by the intellectual leadership of Roger Douglas, the new minister of finance, who had been arguing for these reforms for some time.[4] The government had the political will to implement these reforms at least in part because of the poor performance of the economy for decades before the election. In 1938, New Zealand's gross national product per capita was equal to 92 percent of that in the United States. It had dropped to 70 percent of the U.S. level by 1950 and to 50 percent five decades later. Though government expenditures relative to the size of the economy were not large compared with those of many other rich countries, government control over the economy was more pervasive. It included regulation of wages, imports, foreign currency, some commodity prices, and the sale of exports abroad. Like many poor countries, New Zealand had a policy of import substitution and it protected domestic industry from import competition. The government also owned the dominant enterprises in banking, health, education, transport, energy, and utilities.

233

The government's ability to implement such far-reaching reforms was helped because the business community began to support these reforms. Previously, like the private sector in many poor countries, business leaders supported government policies that provided them with subsidies, protection from competition, and other benefits. Businesses competed with each other for government favors rather than for the market, in other words, rent seeking. Business leaders in New Zealand, however, began to realize that though past policies might benefit them individually in the short run, they were harming the overall economy and thus harming them in the long run.[5]

Privatization

As was the case in New Zealand, inefficient state-owned companies often dominate the economies of poor countries, thus reducing economic growth. There is a growing consensus that such companies should be transferred to private ownership, that is, privatized. International experts, however, often accept without question or even encourage governments to adopt complicated methods of privatization with confused and contradictory objectives.

In this book, I argue that the primary objective of privatization should be to find the private owner who is most likely to improve the performance of the company. The best method for doing so is to sell 100 percent of the company to the highest cash bidder in an international competition open to all investors. The investor willing to pay the highest price is the one most likely to have the best plan for improving company performance. In addition, this method will maximize the revenue to the government from the sale.

Instead of this simple method of privatization, governments often use complicated criteria for selecting the winning bidder, impose conditions on how the new owners can manage the company, sell only part of the company thereby allowing the government to continue to intervene in management, restrict or prohibit foreign investors from bidding, sell the company's shares to many small domestic investors (a share flotation or initial public offering) who have little ability to improve performance or control the managers, and allow workers and managers to buy the company on preferential terms not available to others.

The Labour Party government in New Zealand followed this preferred method of privatization perhaps more than any other country.

The government first tried to improve the performance of state-owned enterprises and had one of the best systems to manage them. This system was called "corporatization" because ministries or agencies that engaged in commercial activities were converted into corporations whose shares were owned by the state. The emphasis was on forcing these new companies to operate in an environment that was as close as possible to that faced by a private firm. Industries previously dominated by these companies were opened up to competition from both domestic and foreign firms. These companies were given a capital structure similar to that of private firms, were expected to borrow on commercial terms from banks, and their debt was not guaranteed by the government.

Most important, these state-owned enterprises were to focus only on the normal commercial objective of a private firm, which is to be as profitable as possible. They were to have no social or political objectives with one exception. The law on state-owned enterprises said that the government could require such an enterprise to take on a noncommercial activity but only if the government paid the enterprise for the extra cost that this entailed.

As a result, the commercial performance of most state-owned enterprises under this regime improved. For example, employment in the national telephone company declined by about 30 percent under state ownership. In spite of this improvement, the government concluded that privatization would improve their performance even more. Also, if these companies were not to have any social or political objectives and were to function as much as possible like private companies, there seemed to be little rationale for keeping them in state ownership. In poor countries with less ability to manage state-owned enterprises, the case for privatization is even stronger.

The government examined which methods of privatization would most likely result in the greatest improvement in the performance of these enterprises. The government generally sold the entire enterprise to the highest bidder in a competitive auction in which all of the investors, both domestic and foreign, could participate. In many cases, the highest bidder was a foreign company or a consortium of foreign and domestic companies. For example, the national telephone company was sold to a joint venture of two U.S. telephone companies plus a local investor, two state-owned banks were sold to Australian banks, the state insurance company was sold to a

British firm, and the tourist hotel company was sold to a U.S. hotel company. The government typically did not ask bidders to submit their business plans for review or impose conditions on how the new owners could manage the enterprises.[6]

There were some exceptions to this method, notably the sale of the telephone company. Though increasing the size of the New Zealand stock market was not a high priority, the government did require the initial purchasers of the telephone company to sell some of their shares on the stock market to reduce their ownership of the company. However, the owners had a number of years to improve profitability before they were required to sell. If they were successful, they could capture the resulting increase in value when they sold their shares. Thus, their incentive to improve company performance was not significantly reduced compared with a situation in which shares are sold on the stock market at the same time as shares are sold to a strategic investor.

Also, the government included a provision in the sale that placed an upper limit on the prices that the new owners could charge for telecommunications services for a number of years. It did this instead of establishing an industry-specific regulatory agency for telecommunications. The provision may have actually reduced regulatory risk for the new owners and increased their bid to buy the company because they had an explicit government contractual commitment establishing what price increases would be permitted. The owners did not have to rely on uncertain future decisions of a newly created regulatory agency.

A number of enterprises remain in state ownership for a variety of reasons. One is that some still have a mixture of commercial and social objectives, and the government has not been able to determine how or whether they should be separated to allow privatization. For example, these enterprises include the company that manages the air traffic control system, the meteorological service, and the national television and radio companies.

Recent governments, however, seem more inclined to accept state ownership. After the national airline, Air New Zealand, was privatized in 1989, it ran into financial difficulties due to a poorly conceived plan to purchase an Australian airline. Out of concern that liquidation of Air New Zealand would harm trade and tourism, the Labour-led government in late 2001 injected $700 million of new capital through loans and by purchasing an 82 percent stake in the company. Other countries have felt compelled to provide financial assistance to their private airlines in recent years because of the impact of terrorism but not usually by nationalizing them. The government is now looking for another airline, possibly Qantas, to buy at least part of Air New Zealand.

Banking

With regard to the financial sector, New Zealand did not suffer from mismanagement of its state-owned banks as disastrously as many poor countries did. In my view, this mismanagement is probably the biggest reason why economic growth has been slow in poor countries. If well managed, banks can channel the savings of the public to those businesses with good investment plans, thus contributing to economic growth. Instead, banks in most poor countries and even some rich countries have become giant pyramid or Ponzi schemes in which the public's savings have been squandered on bad investments or simply stolen by bank managers, owners, and the government. In many cases, governments or powerful politicians have required banks to lend to loss-making state-owned enterprises to keep them operating and to cronies and supporters of the party in power. Because governments in most countries guarantee bank deposits, these pyramid schemes can continue for years or even decades before the banks collapse under the burden of a high proportion of bad loans.

Banks can often hide the extent of these bad loans until they become illiquid. The result is then a financial crisis that forces the government to bail out the banks by replacing the bad loans with government securities. Though banks are state owned in most poor countries, privatization of the banks is not a foolproof solution. Often the new private owners also loot the banks. Over the past 20 years, 105 poor countries have experienced one or more banking crises. The cost to the government of bailing out the banks averaged about 13 percent of gross national product and was sometimes more than 50 percent. If banks do not perform better, poor countries would be better off without them and instead should rely on traditional or less sophisticated methods of financial intermediation.

State-owned banks in New Zealand had performed better than many banks in poor countries because of its strong government and political institutions that limited to some extent the ability of the government to use these banks for various social or political purposes. Nevertheless, the government still found that it had to recapitalize state-owned banks because of bad loans. Consequently, it decided to privatize its four state-owned banks as well as other financial institutions such as the State Insurance Office and to develop a better regulatory regime for this sector. As a result of privatization, foreign investors own three of the former state-owned banks, and domestic investors own the fourth.

The current government, however, decided once again to create a state-owned bank. Named the Kiwibank, it is part of the state-owned postal company. The rationale for its creation is that the private banks are alleged to charge high fees particularly to small savers, do not provide adequate service in rural areas, and charge excessive interest on home mortgages.

As discussed in Chapter 6, some argue in favor of creating a state savings bank but only if it is limited to investing in government securities, a so-called narrow bank. The risk, however, is that private businesses will pressure the government to let it make loans to them and once again create the conditions for a bank pyramid scheme and the buildup of bad loans. Unfortunately, it seems that the Kiwibank will be allowed to make loans such as mortgages to the private sector. Thus, it may find itself becoming a tool of the government to allocate capital to achieve social or political objectives, thereby leading to bad loans just as occurred with the previous state-owned banks in New Zealand and many other countries. In its recent review of the New Zealand economy, the OECD states that the creation of Kiwibank ". . . does not seem to have represented an efficient allocation of public funds, as it did not address any evident market failure."[7]

Banking experts trained in the rich countries argue that the solution to the problem of bank pyramid schemes is for a government regulatory agency to supervise the management of the banks coupled with providing government deposit insurance or guarantees to avoid bank runs. This solution has not worked particularly well in the high-income OECD countries as evidenced by the fact that two-thirds of such countries have also had one or more banking crises over the past 20 years (for example, the massive failure of U.S. savings and loan banks). Given the much weaker government institutions and high levels of corruption in poor countries, this solution is likely to be ineffective in those countries.

New Zealand offers a different solution that is more likely to be effective. Deposits in banks are treated like any other financial security such as stocks or bonds. New Zealand requires banks to disclose information about their finances so that depositors can make an informed choice about the risk of making a deposit. Bank directors are personally liable for the losses of depositors if false information is provided. Like other securities, the government does not guarantee bank deposits. The hope is that depositors and other bank creditors will do a better job of monitoring the financial soundness of banks compared with government officials and will force banks to be better managed or else go out of business. The banking system in poor countries should also be open to entry by banks from the rich countries that have an incentive to maintain their reputations as honest, well-managed banks. Thus, if depositors do not trust locally owned banks, they can turn to branches of foreign banks.

Bankruptcy

All countries have to create procedures to deal with insolvent companies that cannot pay their creditors (banks, bondholders, suppliers, etc.). Historically, most countries allowed only two procedures. The company could negotiate a restructuring plan with its creditors so that it could continue to operate and pay at least some of its debts. If the creditors, however, believed that selling its assets would give them a greater return, they could force the company into liquidation. In this case, the government or the courts would shut down the company, sell its assets, and distribute the proceeds to creditors according to priorities established by law.

In general, these two procedures worked well because creditors supported the restructuring of viable companies who could pay off a larger share of their debts if they remained in business. However, the creditors forced into liquidation those companies that were worth more dead than alive. This outcome is economically efficient because the company's assets will be used where they have the most value either by the bankrupt firm after restructuring or by other firms who buy the assets in a liquidation sale.

In recent years, however, concern about preserving jobs if companies are liquidated has resulted in governments creating a third procedure. This procedure is a government or court-managed restructuring of a company so that it can continue to operate (e.g., Chapter 11 bankruptcy in the United States). Experts on bankruptcy, including those from the IMF, the World Bank, and the Asian Development Bank, usually recommend that poor countries also adopt this third procedure.

Though one can question whether government-managed restructuring of bankrupt companies has worked well in the rich countries, it is likely to be a disaster in poor countries with weak government institutions. Special-interest groups such as labor unions and wealthy businesspeople with close ties to the ruling politicians will pressure the government to use this procedure to write off past debts and to provide additional capital so that companies can continue to operate that ought to be liquidated. A large share of the nation's productive assets and workforce may be locked up in inefficient and unprofitable companies. This procedure also imposes greater losses on the financial system than liquidation would and thus raises interest rates for all borrowers.

Seeing the trend around the world for governments to adopt some variation of this third procedure, New Zealand also considered doing so but for the time being has not taken any action because there does not seem to be a compelling need for change. New Zealand does have a cramdown procedure to assist privately negotiated restructurings. If 75 percent of the creditors agree on a restructuring, then the courts can enforce the restructuring on all creditors.

The Law Commission that advises the government on the need for changes in the law recommended adopting procedures closer to those used in other countries but admitted that there was not a large demand from the private sector for a change. Some people argue that one benefit of a government or court-managed restructuring is that it can stop secured creditors from seizing their collateral and eliminating any chance of a successful company restructuring. The Law Commission could find no examples in which a restructuring ". . . had failed solely due to the lack of an automatic stay against secured creditors."[8] Another consultant report concluded that no market failure had been identified to justify the proposed changes.[9]

Competition Policy

Privately owned businesses will only function well if they are subjected to fierce competition. Recent studies of Japan, Russia, and

India show that many of their companies are poorly managed and inefficient because they are protected from competition and face little pressure to improve. Unfortunately, the greatest opponents of increased competition are companies and their labor unions that pressure governments to erect a wide variety of barriers to competition (e.g., tariffs, licensing, legal monopolies, and restrictions on foreign investment and ownership). Because government barriers are backed by the force of law, they are far more effective than attempts by companies themselves to reduce competition (for example, cartels, price-fixing agreements, predatory pricing, and mergers). The best way to improve the performance of private business is to eliminate government barriers to competition.

Following the advice of competition experts from the rich countries, governments instead mistakenly focus on creating a competition agency that will attempt to stop anti-competitive activities by the private sector. It is difficult for experts to determine when a private activity reduces competition, and they frequently disagree. A competition agency has to examine the specific circumstances of each case and attempt to determine if, on balance, the activity is reducing competition. In other words, the agency has to have broad discretion to use its judgment in deciding cases. Such broad discretion, however, is dangerous when government agencies are weak and subject to corruption. This problem is worsened if the agency is given a variety of objectives in addition to increasing competition that occurs in many countries.

As a result, such agencies are usually ineffective or, even worse, are captured by the private sector and become a tool for reducing competition rather than increasing it. For example, if a company is concerned that it will face greater competition if two of its rivals merge, it will complain to the agency that the merger will actually reduce competition. If a company is unhappy that a rival is charging low prices, it will complain that it is engaging in predatory or discriminatory pricing. Poor countries with weak institutions should not establish competition agencies.

With the reforms beginning in 1985, New Zealand focused on removing government barriers to competition and liberalizing the economy. The goal was an economy whose future structure and direction would be determined by competitive market forces rather than by government planning, regulations, or subsidies. By March

1985, the Labour Party government removed all controls on prices, wages, interest rates, and access to foreign exchange. Import quotas were eliminated, tariffs reduced, and restrictions on foreign ownership were reduced but not entirely eliminated. Industries previously dominated by state-owned enterprises were opened up to competition and entry by private firms. Subsidies to particular industries, notably agriculture, were largely eliminated.

With regard to business regulation, a recent review of the New Zealand economy by the OECD states that government "[e]fforts have focused both on ensuring that complying with new laws and regulations is not unnecessarily burdensome and on reducing the costs derived from existing regulations."[10] One remaining problem, however, is that local governments have implemented environmental regulations inconsistently and have caused long delays. Also, some businesses have lodged complaints under these regulations apparently for the purpose of hindering their competitors rather than improving the environment.[11]

The Labour Party government did not attempt to liberalize labor markets, no doubt because of its traditional support by labor unions. The succeeding National Party government, however, replaced centralized bargaining between unions and employers with decentralized enterprise by enterprise bargaining.

In spite of the removal of most government barriers to competition, the government still perceived the need to create a competition agency, the Commerce Commission, to enforce its competition law, the Commerce Act. One reason is that, at least initially, the government did not create agencies to regulate infrastructure sectors such as electricity and telecommunications, though such agencies are commonly found in most other rich countries. Instead, the government planned to use general competition law enforced by the Commerce Commission to deal with any monopoly problems in these sectors. In establishing the Commerce Commission, the government at least did not give it a variety of objectives as has occurred in other countries. The only objective of the Commerce Act is "to promote competition in markets for the long-term benefit of consumers"[12] In contrast to many poor countries, government institutions in New Zealand are honest and competent, thus reducing the potential that the Commerce Commission might reduce competition rather than increase it.

Were the New Zealand Reforms Successful?

The end result of these reforms is that New Zealand has one of the most liberal economic systems guided primarily by market forces with a minimal role for government. The Index of Economic Freedom prepared by the Heritage Foundation and the *Wall Street Journal* gives New Zealand the fourth highest rating after Hong Kong, Singapore, and Luxembourg.[13] A similar report published by the Fraser Institute lists New Zealand as the fourth freest economy in the world after Hong Kong, Singapore, and the United States.[14] The arguments for this type of economy are even greater in poor countries with much weaker government institutions.

The Labour-led government of New Zealand in office since 1999, however, seems inclined to reverse some of these past policies and to intervene more in the economy. Noted earlier were the government decisions to create a state-owned bank and to renationalize Air New Zealand. The government has also created an organization, Industry New Zealand, to assist business startups, provide information and education to entrepreneurs and small firms, and support regional development initiatives. Fortunately, its budget is modest. Also, in an attempt to create a venture capital market, the government is setting up privately managed closed-end funds with a mixture of private and public capital. After reviewing these initiatives, the OECD concluded that it is unclear what gaps in private markets they are meant to fill.[15]

These reforms were not an end in themselves but were introduced to increase the rate of economic growth and, thus, income levels. During the first five or six years after the reforms began in 1985, growth rates were low. Perhaps this is not surprising because of the large adjustments that the economy had to make to the new business environment. Industries that were profitable when protected from competition or subsidized declined after 1985, and resources had to move to other growing industries that could compete. Over the last decade, however, growth rates have exceeded the average level of other rich countries. New Zealand now seems to be catching up rather than falling further and further behind as was the case for most of the 20th century.

Two Final Examples

This book does not attempt to deal with all elements of the business environment. It focuses on those for which the policies recommended by most experts are not appropriate for poor countries with

243

weak government institutions. Let me, however, briefly discuss two other examples that support the general conclusions of this book— the business environment for agriculture and the legal and judicial system.

Many discussions of economic development give little importance to agriculture and instead focus on industry or services. They are considered to be the modern, dynamic sectors that will contribute the most to economic growth. Making computer chips seems more glamorous, modern, and "high tech" compared with growing potatoes. Yet, agriculture still accounts for about 25 percent of gross national income and a higher percentage of employment in poor countries, and large improvements in agricultural productivity are possible. For example, the agricultural sector in the United States arguably has had the largest increase in productivity of any sector and is the most technically advanced in the country. Some countries such as Chile and New Zealand have achieved high levels of income even though their economies are largely based on agricultural exports.

In spite of the size and importance of agriculture in most poor countries, the business environment for this sector is perhaps the worst of any sector. In both poor and rich countries, government policies for agriculture still emphasize subsidies and heavy-handed regulation that are no longer acceptable in other sectors. In my own country, the United States, I am appalled that the government still provides large subsidies to this sector and protects it from foreign competition. The European Union and Japan are probably even worse in this regard. Farmers are a powerful voting block, which again illustrates that democracy is not a perfect form of government.

An important weakness in the business environment for agriculture in poor countries not usually found in other sectors is that farmers frequently lack clear property rights over their land. Hernando de Soto argues persuasively that this may be the single most important obstacle to economic development.[16] I cannot add to the arguments and evidence provided in de Soto's books and speeches except to give my one limited experience with this issue.

I had the opportunity to discuss land ownership with a senior official in the Sri Lankan Ministry of Agriculture. The government still owns large areas of agricultural land though it has been under long-term lease to private farmers for many years. Also, the government still regulates what farmers can grow on their land. I asked the official why the government does not turn over ownership of the land to these long-term tenants. The official was shocked at my suggestion. He said that if farmers had ownership, they might do bad things with the land, for example, sell it, divide it, mortgage it, or grow different crops. The government must control these activities because the government and, in particular, his ministry knows better than these unsophisticated peasant farmers how to manage the land.

Another important element of the business environment is the legal and judicial system. It protects the property rights of businesses and helps to adjudicate commercial disputes. This system is weak in many poor countries and of limited use to businesspeople. Even in countries with relatively good legal and judicial systems, business-people settle most of their commercial disputes out of court because of the cost and delay of using the courts.

I won't attempt a comprehensive analysis of government policies in this area, but would like to mention one frequent complaint of businesspeople in poor countries. They complain that judges are hired after graduating from law school and spend the rest of their careers in the civil service system. They are automatically promoted on the basis of seniority and not on their knowledge and ability. Thus, there is little incentive for them to learn the complex elements of the new commercial or business law that many poor countries have typically modeled after the laws in the rich countries.

To solve the problem of poor judges, some experts argue that more training must be provided for judges. International development institutions have funded a number of judicial training centers in poor countries. This response is typical when experts are asked how a weak government institution can implement the policies that they recommend.

Two alternatives might be more effective. The first is to change the way that judges are hired and promoted so that they have an incentive to obtain the necessary skills. But this involves fundamental changes in the civil service system and is opposed by existing government officials.

The second, advocated by a few experts, is to adopt laws that are more suited for a weak judicial and legal system. The *Harvard Law Review* article, "A Self-Enforcing Model of Corporate Law," examines the type of corporate law that would be better for poor countries instead of their simply adopting the corporate law that exists in the

United States, the European Union, or some other rich country.[17] One recommendation is that corporate law should whenever possible use "... bright-line rules, rather than standards, to define proper and improper behavior. Bright-line rules can be understood by those who must comply with them and they have a better chance of being enforced. Standards, in contrast, require judicial interpretation, which is often unavailable in emerging markets, and presume a shared cultural understanding of the regulatory policy that underlies the standards, which may also be absent."[18]

Weak Governments Cause Poverty

In the debate about the relative role of government and the private sector in increasing the rate of growth in poor countries, advocates for a greater government role complain about the many failings of the private sector. Though these complaints are often valid, the underlying cause is usually inept and corrupt governments that do not create an environment that would force private businesses to perform better. The major reason why poverty continues in so many countries of the world is that their governments do not function well. The few countries over the past 50 years that have managed to raise most of their citizens out of poverty (e.g., Korea, Taiwan, Singapore, and Hong Kong) have been blessed with good though not perfect governments.[19] In spite of the recent setbacks caused by the East Asian financial crisis, their governments have put in place the policies and institutions that forced private businesses to perform better and thus have increased the rate of economic growth and raised incomes.

A partial solution to the pervasive problem of weak governments emphasized here is to tailor policies to fit the capacity of these governments. This book describes policies in the areas of banking, privatization, corporate governance, competition, and bankruptcy that weak government institutions are more likely to implement successfully. These policies also do not require a large commitment of government resources that are in such limited supply in poor countries, most important, competent and honest civil servants. The resources saved by adopting the *light-handed* policies recommended here can instead be used to improve the ability of governments to carry out those functions that only the government can perform, for example, law and order, national defense, the legal system, roads, and welfare programs to help the poor. Though how to improve the functioning of business is the subject of this book, I have to admit that a far more important subject is how to improve the functioning of governments in poor countries.

Notes

Chapter 1

1. It is commonly believed that this phrase is in the Hippocratic oath taken by those about to begin medical practice. These exact words are not found in any version of the oath. The closest phrase is a physician's promise to "abstain from whatever is deleterious and mischievous."

2. What Winston Churchill said about democracy in a speech in the House of Commons, November 11, 1947, was "No one pretends that democracy is perfect or all-wise. Indeed, it has been said that democracy is the worst form of government except all those other forms that have been tried from time to time."

3. Raghuram G. Rajan and Luigi Zingales, *Saving Capitalism From the Capitalists: Unleashing the Power of Financial Markets to Create Wealth and Spread Opportunity* (New York: Crown Business, 2003).

4. David Ransom, "Bread and Roses: The Trade Union Revival," *New Internationalist*, December 2001, p. 7.

5. William D. Nordhaus and Paul A. Samuelson, *Economics* (New York: McGraw-Hill, 1985).

6. This discussion of Soviet growth is based on Paul Craig Roberts, *Meltdown Inside the Soviet Economy* (Washington: Cato Institute, 1990), pp. 1–3.

7. Daniel Yergin and Joseph Stanislaw, *The Commanding Heights: The Battle for the World Economy* (New York: Touchstone, 1998), pp. 234–238.

8. Ibid., pp. 139–185.

9. Yoshiro Miwa and J. Mark Ramseyer, "Capitalist Politicians, Socialist Bureaucrats? Legends of Government Planning from Japan," Discussion Paper No. 385, Harvard University, John M. Olin Center for Law, Economics, and Business, 2002.

10. Andrei Shleifer and Robert W. Vishny, *The Grabbing Hand: Government Pathologies and Their Cures* (Cambridge, Mass.: Harvard University Press, 1999).

11. Joseph E. Stiglitz, "The Role of the State in Financial Markets," *Proceedings of the World Bank Annual Conference on Development Economics 1993* (Washington: World Bank, 1993), p. 19.

12. Jaime Jaramillo-Vallejo, "Comment on 'The Role of the State in Financial Markets' by Stiglitz," *Proceedings of the World Bank Annual Conference on Development Economics 1993* (Washington: World Bank, 1993), p. 53.

Chapter 2

1. United Nations, "United Nations Millennium Declaration." Resolution Adopted by the General Assembly. A/55/L.2., September 8, 2000.

2. United Nations, "Road Map towards the Implementation of the United Nations Millennium Declaration: Report of the Secretary General," A/56/326, September 6, 2001.

3. United Nations, "United Nations Millennium Declaration." op. cit., p. 2.

4. United Nations, "Road Map . . . ," op. cit., p. 18.

5. Ibid., p. 26.

6. World Bank, September 23, 2003, http://www.developmentgoals.org

7. World Bank, "World Bank Estimates Cost of Reaching the Millennium Development Goals at $40–$60 billion Annually in Additional Aid," News Release No. 2002/212/S, February 20, 2002.

8. Shantayanan Devarajan, Margaret J. Miller, and Eric V. Swanson, "Goals for Development: History Prospects, and Costs," Policy Research Working Paper 2819, World Bank, April 2002.

9. For example, see Doug Bandow and Ian Vásquez, eds., *Perpetuating Poverty: The World Bank, the IMF, and the Developing World* (Washington: Cato Institute, 1994).

10. World Bank, *Assessing Aid: What Works, What Doesn't, and Why*, Policy Research Report (Washington: Oxford University Press, 1998).

11. When I was working at the World Bank, there was a tendency to also evaluate specific loans and projects according to whether they directly benefited the poor. This seems to have been because the Bank had changed its public objective from economic development to a new objective of reducing poverty. I see little difference between these two objectives. Economic development was desired not for its own sake, but because it would increase incomes and reduce poverty. This change may have been implemented mostly for public relations purposes because the general public is more likely to understand and support the new objective. However, one consequence was that it was easier for managers to obtain approval for a new loan or project if they could show a direct impact on the poor and thus clearly meet the Bank's objective of reducing poverty. It seemed out of fashion to evaluate projects according to whether they increased the rate of economic growth. For example, staff in favor of a project that would build a new road would argue that it would allow the poor to bring their products to market. They did not argue that it would reduce transportation costs for everyone, improve the business environment for the private sector, and thus increase the rate of economic growth.

12. These dollar values are based on purchasing power parity exchange rates rather than market exchange rates. This is because one dollar after conversion into Indian rupees at market exchange rates will buy more in India than a dollar will buy in the United States. Using market exchange rates would increase the estimated number of poor people in India.

13. This estimate of the Total Poverty Gap is derived from the mean or average Poverty Gap given in Table 2.6, p. 59, of the *World Development Indicators*, World Bank, 2003. According to p. 61 of the *World Development Indicators*, the mean or average Poverty Gap ". . . is the mean shortfall below the poverty line (counting the non-poor as having zero shortfall) expressed as a percentage of the poverty line. This measure reflects the depth of poverty as well as its incidence." This value for India in 2001 is 8.2 percent for the $1 per day benchmark. Multiplying this number times the total population of 1,032 million and times the benchmark income level of $365 per year equals the Total Poverty Gap of $31 billion for this benchmark. A similar calculation can be done for the $2 per day benchmark. In this case, the mean or average Poverty Gap is 35.3 percent and the total Poverty Gap is $266 billion. Also see Table 2-1.

14. David Dollar and Aart Kraay, "Growth Is Good for the Poor," Development Research Group Working Paper 2587, World Bank, March 2000.

15. Surjit S. Bhalla, *Imagine There's No Country: Poverty, Inequality, and Growth in the Era of Globalization* (Washington: Institute for International Economics, 2002).

Chapter 3

1. The company does have a Web site on the World Wide Web (http://www.mars.com), but this seems to be designed primarily to help recruit new employees. It describes what the company does and the location of some of its subsidiary companies but it does not mention the office near Washington or who the current owners of the company are.

2. For example, see the mission statement of the Global Corporate Governance Forum created by the World Bank and the Organization for Economic Cooperation and Development available on the World Wide Web (http://www.gcgf.org/about.htm).

3. World Bank, *World Development Report 2001: Building Institutions for Markets* (New York: Oxford University Press, 2001), p. 58.

4. Stijn Claessens, Simeon Djankov, Joseph P. H. Fan, and Larry H. P. Lang, "Corporate Diversification in East Asia: The Role of Ultimate Ownership and Group Affiliation," Policy Research Working Paper No. 2089, World Bank, March 1999.

5. See the Web site for the Global Corporate Governance Forum (http://www.gcgf.org/about.htm).

6. Magdi R. Iskander and Nadereh Chamalou, *Corporate Governance: A Framework for Implementation* (Washington: World Bank, 2000), p. 2.

7. ADB, *Corporate Governance and Finance in East Asia: A Study of Indonesia, Republic of Korea, Malaysia, Philippines, and Thailand: Volume One (A Consolidated Report)*, (Manila: Asian Development Bank, 2000), p. 1.

8. Adolf Berle and Gardiner Means, *The Modern Corporation and Private Property* (New York: Macmillan, 1932).

9. A somewhat broader definition of corporate governance would also include the role of the suppliers of debt (banks, bondholders, and other creditors) in monitoring and controlling the managers of a company to ensure that debt is repaid. In other words, corporate governance deals with how all suppliers of capital, both equity and debt, monitor and supervise the managers of the company. This definition is used by Andrei Shleifer and Robert W. Vishny, "A Survey of Corporate Governance," *Journal of Finance* 52 (1997): 737–783. I am not including the suppliers of debt in the discussion of corporate governance here because the role of the most important holder of debt in poor countries, namely, banks, is discussed in other chapters.

10. World Bank, *Finance for Growth: Policy Choices in a Volatile World* (Washington: World Bank, 2001).

11. This discussion of the causes of the East Asian crisis draws heavily on Steven Radelet and Jeffrey Sachs, "What Have We Learned, So Far, from the Asian Financial Crisis," Working Paper, National Bureau of Economic Research, January 4, 1999. Available on the World Wide Web (http://www.nber.org /~confer/2000/korea00/radelet+sachs2.pdf).

12. Michael P. Dooley and Inseok Shin, "Private Inflows When Crises Are Anticipated: A Case Study of Korea," Working Paper, 2000, p. 4. Available on the World Wide Web (http://econ.ucsc.edu/~mpd/).

13. Asian Development Bank, op. cit., p. 51.

14. For a more detailed explanation, see Dooley and Shin, op. cit., and Michael P. Dooley, "A Model of Crises in Emerging Markets," *The Economic Journal* 110 (January 2000): 256–272.

15. For a discussion of this option, see Stanley Fischer, "On the Need for an International Lender of Last Resort." Working Paper International Monetary Fund, 1999. Available on the World Wide Web (http://www.imf.org/external/np/speeches/1999/010399.htm). This is a slightly revised version of a paper prepared for delivery at the joint luncheon of the American Economic Association and the American Finance Association on January 3, 1999.

16. For a review of the performance of banks in East Asia, see Asian Development Bank, op. cit., pp. 40–43.

17. Executive Summary provided by the editor on p. 2 of Mark J. Roe, "The Political Roots of American Corporate Finance," *Journal of Applied Corporate Finance* 9, no. 4 (Winter 1997): 8–22.

18. F. H. Buckley, "The Canadian Keiretsu," *Journal of Applied Corporate Finance* 9, no. 4 (Winter 1997): 46–56.

19. Rafael La Porta, Florencio López-de-Silanes, Andrei Shleifer, and Robert Vishny, "Investor Protection and Corporate Valuation," *Journal of Finance* 57, no. 3 (June 2002): 1147–1170.

20. Stijn Claessens, Simeon Djankov, Joseph P. H. Fan, and Larry H. P. Lang, "Disentangling the Incentive and Entrenchment Effects of Large Shareholdings," *Journal of Finance* 57, no. 6 (December 2002): 2741–2771.

21. For a survey, see Andrei Shleifer and Robert W. Vishny, "A Survey of Corporate Governance," *Journal of Finance* 52 (1997): 737–783.

22. W. Bruce Johnson, Robert Magee, Nandu Nagarajan, and Harry Newman, "An Analysis of the Stock Price Reaction to Sudden Executive Deaths: Implications for the Management Labor Market," *Journal of Accounting & Economics* 7 (1985): 151–174.

23. See, for example, Organization for Economic Cooperation and Development, *OECD Principles of Corporate Governance* (Paris: OECD, 1999), p. 42.

24. Personal conversation with staff at Towers Perin suggests that they do have data on executive compensation for larger companies in both the United States and other countries. However, providing comparisons would disclose information that the companies have provided to them in confidence because of the small number of large companies in some countries. Thus, the user of these data if published might be used to determine compensation levels for particular companies that would violate confidentiality agreements with these companies.

25. Pearl Meyer & Partners, "Executive Pay Trends: Looking Forward and Bank," 2002. Available on the World Wide Web (http://www.execpay.com).

26. "Are CEOs Worth Their Salaries," *Washington Post*, October 2, 2002, p. E1.

27. Lucian Arye Bebchuk, Jesse M. Fried, and David I. Walker, "Managerial Power and Rent Extraction in the Design of Executive Compensation," Discussion Paper No. 366, Harvard Law School, 2002, p. 96. Available on the World Wide Web (http://www.law.harvard.edu/programs/olin_center).

28. Ira W. Lieberman and Robert Ferguson, "Overview of Privatization and Emerging Equity Markets," in Ira W. Lieberman and Christopher D. Kirkness, eds., *Privatization and Emerging Equity Markets* (Washington: World Bank and Flemings, 1998), p. 9.

29. Some of the most recent studies include G. Bekaert and C. R. Harvey, "Foreign Speculators and Emerging Equity Markets," *Journal of Finance* 55, no. 2 (2000): 565–613; Jeffrey Wurgler, "Financial Markets and the Allocation of Capital," *Journal of Financial*

Economics 58, no. 1 (2000): 187–214; and T. Beck, R. Levine, and N. Loayza, "Finance and the Sources of Growth," *Journal of Financial Economics* 58, no. 3 (2000): 261–300.

30. Thorsten Beck and Ross Levine, "Stock Markets, Banks, and Growth: Correlation or Causality," Policy Research Working Paper 2670, World Bank, July 2001.

31. Board of Governors of the Federal Reserve System, "Flow of Funds Accounts of the United States: Flows and Outstandings Fourth Quarter 2002," Federal Reserve Statistical Release, 2003, p. 18.

32. Cherian Samuel, "The Stock Market as a Source of Finance: A Comparison of U.S. and Indian Firms," Policy Research Working Paper 1592, World Bank, April 1996, p. 27.

33. World Bank, *World Development Report 2001–2002: Building Institutions for Markets* (New York: Oxford University Press, 2001), p. 70.

34. International Finance Corporation, http://www.ifc.org/sme/html/the_case_for_smes.html

35. Milton Friedman, *Capitalism and Freedom* (Chicago: University of Chicago Press, 1962), p. 67.

36. I am surprised that not more people, in particular those from the business community, are concerned about this movement by private organizations to specify standards of corporate social responsibility. One of the few dissenting voices is David Henderson, *Misguided Virtue: False Notions of Corporate Social Responsibility* (Wellington, N.Z.: Business Roundtable, 2001). He argues that adopting this concept would reduce competition and economic freedom and undermine the market economy.

37. Michael C. Jensen, "Value Maximization, Stakeholder Theory, and the Corporate Objective Function," *Journal of Applied Corporate Finance* 14, no. 3 (Fall 2001): 18.

38. Ministry of Social Affairs (Denmark), "Social Index: Measuring a Company's Social Responsibility," EMPL-2000-01413-00-00-EN-TRA-00 (DA), p. 1. Available on the World Wide Web (http://europa.eu.int/comm/ dgs/employment_social/lisbon-conf2000/berrit.pdf).

Chapter 4

1. For a recent survey of these studies, see Sunita Kikeri and John Nellis, "Privatization in Competitive Sectors: The Record So Far," Background Paper for World Bank Private Sector Development Strategy, October 29, 2001. Available on the World Wide Web (http://rru.worldbank.org/Strategy/Discussions.asp).

2. Ibid., p.21.

3. Pierre Guislan, *The Privatization Challenge: A Strategic, Legal, and Institutional Analysis of International Experience, World Bank Regional and Sectoral Studies* (Washington: World Bank, 1997), p.20.

4. In the discussion that follows these methods, I will assume that the state-owned enterprise has the legal form of a company, and thus the government is transferring ownership of the company's shares. The alternative is for the government to sell specific assets of the enterprise (e.g., land, buildings, and equipment) rather than the entire enterprise as a legal entity. Though selling assets is often a good method of privatization, I will use the example of a government selling shares in a company because many of the methods of privatization can only be implemented by selling shares.

5. If the government is fortunate enough to have many investors interested in bidding for a particular state-owned enterprise, it may be desirable to reduce the number of bidders in order to reduce the costs of carrying out an auction for all of the parties involved (the bidders, the government, and the state-owned enterprise). It is expensive for investors to make a bid because of the detailed information that they must obtain about the enterprise before they can prepare a bid (often referred to as *due diligence*). It is also expensive for the enterprises to provide this information to many bidders and for the government to evaluate many bids. A two-stage process can be used to reduce costs without significantly reducing the competitiveness of the auction. In the first stage, those investors who are unlikely to offer the highest price can be eliminated. These could be the ones that have little previous experience in the industry or are small and lack access to capital. In the second stage, the remaining investors will go through the expensive process of preparing and submitting their bids. The purpose of this process is not to evaluate the qualifications or business plans of the bidders but simply to make the auction more efficient by eliminating obviously less-qualified bidders.

6. Stoyan Tenev and Chunlin Zhang, *Corporate Governance and Enterprise Reform in China: Building the Institutions of Modern Markets* (Washington: World Bank and International Finance Corporation, 2002), p. 76.

7. Jacques Rogozinski, *High Price for Change: Privatization in Mexico* (Washington: Inter-American Development Bank, 1998), p. 83.

8. Oliver Campbell White and Anita Bhatia, *Privatization in Africa*, Directions in Development series, World Bank, 1998, p. 31.

9. Ibid., pp. 32–33.

10. Ibid., p. 63.

11. Simeon Djankov and Peter Murrell, "Enterprise Restructuring in Transition: A Quantitative Survey," Mimeo, World Bank, February 8, 2002.

12. Florencio López-de-Silanes, "Determinants of Privatization Prices," National Bureau of Economic Research Working Paper 5494, March 1996. Available on the World Wide Web (http://papers.ssrn.com/sol3/papers.cfm?abstract_id=7405).

13. Narjess Boubakri and Jean-Claude Cosset, "The Financial and Operating Performance of Newly Privatized Firms: Evidence from Developing Countries," *The Journal of Finance* 53, no. 3 (June 1998): 1081–1110.

14. Juliet D'Souza, William Megginson, and Robert Nash, "Determinants of Performance Improvements in Privatized Firms: The Role of Restructuring and Corporate Governance," *Journal of Economic Literature* 39, no. 2 (June 2001).

15. *Supplier credits* can also be used in a similar way. The power company buys new equipment from a foreign supplier who agrees to finance the purchase instead of requiring immediate payment. The supplier, however, often insists that the government guarantee the payment. The foreign supplier may be compensated for the risk involved in lending to the purchaser by charging higher prices for the equipment. For an analysis of the use of supplier credits in one poor country, see World Bank, *Bangladesh Suppliers' Credit as External Finance: Challenges for Fiscal and External Debt Management* (Washington: World Bank, 2000). This report concludes that development assistance such as low interest rate loans from the World Bank has been declining because the government has not undertaken needed economic reforms. The government has compensated for this decline by increasing the use of supplier credits and government-guaranteed foreign investment such as independent power projects (Ibid., p. 3).

16. World Bank, http://www.worldbank.org/html/fpd/guarantees/html/projects_completed.html.

17. Privatization can be viewed as a large adjustment to the hypothetical balance sheet of both the government and the private sector. Before privatization, the typical government (except for the transition economies) had a large amount of real assets (state-owned enterprises) on the asset side of its balance sheet but also large debts, for example, bonds sold to the private sector, on the liability side. These bonds appeared on the balance sheet for the private sector as financial assets. Because of privatization, the total assets on the government's balance sheet was reduced. If government used the proceeds from privatization to pay off some of its debt (government bonds), as is usually recommended, its total liabilities would be reduced by an equal amount and thus its balance sheet would remain in balance. At the same time, the real assets of the private sector are increased because private investors purchased former state-owned enterprises, and its financial assets (government bonds) are reduced by an equal amount. In effect, the end result is that the private sector is selling government bonds back to the government to buy the state-owned enterprises. In the transition economies, however, governments typically had little debt owed to their private sectors. What domestic debt that these governments had was wiped out by hyperinflation in the early 1990s. Consequently, the private sectors had almost no financial assets that they could use to buy state-owned enterprises.

18. Some critics of privatization in the transition economies argued that privatization should have been delayed until a market-supporting infrastructure (legal system, regulation, property rights, minority shareholder protection, etc.) was in place. For example, see Joseph E. Stiglitz, *Globalization and Its Discontents* (New York: W. W. Norton, 2002), p. 157. I agree that the performance of newly privatized firms would have been improved if this infrastructure had been in place, or in other words, the business environment had been improved. The problem with delaying privatization, however, is that the government had largely given up trying to control the managers of state-owned enterprises. Central planning in the former communist economic system did exercise some control over managers and held them accountable for their performance. This control limited to some extent their outright theft of state assets. Once central planning was eliminated and state-owned enterprises were allowed to operate more freely in the new market economy (a process sometimes called *commercialization*), government controls over the managers were weakened and they proceeded to steal the more valuable assets. The unpleasant choice facing governments was whether to allow the managers to steal the assets or to give them the assets by using some type of management buyout.

Chapter 5

1. One important function of banks that I will not discuss here is that they facilitate making payments, for example, payment using checks or bank drafts instead of paper currency.

2. Pyramid schemes were common in most of the countries in Central and Eastern Europe after the fall of communism. In Albania, for example, almost every citizen had invested in one or more such schemes and lost money when they crashed. Perhaps citizens of these countries were more gullible than in other countries because they naively believed that the replacement of communism with a market economy

would immediately make everyone rich. They believed that these pyramid schemes were the vehicle to bring the imagined wealth of capitalism to everyone.

3. Though this book only analyzes the banking sector, many of the conclusions and recommendations apply to other state-owned financial institutions. In many poor countries, the government also owns insurance companies, pension funds, and investment (mutual) funds. Such institutions typically take in investments similar to bank deposits and then re-invest the money. In other words, they are also financial intermediaries. If well managed, they can be a major source of financing for capital investment. For example, insurance companies and pension funds can provide long-term loans to a company because they will not need the money for many years (for example, when their customer dies or retires). Unfortunately, they are also prone to become pyramid schemes because politicians control how they make investments. Like banks, detailed examination of many of these financial institutions will show that they are insolvent even though they are still liquid.

4. Sometimes economists are blunter about what is going on in many banks. For example, see George A. Akerlof and Paul M. Romer, "Looting: The Economic Underworld of Bankruptcy for Profit," *Brookings Papers on Economic Activity* 2 (1993): 1–68.

5. The unwillingness of politicians to deal with the bad loans made by banks to enterprises occurs in rich countries as well. Recently, news reports suggest that the Japanese bank regulatory agency is pressuring private banks to be lenient on borrowers, for example, not forcing them to repay their loans or forcing them into bankruptcy. No doubt one reason is that the government is concerned about the resulting unemployment that this might cause. According to a *Wall Street Journal* article, "Shinsei Bank Pressured to Keep Shaky Loans," on September 26, 2000, "Arm twisting of bankers by politicians and regulators to support deadbeat borrowers is a major reason why Japan's lenders have been crippled by bad loans for a decade."

6. Dominic Ziegler, "Casino Capital," in "A Survey of Asian Finance," *The Economist*, February 8–14, 2003, p. 12.

7. This example is based on personal discussions with businesspeople and government officials in Pakistan.

8. Rafael La Porta, Florencio López-de-Silanes, and Guillermo Zamarripa, "Related Lending," Mimeo, 2001. Available on the World Wide Web (http://papers.ssrn.com/sol3/papers.cfm?abstract_id=302128).

9. Savings and loan associations were specialized banks that previous to the crisis primarily made mortgage loans to homebuyers.

10. Gerard Caprio Jr. and Daniela Klingebiel, "Episodes of Systemic and Borderline Financial Crises," World Bank, January 2003, Annex II, p. 5.

11. See, for example, Stephen Pizzo, Mary Fricker, and Paul Muolo, *Inside Job: The Looting of America's Stavings and Loans* (New York: McGraw-Hill, 1989).

12. Thomas Perry, *Dance of the Dead* (New York: Random House, 1996), pp. 62–68.

13. Sergio de la Cuadra and Salvador Valdés, "Myths and Facts about Financial Liberalization in Chile: 1974–1983," in Philip Brock, ed., *If Texas Were Chile: A Primer on Banking Reform* (San Francisco: ICS Press, 1992).

14. Gerard Caprio Jr. and Daniela Klingebiel, "Bank Insolvency: Bad Luck, Bad Policy, or Bad Banking," *Annual World Bank Conference on Development Economics* (Washington: World Bank, 1996), p. 91.

15. Patrick Honohan and Daniela Klingebiel, "Controlling the Fiscal Costs of Banking Crises," Policy Research Working Paper 2441, World Bank, September 2000, p. 3.

16. As shown in Table 6.10 (p. 340) of *World Development Indicators*, World Bank, 2003, official development assistance to low- and middle-income countries totaled $57.2 billion in 2001.

17. For an official description of this new role, see International Monetary Fund, "IMF Surveillance Enhances Members' Ability to Take Corrective Policy Actions," IMF Survey Supplement 30, September 2001.

18. Charles W. Calomiris, "The IMF's Imprudent Role as Lender of Last Resort," *The Cato Journal* 17, no. 3 (1998): 276–294.

19. Christopher Swann, "Japan Seeks Compromise on IMF Assessors," *Financial Times*, September 4, 2001.

20. International Monetary Fund, "IMF Surveillance Enhances Members' Ability to Take Corrective Policy Actions," op. cit., p. 6.

21. Rafael La Porta, Florencio López-de-Silanes, and Andrei Shleifer, "Government Ownership of Banks," Mimeo, November 2000. Available on the World Wide Web (http://papers.ssrn.com/sol3/papers.cfm?abstract_id=236434).

Chapter 6

1. One possible weakness of quality regulation is that the government may set the minimum standard too high. This standard forces consumers to buy a higher quality product than they need or can afford. For example, some believe that governments in the United States have set the minimum standard too high for licensing childcare services. This high standard raises the cost of childcare to levels that many cannot afford and encourages working parents to use unlicensed and illegal childcare services that they can afford.

2. For a good description of the origins of deposit insurance in the United States, see Eugene White, "Deposit Insurance," Policy Research Working Paper 1541, World Bank, 1995.

3. U.S. Senate, *Amendments to Federal Deposit Insurance Act*, Hearings before subcommittee of the Committee on Banking and Currency, 81st Cong., 2d sess., January 30, 1950, pp. 87–88.

4. Greg Ip, "Small Banks Push Deposit-Insurance Boost," *Wall Street Journal*, April 29, 2002.

5. When I was living in Illinois in the early 1970s, there was a controversy about the new concept of drive-in banking facilities that could be used without leaving one's automobile. Illinois did not allow branch banking within the state. Regulatory authorities insisted that any new drive-in facility must be located within a short distance from the bank's office to make certain that the bank was not establishing a separate branch in violation of the law.

6. World Bank, *Finance for Growth: Policy Choices in a Volatile World* (Washington: World Bank, 2001), p. 82

7. To use a medical analogy, are widespread bank failures like a flu epidemic in which a sick person infects a healthy person? Alternatively, are they like three fat middle-aged smokers who happen to have chest pains at the same time? I think that the latter is a better analogy.

8. David C. Wheelock, "Regulation, Market Structure, and Bank Failures of the Great Depression," Federal Reserve Bank of St. Louis, *Review* 77, no. 2 (1995): 27–38.

9. Many experts believe that the central bank for the United States, the Federal Reserve, failed to do this in the Great Depression out of fear that its own solvency

might be impaired. This failure greatly worsened the Great Depression. The behavior of the Federal Reserve is a little bit like a firefighter refusing to fight a fire out of concern that he might suffer a burn. See Milton Friedman and Anna Jacobson Schwartz, *The Great Contraction, 1929–1933* (Princeton, N.J.: Princeton University Press, 1965).

10. Asli Demirgüç-Kunt and Enrica Detragiache, "Does Deposit Insurance Increase Banking System Stability?" International Monetary Fund Working Paper WP/00/03, January 2000, Abstract, p. 1.

11. World Bank, *World Development Report: Building Institutions for Markets* (New York: Oxford University Press, 2001), p. 80.

12. For a good discussion of the various arguments concerning competition and the entry of foreign banks, see ibid., Section 4.4.

13. For more detailed information see Peter Ledingham, "The Review of Bank Supervision Arrangements in New Zealand: The Main Elements of the Debate," *Reserve Bank Bulletin* 58, no. 3 (1995): 163–171, or Peter Nicholl, "Regulating Banks through Public Disclosure—The Case of New Zealand," World Bank, *Viewpoint*, no. 94 (October 1996).

14. Maria Soledad Martinez Peria and Sergio L. Schmukler, "Do Depositors Punish Banks for 'Bad' Behavior?: Market Discipline in Argentina, Chile, and Mexico," Policy Research Working Paper 2058, World Bank, February 1999.

15. Pankaj Ghemawat and Tarun Khanna, "The Nature of Diversified Business Groups: A Research Design and Two Case Studies," *The Journal of Industrial Economics* 46, no. 1 (March 1998).

16. Y. W. Lee and J. D. Stowe, "Product Risk, Asymmetric Information, and Trade Credit," *Journal of Financial and Quantitative Analysis* 28 (1993): 285–300.

17. Sabapathy Thillairajah, "Development of Rural Financial Markets in Sub-Saharan Africa," Discussion Paper No. 219, World Bank, June 1994, p. 70.

18. Abhijit Banerjee, Timothy Besley, and Timothy Guinnane, "Thy Neighbor's Keeper: The Design of a Credit Cooperative with Theory and a Test," *Quarterly Journal of Economics* 109, no. 2 (1994): 491–515.

19. Ziegler, p. 11.

Chapter 7

1. Strictly speaking, this is not an entirely correct use of the term *viable*, but I could not think of anything better. *Viable* means capable of living. A company that is restructured by the government even though its going concern value is less than its liquidation value is capable of living if the government forgives all or part of its debts and thus the company is no longer insolvent.

2. Stuart C. Gilson, "Investing in Distressed Situations: A Market Survey," *Financial Analysts Journal* 51, no. 6 (November/December 1995).

3. Stuart Gilson, Kose John, and Larry Lang, "Troubled Debt Restructurings: An Empirical Study of Private Reorganization of Firms in Default," *Journal of Financial Economics* 27, no. 2 (October 1990).

4. International Monetary Fund, "Orderly and Effective Insolvency Procedures," IMF Legal Department, 1999, p. 10.

5. This is also an example of the *Coase Theorem* attributed to the Nobel Prize–winning economist Ronald Coase. According to the theorem, if the property rights of all the parties are well established and if transactions or bargaining costs are low, negotiations between the parties will result in an efficient use of resources regardless

of how the property rights are established. In the case of an out-of-court restructuring of an insolvent company, the parties will negotiate an efficient outcome if their rights in the alternative of a liquidation are well established and if bargaining costs are not high. Thus, the merits of relying on an out-of-court restructuring instead of a government-managed restructuring depends largely on whether the bargaining or negotiating costs are high.

6. "A Matter of Life and Death," *The Economist*, November 3, 2001, pp. 72–73.

7. The Turnaround Management Association has a Web site at http://www.turnaround.org/abouttma/.

8. The Recovery Group.

9. Though I am not certain, I suspect that the term *cramdown* is derived from the idea that it may be necessary for unpleasant food or medicine to be crammed down the throat of an unwilling person.

10. Michael Bradley and Michael Rosenzweig, "The Untenable Case for Chapter 11," *Yale Law Review* 101 (1992): 1043–1089.

11. Use of the bankruptcy process by managers to benefit themselves at the expense of the shareholders is another example of weak corporate governance in U.S. companies with dispersed ownership as discussed in Chapter 3.

12. A survey of the use of restructuring or workout intermediaries can be found in David Woo, "Two Approaches to Resolving Nonperforming Assets during Financial Crises," Working Paper WP/00/33, International Monetary Fund, March 2000.

13. Bruno M. Kübler and Karsten Otte, "Insolvency Proceedings," *Business Transactions in Germany*, Bernd Rüster, ed., Chapter 17, Release 24, December 2000, Mathew Bender & Co., p. 17–6.

14. Ibid., p. 17–7.

15. Izak Atiyas, "Bankruptcy Policy," PSD Occasional Paper No. 14, World Bank, February 1996, p. 36.

16. Ariane Lambert-Mogiliansky, Constantin Sonin, and Ekaterina Zhuravskaya, "Capture of Bankruptcy: Theory and Evidence from Russia," Discussion Paper No. 2488, Centre for Economic Policy Research, 2000.

17. International Monetary Fund, "Orderly and Effective Insolvency Procedures," IMF Legal Department, 1999, p. 44.

18. Shawn W. Crispin in Bangkok and Todd Zaun in Tokyo "Thai Policy Worries Crucial Investors," *Wall Street Journal*, September 3, 2003.

19. Thomas O'Brian and Christian Filipov, "The Current Regulatory Framework Governing Business in Bulgaria," Technical Paper No. 513, World Bank, 2001, p. 48.

20. Malcom Rowat and José Astigarrago, "Latin American Insolvency Systems: A Comparative Assessment," Technical Paper No. 433, World Bank, 1999.

21. Joseph A. Schumpeter, *Capitalism, Socialism and Democracy* (New York: Harper, 1975), p. 82.

Chapter 8

1. World Bank, *World Development Report 2001: Building Institutions for Markets* (New York: Oxford University Press, 2001), p. 133.

2. Economists sometimes refer to a market with few sellers but low barriers to entry as a *contestable* market as opposed to a *competitive* market.

3. A third impact that I will not discuss in detail is what economists call allocative inefficiency. Though not widely understood outside of the economics profession,

allocative inefficiency results because the price consumers have to pay for a product or service sold in an uncompetitive market is above the cost of production (cost includes a normal profit to compensate the suppliers of capital). As a result, some consumers reduce their purchases of the product or service due to the high price even though the value they would receive from its consumption would exceed the cost to society of producing it. The difference between the value to consumers and the cost of production is called the consumer surplus. Monopoly pricing reduces consumer surplus and thus the overall welfare or standard of living of society.

4. For a summary of these studies, see World Bank, *World Development Report: Building Institutions for Markets* (New York: Oxford University Press, 2001), p. 134.

5. Fred Gale, "Regions in China: One Market or Many?" in *China's Food and Agriculture: Issues for the 21st Century* by Fred Gale, Francis Tuan, Bryan Lohmar, Hsin-Hui Hsu, and Brad Gilmour, U.S. Department of Agriculture, Economic Research Service, Agricultural Information Bulletin No. AIB775, April 2002, pp. 20–23.

6. McKinsey Global Institute, *Why the Japanese Economy Is Not Growing: Micro Barriers to Productivity* (Washington: McKinsey Global Institute, 2000).

7. McKinsey Global Institute, *The Growth Imperative* (Mumbai, India: McKinsey Global Institute, 2001).

8. McKinsey Global Institute, *Unlocking Economic Growth in Russia*, (Moscow: McKinsey Global Institute, 1999).

9. For more information on how the World Bank conducts these surveys, see its Web site (http://www.world bank.org/privatesector/ic/icica.htm).

10. To confuse the noneconomist even more, economists also call the excess profits from exploiting a natural resource such as oil a *rent*. The rent is equal to the difference between the value of the resource when sold in a competitive market and the cost of producing it. In the case of a large oil field, for example, the cost of exploring, producing, and refining the oil may be just a few dollars per barrel but it can be sold for $20 per barrel or more.

11. The reader may not be surprised to learn that I was employed for some time by the U.S. Department of the Interior that managed the leasing of oil and gas resources on federal government land using the bonus-bid method.

12. International Monetary Fund and World Bank, "Market Access for Developing Countries' Exports," Mimeo, April 27, 2001, p. 20

13. Ibid.

14. Ibid., p. 34.

15. World Trade Organization, "Market Access: The WTO's Unfinished Business: Post-Uruguay Round Inventory and Issues," Geneva, WTO, 2001, Table II.8.

16. A humorous example of this process occurred in the Czech Republic. One government agency responsible for regulating investment funds required them to change their legal status. The funds did not support this requirement but they had to comply. To do so, a fund had to register its new legal status and obtain approval from another government agency. This process could take many months unless the applicant was willing to offer "speed money" to the right officials. The officials of the first agency supposedly complained that the funds were taking too long to change their status because they were unwilling to bribe the officials of the second agency as was customary.

17. Simeon Djankov, Rafael La Porta, Florencio López-de-Silanes, and Andrei Shleifer, "The Regulation of Entry," *The Quarterly Journal of Economics* 117, no. 1, February 2002, p. 37.

18. James J. Emery, Melvin T. Spence Jr., Louis T. Wells Jr., and Timothy S. Buehrer, "Administrative Barriers to Foreign Investment: Reducing Red Tape in Africa," Occasional Paper 14, U.S. Foreign Investment Advisory Service, 2000.

19. Canadian Chamber of Commerce, "Foreign Investment Barriers," prepared in partnership with Industry Canada, Ottawa, March 31, 2000.

20. Marianne Bertrand and Francis Kramarz, "Does Entry Regulation Hinder Job Creation?: Evidence from the French Retail Industry," National Bureau of Economic Research Working Paper 8211, Cambridge, Mass., April 2001.

21. Emery et. al., op. cit., p. 33.

22. Economists refer to products or services that cannot be imported for physical reasons as *nontradables*.

23. World Bank, *World Development Report: Building Institutions for Markets* (New York: Oxford University Press, 2001), p. 139.

24. World Bank and Organization for Economic Cooperation and Development, *A Framework for the Design and Implementation of Competition Law and Policy* (Washington: World Bank and OECD, 1999): 1–2.

25. Robert H. Bork, *The Antitrust Paradox: A Policy at War with Itself: With a New Introduction and Epilogue*, 2d ed. (New York: Macmillan, 1993), p. x.

26. Kalypso Nicolaidis and Raymond Vernon, "Competition Policy and Trade Policy in the European Union" in Edward M. Graham and J. David Richardson, eds., *Global Competition Policy* (Washington: Institute for International Economics, 1997), p. 272.

27. World Bank and Organization for Economic Cooperation and Development, *A Framework for the Design and Implementation of Competition Law and Policy* (World Bank and OECD, 1999), p. 29.

28. F. M. Scherer and David Ross, *Industrial Market Structure and Economic Performance* (Boston: Houghton Mifflin, 1990), p. 198.

29. Ibid., p. 569.

30. Ibid., p. 508.

31. Kotaro Suzumura, "Formal and Informal Measures for Controlling Competition in Japan: Institutional Overview and Theoretical Evaluation" in Edward M. Graham and J. David Richardson, eds., *Global Competition Policy* (Washington: Institute for International Economics, 1997), p. 447.

32. Korea Fair Trade Commission, "Annual Report on Competition Policy Developments in Korea," 1999.

33. Office for the Protection of Economic Competition in the Czech Republic, "Annual Report on Competition Policy," 1999.

Chapter 9

1. For example, a comprehensive review of what needs to be done in poor countries can be found in World Bank, *World Development Report: Building Institutions for Markets* (New York: Oxford University Press, 2001).

2. For examples of such a survey, see Andrew H. W. Stone, Daniel Kaufmann, and Geeta Batra, *Investment Climate around the World: Voices of the Firms from the World Business Environment Survey* (Washington: World Bank, 2003).

3. These studies are based in part on a presentation at a World Bank seminar on April 24, 2002, by Vincent Palmade from the McKinsey Global Institute.

4. The discussion of the New Zealand reforms is based on Lewis Evans, Arthur Grimes, and Bryce Wilkinson, "Economic Reform in New Zealand 1984–95: The Pursuit of Efficiency," *Journal of Economic Literature* 34, no. 4 (December 1996).

5. One influential business organization that supports this view is the New Zealand Business Roundtable, which according to its Web site, (http://www.nzbr.org.nz/index.html) ". . . is an organization of Chief Executives of major business firms who meet to discuss and develop points of view on matters of common interest, and particularly public policy issues."

6. Sometimes an initial screening of the qualifications of bidders was done to reduce the number of bidders to a manageable size and to reduce the cost of carrying out an auction.

7. Organization for Economic Cooperation and Development, "OECD Economic Surveys: New Zealand," 2002, p. 14.

8. New Zealand Law Commission, "Insolvency Law Reform: Promoting Trust and Confidence: An Advisory Report to the Ministry of Economic Development," Study Paper 11, 2001, p. 71. Available on the World Wide Web (http://www.law-com.govt.nz/insolv.htm).

9. Charles River Associates, "Review of the Law Commission Report 'Insolvency Law Reform: Promoting Trust and Confidence,'" June 8, 2001, p. 33, http://www.med.govt.nz/ri/insolvency/tiertwo/lawcomreview/index.html.

10. Organization for Economic Cooperation and Development, "OECD Economic Surveys: New Zealand," 2002, p. 89.

11. Ibid., p. 90.

12. For a description of competition policy in New Zealand, see New Zealand Commerce Commission, *Anti-Competitive Practices Under Part II of the Commerce Act* (Wellington, New Zealand: Commerce Commission, 2002).

13. Gerald P. O'Driscoll Jr., Edwin J. Feulner, and Mary Anastasia O'Grady, "The 2003 Index of Economic Freedom," Heritage Foundation and *Wall Street Journal* (2002).

14. James Gwartney and Robert Lawson with Neil Emerick, *Economic Freedom of the World: 2003 Annual Report* (Vancouver: Fraser Institute, 2003).

15. Organization for Economic Cooperation and Development, "OECD Economic Surveys: New Zealand," 2002, pp. 11–12.

16. Hernando de Soto, *The Other Path* (New York: Harper & Row, 1989) and *The Mystery of Capital: Why Capitalism Triumphs in the West and Fails Everywhere Else* (New York: Basic Books, 2000).

17. Bernard Black and Reinier Kraakman, "A Self-Enforcing Model of Corporate Law," *Harvard Law Review* 109 (June 1996): 1911–1982.

18. Ibid., p. 1916.

19. Another small group of countries, for example, Saudi Arabia, Kuwait, and Dubai, have been blessed with abundant supplies of petroleum that could be sold to provide high incomes for most of its citizens despite a terrible business environment that does not encourage private firms to perform well.

Index

About the Author

Robert E. Anderson is an economic development expert and has extensive experience with government policies and programs to help private business. During his 10 years at the World Bank, Anderson worked in more than 15 countries, including Kazakhstan, Slovakia, Pakistan, and Tanzania. Earlier, he worked for the Treasury of New Zealand, the State Property Committee of Russia, and the Yugoslav Ministry of Industry. He was also manager for economic analysis at the Federal Energy Regulatory Commission. Anderson holds degrees in economics from Stanford University and Johns Hopkins University and has taught at the University of Illinois (Urbana). He lives in Falls Church, Virginia.

Cato Institute

Founded in 1977, the Cato Institute is a public policy research foundation dedicated to broadening the parameters of policy debate to allow consideration of more options that are consistent with the traditional American principles of limited government, individual liberty, and peace. To that end, the Institute strives to achieve greater involvement of the intelligent, concerned lay public in questions of policy and the proper role of government.

The Institute is named for *Cato's Letters*, libertarian pamphlets that were widely read in the American Colonies in the early 18th century and played a major role in laying the philosophical foundation for the American Revolution.

Despite the achievement of the nation's Founders, today virtually no aspect of life is free from government encroachment. A pervasive intolerance for individual rights is shown by government's arbitrary intrusions into private economic transactions and its disregard for civil liberties.

To counter that trend, the Cato Institute undertakes an extensive publications program that addresses the complete spectrum of policy issues. Books, monographs, and shorter studies are commissioned to examine federal budget, Social Security, regulation, military spending, international trade, and myriad other issues. Major policy conferences are held throughout the year, from which papers are published thrice yearly in the *Cato Journal*. The Institute also publishes the quarterly magazine *Regulation*.

In order to maintain its independence, the Cato Institute accepts no government funding. Contributions are received from foundations, corporations, and individuals, and other revenue is generated from the sale of publications. The Institute is a nonprofit, tax-exempt, educational foundation under Section 501(c)(3) of the Internal Revenue Code.

CATO INSTITUTE
1000 Massachusetts Ave., N.W.
Washington, D.C. 20001
www.cato.org